ILLUSTRATED ENCYCLOPEDIA
OF STAMP COLLECTING

ILLUSTRATED ENCYCLOPEDIA OF STAMP COLLECTING

Otto Hornung

PHOTOGRAPHS
by Zdeněk Humpál

HAMLYN LONDON · NEW YORK · SYDNEY · TORONTO

AUTHOR'S ACKNOWLEDGMENT

The author has been offered great help, advice and assistance by many outstanding philatelists in Britain and elsewhere while working on this book. He wishes especially to express his deepest gratitude to the following: Mr H.R. Holmes, Mr I.J. Glassborow, Mr C.H.C. Harmer, Major E.D. Fairweather, Ing. L. Dvořáček, Dr P. Lavrov, Dr S. Zrubec, Mr P. Borek, and the late Mr K. Basika.

Designed and produced
by Artia
Published by THE HAMLYN PUBLISHING GROUP LIMITED
Hamlyn House, Feltham, Middlesex, England
Graphic design by Milan Albich
© *Copyright by Artia 1970*
ISBN 0 600 01797 4
Printed in Czechoslovakia by Svoboda, Prague
S 2755

FOREWORD

The author of this book has honoured me with an invitation to write a foreword to his work, and I do so with the greatest pleasure. Many books have been published extolling the delights of stamp collecting since the first one appeared more than one hundred years ago, but Otto Hornung's book is different from all that have gone before. Over the years the hobby has developed from the mere collecting of stamps into an intellectual pastime calling for close application and study, requiring a knowledge of the various printing processes, the inks and colours used, as well as the varying qualities of the papers on which the stamps are printed. Moreover, philately now embraces the study of postal history which takes the collector back to the origins of the postal system, several hundred years before the issue of the first adhesive postage stamps in 1840. Another aspect of the hobby is the collection of everything pertaining to the carriage of mail by air (aerophilately), and this takes into account not only the employment of the modern aeroplane for the service, but also pigeon posts, balloon posts, and mail carried by the now discarded airships.

A modern branch of philately is the collection of stamps illustrating a particular subject, e.g. trains, ships, etc.; this is called thematic collecting by some, topical collecting by others, and it is a method of collecting that has attained great popularity. Those who read Mr Hornung's book will quickly learn how to enjoy the hobby, and how to restrict or expand their interests, for he deals with all aspects of stamp collecting.

H. R. HOLMES
Former President of the Royal
Philatelic Society, London

CONTENTS

INTRODUCTION
LADY GOMM'S GREAT IDEA

The name of Mauritius is known throughout the world, but not everybody connects it with an island in the Indian Ocean. What is well known, however, is that Mauritius is a stamp, and a most valuable stamp, sought after and treasured above all others.

Lady Gomm was a woman of some distinction. Her husband, Sir W. Maynard Gomm, had reached the rank of Lieutenant-General, and was a much respected man at home in London; and it was no small thing to be appointed Lieutenant-Governor, even though Mauritius was only a pinpoint on the map of the British Empire.

The annual ball given by Lady Gomm was a sensation, the talk of Port Louis and the whole of Mauritius, and a social event of such importance that even the London Times took notice of it.

A Fancy Dress Ball at Government House was planned for 30 September, 1847. Everything was arranged and prepared for the great occasion; only one thing was missing, one that would give the ball the mark of originality and novelty. Suddenly Lady Gomm had a wonderful idea.

Letters were arriving from England with strange labels showing the serious young Queen looking out on to the world. The Governor also had received such letters. 'That's it!' exclaimed Lady Gomm when she went through her mail. She immediately told the General, and as soon as he took the idea to his council things began to happen. The next day a Mr Barnard was called to Government House.

Joseph Barnard was the local jeweller, watchmaker and odd-job man. His eyesight was poor but nobody else in the whole of Mauritius would have been able to produce stamps. Mr Barnard bowed courteously and promised to do his best. 'Don't forget, the ball is on 30 September,' said Lady Gomm when he took his leave.

Joseph Barnard took a copper plate used for visiting cards and engraved two copies of the English stamps — a Penny stamp and a Twopenny. To make it easy for everyone he added on the right-hand side the word 'Mauritius' and on the left 'Post Office'. Without delay he printed five hundred copies each of the orange-red Penny and the deep-blue Twopenny; every single stamp separately, as there was only one plate.

Lady Gomm was greatly pleased. She saw to it personally that the stamps were carefully stuck on all the invitations: 'Lady W. Maynard Gomm and the Lieutenant-Governor of Mauritius request the pleasure . . .' In all the excitement preceding the Great Ball nobody spotted Barnard's error, for instead of 'Post paid' he had engraved 'Post Office'.

The invitations carried the portrait of Queen Victoria to all corners of the island. Unfortunately not one of these invitations has survived. Luckily a few of the stamps remained at the post office, and these sailed on the next ships to Europe and to India.

When the supply of stamps was exhausted Mr Barnard engraved new and different plates, mainly because of the error, of course, but

1 The famous Penny *Post Office Mauritius* stamp.

also because it was very expensive and cumbersome to print stamps
two by two. This time there were twelve stamps on a plate, and each
of them bore the correct inscription POST PAID.

Even these stamps are a thrill for any philatelist, but they do not
approach the popularity of the first ones. The famous 'Post Office
Mauritius' became a philatelic legend. All in all some fourteen copies
of the orange-red stamp and twelve of the deep-blue have survived.
The rarest of rarities are, of course, entire letters and covers bearing
the first stamps of Mauritius. One of these even exists franked with
both values, the Penny and Twopenny. This letter was sent to the
address of M. Lurguie at Bordeaux in France. For many years it
remained in the collection of tobacco king Maurice Burrus in Switzerland. Four years after his death this letter was sold, in 1963, in
a Robson Lowe auction in London, for the handsome sum of £28,000.

The greatest Mauritius sensation, however, came five years later.
Alfred F. Lichtenstein was one of the most famous philatelists of our
time. He had a number of outstanding items in his collection including
rare 'Post Office Mauritius' stamps. He left his collection to his
daughter Louise Boyd Dale, who continued his work and built up the
Mauritius section. She died in 1967, and on 21 October 1968 the
Mauritius collection came up for sale at H. R. Harmer's, Inc., in
New York.

It was expected that the most beautiful item of the collection,
a cover bearing two copies of the One Penny orange-red, would fetch
a high price. The result of the sale was a surprise and, for the whole
world of philately, an all-time record — $380,000! The reason for
this was that the two stamps on the cover are really superb, in perfect
condition, with wide margins and unbelievably fresh colours. Almost
all the other 'Post Office Mauritius' stamps are damaged to some
extent, or cut to the frame lines.

2 Highly-prized
cover bearing
two Penny *Post
Office Mauritius*
stamps.

8

When a 'Post Office Mauritius' stamp goes on sale something is bound to happen, something which belongs to the legend of famous stamps. The bidding for the unique cover was very keen, with jumps in the bidding going from $5,000 to $10,000 and finally to $20,000. Five competitors were in the race: the Raymond H. Weill Co. of New Orleans, Stanley Gibbons Ltd of London, Renato Mondolfo of Italy, Robert Siegel of New York and the auctioneer bidding on behalf of Giulio Bolaffi of Italy. Only two of these fought right to the end — Mr Michael of Stanley Gibbons and Mr Roger Weill.

Mr Weill, so the story goes, is supposed to have informed the auctioneer that he would be bidding as long as his pencil was raised. Mr Michael, on the other hand, told Mr Bernard Harmer, who was conducting the sale, that he would enter the race at a certain figure (his assistant would be bidding before this), and as long as his pencil pointed downwards he was bidding. When the bidding reached $280,000 Mr Michael's agent dropped out and Mr Harmer in the excitement of the moment overlooked the previously arranged agreement and knocked down the cover to Mr Weill. Mr Michael protested politely, and the auctioneer accepted his objection. 'No wonder one gets a little nervous when a quarter of a million is involved', he said.

And so the bidding continued, a duel between two giants. When Mr Weill offered $380,000, Mr Michael sadly shook his head. 'Going, going, gone' — the hammer fell, and the Raymond H. Weill Co. was the new owner of the precious letter and the two Mauritius stamps. After the sale one of the journalists present asked Mr Weill if he did not mind that in the end he had to pay an extra $100,000 for the letter when it had been already knocked down to him at $280,000.

3 The only existing cover franked with both *Post Office Mauritius* values.

'Oh, we don't mind paying for nice stamps', was the answer.

Mauritius is a synonym for the most famous stamps, but they are not the rarest by any means. Philately knows of other rarities. Only one copy of the One Cent British Guiana stamp of 1856 is known, while there are less than a dozen of the Two Cents Hawaiian 'Missionary' stamps in existence.

But is the idea really to own the most valuable stamp? Only a handful of philatelic rarities exist, but there are millions of ardent philatelists who know well enough that they will never possess these superb rarities. Why, then, do people collect stamps?

Similarly, why do young people engage in sport? Richard Fosbury of the United States cleared 7' 4¼" in the high jump at Mexico; David Hemery of Great Britain won the Gold Medal in the 400 metres in 48.1 seconds. Thousands of young people run, jump and throw day after day on sports fields all over the world, although they know very well that Fosbury's style and Hemery's speed are out of their reach. They practise their sport because it is good for the health, because they love to pit their strength against their competitors', because it expands their lungs and hardens their muscles; above all they do it because it gives them pleasure.

The same applies to philately. Many learned papers have been written about philately broadening man's horizon, bringing people together, widening the knowledge of geography and history, botany and zoology, science and technology, about teaching collectors to be systematic, patient, industrious and tidy.

But there is one more essential fact to be mentioned — philately is a hobby, an obsession, a science, a study, recreation and fun.

In short — philately is pleasure!

I. THE BIRTH OF THE POSTAL SERVICE – STAMPS AND PHILATELY

The earliest form of communication was the spoken, whispered, shouted word. People knew from the beginning of time that a man on his own cannot survive, that he needs help to hunt deer, a friend in his fight for survival, a comrade to build his home. And the spoken word became the link between individuals, the cement of society.

The human voice, though, has its limits. A call will carry far, even across a river, but it cannot carry across a mountain. And so the messenger was born. Whenever a few members of the tribe killed a deer and could not manage it on their own, they simply sent someone for help. The messengers carried good news and bad news; they very often saved their tribe, or their family. The right to send a messenger was naturally the prerogative of the leader and ruler. Since their task was sometimes vitally important the messengers became persons of great respect. No wonder the ancient Greeks promoted a messenger into a god — everybody knows about Hermes, the divine messenger with the winged heels.

HEMERODROMES

The strongest, fastest young runners were chosen to become messengers. They covered fantastic distances and delivered their messages in an unbelievably short time. Probably the most famous was the Greek messenger of Marathon. He covered the distance to Athens in such a short time that he only managed to call 'We are victorious . . .' before he fell and died exhausted. Even today the Marathon course over a distance of 42,195 metres (over 26 miles) is one of highlights of the Olympic Games.

These runners were called Hemerodromes in ancient Greece. It is said that one of them, the Cretan Philonides, who served King Alexander, covered the distance from Elis to Sikyon, being 480 stadia (one stadium equal to about 202 yards), in nine hours. When the Persian army of King Darius invaded Greece the Athenians sent the Hemerodrome Phidippos for help to Sparta. He covered the distance of 1,200 stadia (almost 138 miles) in one day and one night only. The runners took light arms and the barest essentials with them. Historians write about Ladas, one of the messengers serving Alexander the Great, who ran so fast that his feet left hardly discernible foot-marks in the sand.

A messenger had to overcome all sorts of hardships and dangers on his journey. No wonder that it is written in an Egyptian manuscript dating back to the twenty-fourth century BC: 'A messenger, before he starts on his errand to foreign lands, leaves his property to his children out of fear of the Asians and of wild beasts.'

The place of the foot messenger was soon taken by faster messengers — on horseback and on camels; swimmers were used and messengers in boats, depending on what was needed and the conditions of the route.

HOW A MESSAGE WAS KEPT SECRET

Almost at the same time as writing was discovered the first written message was created — the letter. A runner could mix up or forget important parts of the oral message, but a written message always remained the same, exact and eloquent. No doubt the use of written messages was supported by the fact that writing was a great art known only to a select few. Whereas the messenger knew the oral message and could always give it away, a written message was a secret kept from an illiterate man, as long as it did not fall into enemy hands.

Very soon the problem arose of how to keep the message a secret, how to make it impossible for the enemy, even if he should get hold of the letter, to decipher its contents. In ancient times people had already devised very effective ways. In Greece, for instance, they picked a suitable slave and had his head shaved. The message was written on his skull. The growing hair soon covered the writing and during the long journey his hair grew longer and thicker. When the messenger reached his destination it was only necessary to shave the 'letter' and read the message. This method had one more advantage — the slave could not read what was written on his own head.

Another widely used method is described by Plutarch. When Sparta sent a military leader or commander of the fleet to the wars a pair of sticks was made of exactly the same diameter and

4 Egyptian runner delivering a message.

length. These sticks were called *skytales*. One stick remained in Sparta, and the other stick was taken by the commander. When it was necessary to send a letter, a long, thin papyrus leaf was wound around the stick, one ring closely touching the other. The message was then written along the length of the stick in such a way that every letter was on a separate ring of the papyrus. After finishing the first line, the next was written underneath in the same way. Then the leaf was taken off the stick and sent to the field commander. Nobody could read this secret letter unless he had exactly the right stick on to which the leaf had to be wound.

Letters were written on all sorts of material — on papyrus and clay tablets, on bones, stones, splinters, wood and bark. Five thousand years ago in China, later in ancient Mexico and Peru and, until fairly recently, in some Indian and Negro tribes, knot letters were used. The knot letter usually consisted of a main strap from which secondary straps hung down with knots of all shapes and sizes. Each one of the secondary straps represented a certain code. Details were expressed by the colour of the straps, their winding, and, of course, by the knots themselves. Right up to the end of the last century such knot records were used in Peru, where they were called *quipu*. They were used for recording heads of cattle, for instance. The first secondary thread would represent horses, the second horned cattle, the third sheep, and so on. The Incas though, used the quipus for much more important purposes — for sending information about the enemy, for example. The red colour might mean soldiers, the yellow gold, the white silver, the green corn. Every single knot would mean ten, a double knot one hundred and a treble knot one thousand. In the public offices of every Inca town special officials were appointed who could tie quipus and decipher knot messages.

In Assyria *clay tablets* were used for writing. The letters were scratched into the clay surface and the tablets baked. Since the pressure was always stronger when a line was started the typical wedge of cuneiform writing appeared. After baking, the tablets were stored. In Greece, and especially in ancient Rome, tablets covered with a layer of wax were used. A stylus was used for writing. Longer entries or letters were written on two or three joined tablets. Two joined tablets were called a *diptychon*.

At the same time, though, they used *papyrus* in Greece and Rome, too. Papyrus, being the most suitable material for letter writing, soon ousted all other materials. The invention of papyrus is some five thousand years old and comes from ancient Egypt; it was produced from a sort of reed growing in abundance in the Nile Delta. The inner part of the stalk was cut into long, thin slices. The slices were crossed in layers, and by pressing and beating they were joined into thin sheets. The natural juice of the plant served as glue. For writing on papyrus a sharpened piece of reed was used, and also a special black, red or green ink.

In India palm leaves were widely used as writing material, and were so common that the British post accepted *palm letters* for forwarding during the last century. The written letter was not stuck down, but closed with the help of another piece of palm leaf tied across it.

The place of papyrus was later taken by *parchment*, invented

5 A *skytales* stick, used for confidential messages. A strip of papyrus was wound onto the stick and the message written horizontally along it. The papyrus was then detached and sent by messenger to the recipient who possessed a stick of identical diameter.

in the second century BC. Historians tell us that a great rivalry existed between the largest library of the past, in Alexandria, and the library in the town of Pergamon in Asia Minor. The Alexandrians used deceitful means. They arranged for all shipments of papyrus from Egypt to Pergamon to be stopped in order to disable the competing library. No papyrus — no books. But the librarians of Pergamon did not give up. They took animal hides, soaked them, removed all traces of meat and hair, stretched and dried them. A new material for writing was thus discovered — parchment, named after the city of Pergamon. Compared with papyrus, parchment had the advantage that it was more durable and one could write on both sides. On the other hand, it was more expensive.

We could not imagine life today without paper. It was invented in AD 105 in China by Ts'ai Lun, who later became minister of agriculture. The knowledge of paper was for many centuries restricted only to China. When the Arabs took Samarkand in 751, they learned from Chinese artisans how to make paper and the new material became used in the Middle East. Paper came to Europe much later. The first paper mills in Central Europe were built as late as the fourteenth century. The first paper mill in Germany, for instance, was built in 1390 in Nuremberg by Ulman Stromeir.

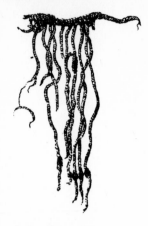

6 A *quipu* or knot letter. Each strand and knot had a prearranged significance.

SEMIRAMIS AND KYROS

Rulers and military commanders soon realized the importance of the fast and safe delivery of messages. Therefore they took great care to organize an efficient body of messengers. Especially in times of war, when the ruler had to leave his capital, it became most important for him to have accurate information, and to be able to direct and rule by written instructions. The first mail routes therefore came into existence. In ancient China a mail route of about a thousand miles existed along the Yangtze-Kiang river. The runners carried a little bell around their neck so that people could be warned of their approach. They were called tshien-fu, strong men, and they were able to cover up to seventy miles a day. Letters were transported along the Chinese rivers, too, on boats and junks. To keep the letters dry they were wrapped in oiled paper.

When Semiramis, the legendary queen of Assyria who built

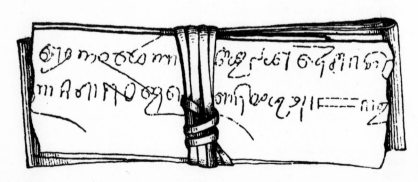

7 Letters written on palm leaves were commonly used in India as late as the nineteenth century.

the famous hanging gardens undertook her expedition into distant India with three million infantrymen, five hundred thousand soldiers on horseback and one hundred thousand chariots, she organized a very reliable courier service which ensured her communications with the Assyrian Empire.

An excellent courier service was established some five thousand years ago in ancient Egypt. In the course of excavations, drawings were discovered showing a messenger handing a letter to the Pharaoh. Instructions for the services of messengers survived, and even lists of their names.

The best courier service in America was built up by the Aztecs. The Spanish conquistadors found out during their campaign against Montezuma in Mexico that this ruler had a special group of runners who were attached to military units. Their task was to inform the Emperor as quickly as possible of the result of every battle and of all important events.

The delivery of messages, mostly oral was not the only duty of Montezuma's runners. They also carried for the Emperor's table fruit, fish and other delicacies from the most remote corners of his land. The runners adapted their behaviour according to the kind of message they were carrying. When they brought news of a victorious battle their hair was tied with red ribbons, they wore a white scarf around their waist, while in the left hand they carried a shield, and a sword in the right hand. When the messenger brought news of a lost battle his hair was dishevelled, he never said a word to anyone on his way, but proceeded to the Emperor to kneel before him and tell him the bad news.

We can see that everywhere, when the organization of the State reached a certain level, it became necessary to construct a courier service in some form.

In this connection there was one ruler of the ancient world who took special care to organize his postal courses and routes. It was King Kyros II, who ruled approximately 558—29 BC and founded the vast Persian Empire. His kingdom had become so large that the speed of runners was no longer good enough. Therefore Kyros introduced a much faster service — horses. The Greek historian Xenophon writes that the King first of all ascertained what distance a horse could cover in a day without feeding. At such points he established stations where spare horses were available. A special official was appointed for every station. He accepted messages from mounted messengers and passed them on to the next one.

The courier service functioned day and night. Xenophon writes that a letter travelled faster than a crane could fly. The Persian mail routes crossed the whole of the country in all the most important directions, so as to make it possible to deliver messages to the royal seats at Susa, Ekbatan and Babylon. The postal relay stations were so well equipped that sometimes even the King used them personally. The whole courier network was a State institution. The Greeks adopted the Persian name of the system and called it *angareion*. Alexander the Great, the conqueror of Persia, kept the courier routes and used them for his own purposes.

8 Chinese messenger equipped for a long-distance journey.

CURSUS PUBLICUS

In Rome it was Caesar who adopted the Persian tradition of transmitting information with the help of mounted messengers. But a perfect organization of the State courier service was introduced only later, by the Emperor Augustus. Courier routes were established along the Roman roads, which were already in excellent condition. In addition to messengers on foot and on horseback, carriages were introduced into the service. All along the military roads stations were built manned by permanent garrisons of messengers, horsemen and carriage drivers. In addition there were spare horses and supplies of fodder and food. The whole establishment was called *cursus publicus* and the individual stations *mansio* or *statio*. Although it was a State institution it was not financed by the State. It was the duty of the villages nearest the station to supply horses, fodder and food.

What importance Augustus attributed to the cursus publicus is evident from the fact that he subordinated it to the commander of his personal guard. In the beginning the cursus publicus was available only to the Emperor and his stepsons, Tiberius and Drusus. Nobody else had the right to use the services of the messengers or travel with the carriages of the cursus publicus. For such a purpose a special, written authorization was necessary, a so-called *diplomata* which was issued by the Emperor only in cases of necessity.

As time passed the cursus publicus was improved and enlarged. But that was not all. Diplomata were issued in more and more cases. The travellers were not only transported free of charge, but in the stations they were also accommodated and fed without fee. It is obvious that the spoiled Roman dignitaries made extravagant demands. So it happened that the cursus publicus became a great and heavy burden on the unfortunate municipalities in the vicinity of the stations. In Rome they realized all these problems and many

10 An Egyptian messenger arrives at the Pharaoh's court. This drawing is about 3,500 years old.

16

3, 4

1 Examples of the postman's uniform through two centuries: a posta
messenger of 1640 (1); a Saxon postmaster of 1719 (2); a Hamburg—Lübeck
postilion of 1828 (3); and a royal Bavarian postilion of about 1850 (4).

◀ A postilion in the second half of the nineteenth century: full-dress uniform
(1) and service uniform (2). Wearing full-dress uniform, he uses his horn to
announce the stage-coach's arrival to watching villagers (3).

11 Roman messenger on horseback.

12 Mounted Roman messenger depicted on a modern French stamp.

an Emperor issued strict orders limiting the use of the cursus publicus, or rather limiting the misuse, but it did not help very much.

In the end Emperor Nerva exempted the Italian municipalities from the heavy burden of supplying the stations. It was such a relief that, for this special occasion, a commemorative coin was struck, a bronze sestertius.

STATIO POSITA IN . . .

Even the word 'post' dates back to Roman times. It became common use to say *statio posita in...*, the station (of the cursus publicus) situated at... This phrase was mutilated with the passing of time until only the word posita remained, and this was eventually changed into posta — post. The word post, in its present meaning, was used for the first time by Pope Honorius III in the thirteenth century, and at about the same time by the Castilian King Alphons X. Marco Polo, in his description of the Chinese courier service, used the expression 'poesta' too.

It is weil understood that in ancient times boats were already being used for the transportation of messages and letters. But it was the Romans who organized a regular ship mail. This was required by the size of the Roman Empire which embraced the whole of the Mediterranean. Small but fast sailing boats were put into the service of the cursus publicus. A mail line led from the

JOURNÉE DU TIMBRE 1963
1ᴱᴿ JOUR D'ÉMISSION

Courrier Romain

JOURNÉE DU TIMBRE 16.3.63 PARIS

JOURNÉE DU TIMBRE 16.3.63 PARIS

Editée par la Fédération des Sociétés Philatéliques Françaises

port of Ostia to Carthage; other lines led from Regia to Sicily, from Brundisium to Illyria and Greece. Boat services were established also in Constantinople, on the island of Rhodes and in Alexandria. From the Spanish port of Gades boat lines led to the coast of North Africa, and from Gessoriacum (Boulogne) to Britain. Naturally, in addition to special State ships, merchant ships sailing in the appropriate direction were used too.

POSTMEN IN MONKS' HABITS

The fall of the Roman Empire also meant the end of the cursus publicus, the most perfect postal network of ancient times. There followed a long period without any organized postal service. After all, the number of people who could read and write and who needed to send letters was very limited. Almost without exception they were influential and rich people. They could afford, if need be, to send a special messenger with a letter.

Only in Gaul were the remains of the Roman cursus publicus preserved. The ruler and the highest officials made use of obligatory services of the municipalities and stations for the transmission of their letters and also on their journeys. Charlemagne probably tried to revive the Roman Post. Some evidence has been discovered from which it is possible to deduce that he established postal lines leading from Auxerres in three directions: via Nevers, Limoges and southern France to Spain; through Autun and Lyons to Italy, and via Paris and Aachen to Germany.

In the Middle Ages monasteries became the centre of literature, and soon they felt the necessity to establish mutual connections. The monasteries used mendicant monks and special messengers for their courier service, and for the transmission of messages and letters. How developed this service was can be seen from the fact that some monasteries went so far as to build special accommodation for travelling monks.

hie bringt man de apt botschaft von
ein dors lag am zürich seiw hiek ze
vänie vn oselb apt begit sat memra
tzehã iime doll die uuige ze lere.

15 In the Middle Ages a courier service grew up among the monasteries of Europe.

The development of the old universities and their growing importance also soon required a courier service. First of all, contacts were needed between different universities, and an exchange of information; secondly, some of the students who were sons from the highest levels of society kept up contacts with their homes, and in this way the messenger service of universities came into existence. The best service was organized by the University of Paris. The students were grouped into four sections according to their countries of origin. Every section elected its own messengers (*messagers*). The messengers had to take an oath, and a chief messenger was in charge of the rest. The messagers had their own brotherhood, and their patron saint was St Carolus. The services of the university messengers and of travelling monks were naturally used by private persons too. The network of university messengers existed right up to the eighteenth century.

WHO WAS THE FIRST TO BLOW THE HORN?

With the great development of the towns in the Middle Ages, with the growth of crafts and the importance of trade, the need for fast links between towns became imperative. The forming of courier services was undertaken by the town administration on the one hand, and by all sorts of corporations on the other. According to surviving documents Strasbourg, for instance, was, as far back as the twelfth century, obliged to place at the bishop's disposal a group of twenty-four runners. A document from 1443 states that the Chief Scrivener of the town was in charge of three runners. They were issued special containers in which to carry letters. In 1484 Strasbourg employed three chief messengers and twenty-one assistant messengers.

The city messengers carried the mail of the citizens but not the letters of the Emperor or the knights. In Cologne, for instance, a special servant always informed the merchants and the general public of the day and hour that a messenger would leave for Brabant, or for central or southern Germany, to give them time to prepare the letters the messenger would carry on his way.

16 Illustration from the sixteenth-century Melantrich Bible showing the arrival of a messenger.

Documents about messenger services of many towns are in existence.

The postal services of the towns developed mainly in the fourteenth century. In those times well-functioning messenger services existed in many towns, for instance in Leipzig, Vienna and Prague. Prague can boast of a special institution — a Jewish postal service. It was introduced on the basis of a request by the Council of the Jewish quarter, Josefov. The head of a Jewish postal collection service was named; he had two Jewish assistants and a Christian assistant for Saturdays. In additions to the normal postal rates he was entitled to charge an additional *kreuzer* for every letter. This was his salary and also that of the assistants. He did not receive any other payment. It is not known when this Jewish post was founded, but a document exists, dated 1757, according to which, after the death of Breynel Taussig, the head of the service, this office was to be given to his widow. In the Jewish State Museum of Prague a painting is exhibited showing the organization of the Prague Ghetto. It also shows a Jewish messenger from Prague on horseback. This figure appears on an Israeli stamp and miniature sheet of 1960.

Some of the guilds organized their own postal services in the Middle Ages; in Germany, for instance, this was done mainly by the butchers. Very often they travelled to buy cattle, not only to the surrounding villages but further afield. People started to use their services for the carrying of mail. In return the butchers were exempted from the payment of communal rates. By joining the individual routes of the butchers, a continuous network emerged, covering a territory of considerable size. The butchers always announced their arrival and departure from the villages by blowing a horn; this is the derivation of the post horn, a symbol inseparable from our image of the stage-coach and the postilion in Europe. To be able to blow the horn well was just as much one of the requirements of a good stage-coach driver as was the ability to master his horses and to drive speedily and safely.

17 Fifteenth-century messenger.

18 Messenger c. 1500.

19 A messenger from Basle, fifteenth century.

A LANTERN SHOWED THE WAY

Postal services were developing in other parts of the world.

A very reliable messenger service existed in Japan. Usually two messengers were sent out. The first runner carried a lantern on a bamboo pole. The lantern not only served to light the road at night but also as a signal from the Emperor's messenger. It was a warning for everybody to clear the road. Behind the first messenger came the second runner, who carried a box with the letters on a pole on his back. When the message was extremely urgent only one runner was sent out and he carried the letter in a cleft stick. Arriving at the courier station he handed the stick to the next runner, who continued. A similar method of transporting a letter — in a cleft stick — was also used in Africa.

By the seventh century the caliphs of Baghdad already had a wide courier network. Towards the end of the ninth century there was the astonishing number of 930 stations in service along the most important roads. Messengers mounted on horseback or on camels could cover a distance of 125 to 190 miles in twenty-four hours. Contrary to all other State postal services of those days the courier service of the caliphs was quite remarkable in so far as it

20 German manuscript describing the life and work of a messenger.

21 Prague postman of 1786.

22 Israeli miniature sheet of 1960 showing a Jewish messenger from Prague, where a special Jewish postal service was introduced.

also accepted letters and messages from private persons. The runners and horsemen of other postal services did take private letters and messages in some cases, but only secretly and risking heavy punishment.

THE ENTERPRISE OF THE THURN AND TAXIS FAMILY

The greatest credit for the development of a modern postal system in Europe, which later spread to the whole world, must go to the Thurn and Taxis family. When Emperor Maximilan I of Austria felt that it had become absolutely necessary for him to have permanent and reliable communications with all the distant parts of his Empire, the Italian nobleman Francesco de Tassis, called Torriani, offered to take care of the carriage of the Emperor's letters from Vienna to the Netherlands free of charge. In exchange he asked for the granting of a privilege of the exclusive use of this service for himself and his heirs. The postal route was opened on 18 January 1505, and the imperial privilege was granted in 1516.

The first route led from Vienna to Brussels. Very soon Tassis stretched his routes from Brussels to France and Spain, and from Vienna to Milan, Mantua, Venice and Rome. In due course subsidiary routes were linked to these main connections. Following the lines of the Roman cursus publicus, stations were established in the cities and their managers had to have horses ready and were responsible for the correct passage of the letter from one messenger to the other.

The descendants of Francesco de Tassis, who later changed their name to Thurn and Taxis, extended their postal network and tried to monopolize the postal service. Many rulers of the small German principalities through which the Taxis postal routes passed welcomed this service. Very often they tried to get their country included in the service. But there were others who had their own

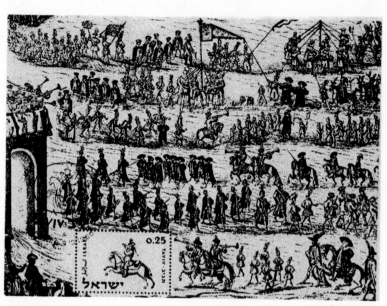

postal service and who derived an income from it. Therefore they resisted the Taxis postal routes. The Thurn and Taxis family fought against the postal services of the towns and guilds. Very often blood was shed and messengers were held up and killed.

In the end the Taxis family succeeded in establishing a continuous postal network which was their monopoly. Towards the end of the sixteenth century this network covered almost the whole of continental Europe. As late as the end of the nineteenth century, when well organized postal services of the individual countries were in existence, the postal empire of Thurn and Taxis covered a territory of over twenty-five thousand square miles, with a population of about four million. In 1867 Prussia finally bought the remaining rights of the Thurn and Taxis family, and their postal network, which had existed for 362 years, disappeared.

On the territory of Austria proper the postal service was in the hands of another family of noblemen — the Paars.

The Thurn and Taxis postal service lasted till 1867, in other words right up to the age of stamps, and therefore classical stamps of Thurn and Taxis can be found. They are most remarkable, as they were not issued by a country but by the postal service of a family of noblemen.

Postal services proved to be a very profitable business and their owners made a huge profit. No wonder, therefore, that in some countries postal services were sold or hired out for fantastic sums of money. In France, for instance, the postal service was leased to

23 Merchants' messenger from Berlin, about 1800.

24 Mounted postal courier.

25 Japanese messengers sometimes worked in pairs, the first carrying a lantern on a bamboo pole.

22

a certain Lazar Patin in 1668 for £1,200,000 per annum. One hundred years later the sum paid for the lease of the postal service had reached £12,000,000 a year.

POSTILIONS AND DILIGENCES

Postal messengers and riders wore special uniforms so that people could recognize them from a distance. The towns started this custom in the Middle Ages. They dressed their messengers in the town's colours. The uniforms of mail runners and postilions became more and more elaborate and colourful. Their purpose now was not only to show the function of the postal messenger, but also the power and importance of his master.

The Taxis postal service at first dispatched messengers on horseback along its lines, but very soon all sorts of carriages were introduced. These carriages were improved all the time, until they achieved the appearance of the well known stage-coach, also called diligence. The post took care not only of the transportation of messages and letters but of travellers and luggage as well.

In those unsettled times travelling by postal stage-coach was anything but a pleasure. The ride itself was tiring, and the stations where the travellers spent the night were in many cases primitive and badly equipped. The post was continually threatened by hold-ups due to weather and highwaymen. The roads, especially during the Thirty Years' War (1618—48), and for a long time after the war, were extremely unsafe on the Continent. Stage-coaches and postal messengers were not only a prey for robbers and highwaymen but also for marauding bands of soldiers and deserters. Many an officer 'added to his income' in this profitable way.

The kings, princes and townspeople were well aware of this

26 African messenger carrying a letter in a cleft stick.

27 Camels were a fast and reliable means of transport for the vast courier network set up by the Caliphs of Baghdad.

28 A fine example of letter writing, executed by Ferdinand Ernst Wallenstein in 1651.

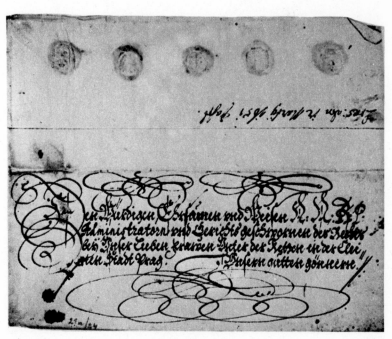

danger, and had to bear the disadvantages of disrupted transportation and communications. Many attempts were made to make the roads safe again, but it was a long time before the stage-coaches were reasonably reliable. One of the methods introduced was that of armed escorts. Towards the end of the Middle Ages an escort was almost the rule. But there were many cases when the escort itself turned into a band of highwaymen.

These were not the only difficulties that regular stage-coach lines

29 Lamoral of Taxis, Imperial Postmaster General from 1615 to 1624.

30 Cover bearing Thurn and Taxis stamps.

31 A French post office during the reign of King Louis XV.

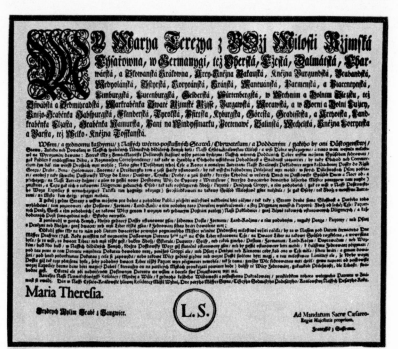

32 Edict of Maria Theresia which in 1750 raised the permitted weight of items for mailing from eight to twenty pounds.

33 Prussian postilion of 1715

34 German postilion of 1871

had to overcome. It was towards the end of the seventeenth century that an English Member of Parliament stated in the House of Commons: 'If someone suggested a regular stage-coach service by which he would carry us in seven days to Edinburgh and in the same time back again, wouldn't we send such a man straight to the madhouse?' But hardly fifty years passed and a stage-coach line was running between London and Edinburgh, and this journey, a distance of three hundred and fifty miles as the crow flies, took exactly the seven days.

Another opponent of the stage-coach declaimed against it thus: 'It cannot be healthy for anyone if he has to crawl out of his bed one or two hours before sunrise to board a stage-coach. With the greatest of speed they carry him till late at night from one place to another. And so he sits all day long in the stage-coach, in summer half choked by dust and heat, in winter half frozen and hungry. And finally in torch-light he reaches the public house. The next day they load him again into the stage-coach so early in the morning that he does not even get time to have his breakfast. Is it good for a man's health or his business if he travels with sick people or crying children; if he has to endure all sorts of moods, if he is bothered by stinking smells and crippled by boxes and bales? Is it good for your health when they overturn the stage-coach on bad roads, when you have to wade through mud and sit in the cold and wait till they bring new horses to drag the stage-coach away? Is it good for your health to travel in rotten carriages till the axle breaks, or the wheel? And then one has to wait for three or four hours or for half a day and one has to travel all night to make up for the lost time.'

The author of this outcry describes very vividly what it was like to travel by stage-coach in those days, but he paints his picture in colours too dark. That was at the beginning of the eighteenth century. By then stage-coaches had already proved their usefulness,

36 Austrian postal 'express' of 1820.

35 Viennese post coach of 1812.

38 Seventeenth-century hold-up.

37 Spanish post near Toledo.

39 Highwaymen attacking a stage-coach.

and nobody could stop the increase in their use. Stage-coaches became the first reliable means of transport available, not only to kings and the rich, but to the general public. They were means of transportation which, on the basis of the technical development of those days and due to the state of the roads, ensured the fastest possible communication.

ON WATER AND ON LAND

Right from the very beginning the transportation of postal items and of persons had to be adapted to suit natural conditions. In Peru, for instance, a 'swimmer post' existed. The most reliable means of communication in the jungle was by river. The postal messenger tied the letters to his head with something like a turban and went

on his way, and, so as not to get tired too soon, he held on to a log in the water.

In India postmen used bicycles as far back as the last century. In France, in the Landes and the Gironde, where the sandy ground is in many places covered by high heather, rural postmen were issued with stilts. In the Vendée postmen were given long poles to enable them to vault across the many channels and ditches.

In the desert regions the camel was as important a means of transportation as the horse was in other parts of the world. Camels were used mainly in the Middle East, but also in Mongolia and China. Towards the end of the nineteenth century, the Turkish post in Baghdad used a special handstamp for mail carried by camel. In Indo-China postal carriages were drawn by buffaloes and zebus.

Stage-sledges took the place of stage-coaches in winter. In Siberia, Canada and other countries of the north, dog and reindeer teams were used.

The development of the postal network and postal services is very closely related to the development of transportation. The invention of the railway soon led to a complete revolution of the

40 German stage-coach on a narrow mountain road.

41 Arrival of the post in a French town.

42 French two-wheeled post carriage of 1825.

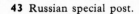

44 Tricycle transport in Paris, 1840.

45 Rumanian post coach
depicted on a stamp . . .

46 . . . and the postilion.

postal system, just as in recent times the development of air transport has done.

Special postal wagons were included in the trains, which meant
a much faster delivery of mail. Letters and other postal items were
sorted during the voyage, and a great deal of time was saved this
way.

Post offices were in due course opened on board large steamers
sailing on regular lines, especially on boats crossing the Atlantic.

47 Turkish carriage of 1840.

48 Swimmer post in Peru. Messages were carried in a form of turban and the swimmer supported himself on a log.

49 Nineteenth-century bicycle postman in India.

'ORPHANS PREFERRED'

Fast communications between the east and west coasts of the United States were soon of vital importance. The journey by ship from New York to San Francisco took months before the Panama Canal was opened. The journey across the continent was also very long and dangerous. The only possible solution was the building of a railway across the continent from ocean to ocean. This need became most urgent when the period of great economic development began after the Civil War. And there was one more fact to be taken into account — the discovery of gold.

One after the other the gold-digger towns sprang up in the West. Their inhabitants had come from afar and obviously they wanted to keep up their contacts with home. The so-called Express

Companies came to their assistance. They supplied the gold diggers with everything they needed, from food and clothing to newspapers, arms and ammunition. They accepted the gold for safe deposit in a bank and they also took care of the mail. A normal stamp had to be put on every letter, but, in addition, the Express Company charged extra for taking the letter to the nearest post office or for its delivery into the hands of the gold prospector. This service was handled by many individuals but also by large companies, like, for instance Wells, Fargo and Co. The payment of the extra charge was at first marked on the letter by hand; later the companies introduced handstamps and even their own stamps and postal stationery such as envelopes and postcards.

Even so, it took a letter from one to three months to get from New York to California. The time of travel depended upon the route, whether via Panama, Nicaragua, Mexico or across the continent. That was the reason why the Express Company Russell,

50 French postman on stilts.

51 German postman in the shallows *(Watten)* of the North Sea.

52 Post rider in Indochina.

53 Two-wheeled cart of the Indian postal service.

54 Sino-Russian camel post of 1860.

56 Handstamp of the Baghdad camel post.

57 Zebu-drawn post carriage in Indochina.

58 Stage-sledge crossing Mont Cenis in 1864.

59 Dog team carrying post in Russia, 1859.

60 Dog post in Hudson Bay, 1873.

61 Russian reindeer post, 1859.

62 Railway sorters at work in an early travelling post office.

63 Mechanization of postal transport, East Germany, 1963.

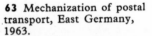

Major and Waddel introduced a special service of postal horsemen. The route was between the railway terminal at St Joseph in Missouri to Sacramento in California. The mail arrived at St Joseph on a train coming from the east coast of the USA, and from Sacramento it travelled by boat to San Francisco. This service of postal horsemen was called the Pony Express. The riders covered the distance of some two thousand miles in about nine days. The record was held by Pony Bob Haslan, whose time was seven days and seventeen hours.

The ablest and most daring young men were chosen as riders for the Pony Express. A poster from those times offered the job to slim young men up to eighteen years of age. 'Orphans Preferred' read the poster. The journey was not only very hard but dangerous, too. The route led through wilderness, and through Indian territory. The rider carried between twenty and thirty-five pounds of mail in four leather bags strapped to his saddle. Every ten to fifteen miles there was a station with fresh mustangs. The horseman had

64 Stage-coach held up by bandits in Colorado.

III The world's first stamps, the British Penny Black and the Twopenny Blue. The Penny Black 'on piece', that is, on part of an envelope, has an attractive red cancellation (1), the other a rare yellow cancellation (2.) Also shown are a strip of five Twopenny Blues 'on cover', that is, an entire envelope (3) and another envelope with Twopenny Blues and one Penny Red, a later issue (4).

1, 2

3

4

IV These early stamps of the German States have no great rarity value, but each of the examples shown here would be a valuable acquisition because of the excellent margins, cancellation, etc.

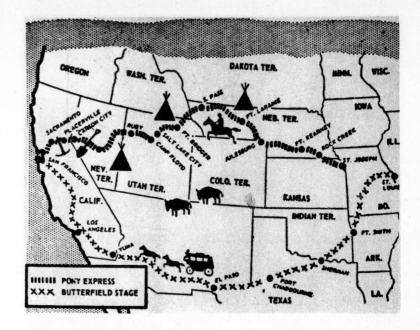

65 Route of the Pony Express across the North American continent.

66 'Orphans preferred', from a Pony Express recruiting poster.

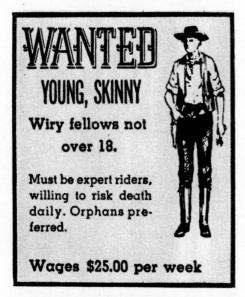

67 US stamp commemorating the centenary of the Pony Express.

only two minutes to change saddles, for the speed was murderous. And for such a job he was paid only twenty-five dollars a week.

But the postal rates were high. A letter weighing up to half an ounce was five dollars, every additional half ounce another dollar.

The most famous rider of the Pony Express was William F. Cody, who started on the route at the age of fifteen. In the Civil War he fought on the side of the Union as a scout. In later years, when he hunted buffaloes for the workers building the trans-continental railway, he was given the nickname which made him famous all over the world — Buffalo Bill.

The Pony Express existed for a period of eighteen months only. The service was discontinued in October 1861 when the construction of a transcontinental telegraph was finished. And when the railway cut across the continent the speedy delivery of mail was assured.

During the eighteen months of its existence the Pony Express carried some thirty-five thousand postal items. This is quite a number, but only a small part of them have survived a hundred years. Collectors owning letters carried by the Pony Express can congratulate themselves, not only because these items are valuable and in great demand, but also because they are the most interesting postal history documents of those times of great adventure.

THERE WERE CHEAPER WAYS THAN BY POST

The development of the post grew in different ways in different countries, always according to the local conditions. The transportation of messages and letters led to the birth of a postal service as we understand it today, only when this was required by the development of the country, the economic conditions, and the

growth of trade. As soon as the great importance of the postal service became evident it was taken over by the ruler or by the State. From modest, private beginnings a well organized service arose with its own staff, means of transportation and buildings.

Those who ran a postal service were doing all they could to make as large a profit as possible, be they private persons, rulers or the State. At first the charges for the delivery of letters was left to the discretion of the carrier and the means of the sender or addressee. Only much later did they develop into postal rates graded according to the weight of the letter and the distance. These rates naturally differed from country to country.

Up to the middle of the last century it was by no means cheap to send a letter. The post was a very profitable business and the users of postal services had to pay for it. People therefore looked for cheaper ways. Shortly before the introduction of stamps a survey was made in England. A merchant confessed that in 1836 he had received through the post 2,068 letters, but through other channels 5,861. Another citizen received 117 letters, but out of this number only seven had come through the State post. And it has to be borne in mind that in England the postal rates were not the highest by a long way. A letter sent a distance of about one hundred miles cost between four and nine pence, and for every additional hundred miles one penny extra.

The illegal mail service was handled mostly by cartmen. It must have been very profitable, as some of them made it their permanent business. One of these cartmen admitted confidentially that out of the twenty thousand times that he had violated the rules of the State monopoly of postal services, he had been caught only once. Practically everybody who undertook a journey took letters with them. This practice made their journey cheaper and sometimes they even made a profit. In England and in many other countries severe laws were passed aimed at stopping this practice, but to no avail. As long as the postal rates were high, people looked for cheaper ways.

The problems became even greater when it was necessary to send a letter abroad. It was practically impossible to pay the postage rate in advance. In many cases nobody could say which way the letter would travel, and the price was calculated according to the real distance the letter had covered. A flooded river or

69 Austrian postal rates of 1803.

a bridge torn away could result in the letter travelling an additional hundred miles. Moreover, whenever a letter had to cross frontiers — and there were a great number, especially in Germany, which was split into many tiny states — the postal rates became higher and higher, due to the transit charges. The postage was therefore almost always collected from the addressee.

An interesting story is told about Sir Rowland Hill, the father of postal reform in England. It is probably no more than a nice story, but it illustrates very well the conditions prevailing in the postal service in the thirties of the last century. It so happened that Rowland Hill was present somewhere in Scotland when the postman brought a letter for a peasant girl and asked for a shilling postage. The girl turned the letter over in her hands but in the end she returned it and refused to pay. When Hill learned that the letter was from the girl's brother he felt sorry for her and paid the shilling on her behalf. But instead of receiving thanks he was reproached. The girl opened the letter and showed him that it was empty, without any writing inside. She explained that she and her brother had agreed upon a secret sign on the reverse telling her that he was all right and doing well. The legend goes on to say that this event gave Rowland Hill the idea to propose a reform of the postal service. But this will be dealt with later.

70 Higher postal rates introduced by decree in Austria in 1808.

71 Title page of a booklet published in 1791 containing a collection of early postal stories.

THE POST DISCOVERS THE HANDSTAMP

The higher the number of items carried by the post, the greater the need became for records and order. In ancient times records of forwarded letters had been kept; the same became a necessity in modern times. It was no longer sufficient just to list the letters; they had to be marked with all sorts of service data, as, for instance, the place, day and hour of posting, the postage rate, and so on. This was done at first by handwritten remarks on the cover, and later by handstamp.

It has long been forgotten who invented the handstamp and where it was used for the first time. The oldest surviving handstamp comes from Venice and dates back to 1435. This handstamp was not printed in ink on the cover, but was embossed on the letter. It is quite possible that the Republic of Venice had accepted this invention from another Italian town.

Neither is it known for certain when handstamps using ink were first introduced. The oldest handstamp printed with ink on a letter also came from Italy in the year 1454. The Sforza family used a handstamp showing the coat of arms of the family surrounded by the text 'Corriere Mediolanum' (Post of Milan). In 1661 Henry Bishop introduced into England a circular handstamp with the month and the year. The London City Post, established by Robert Murray and shortly afterwards taken over by William Dockwra, also used handstamps in about 1680. The triangular handstamp bore the text 'Penny (Post) Paid', and in the centre a sign giving the post office where the letter was posted. Dockwra opened post offices in all London districts. Letters were accepted at the seven borough post offices, at the main office in Lyme Street and at four or five hundred mail collection stations. The London City Post showed such a profit, although the postage was so cheap, that the State did not want to miss the chance of ready income and took it over in 1698.

Postal handstamps were so successful that every postal service in the world accepted them in due course. In Austria-Hungary, for instance, a decree by the Postmaster General of 23 July 1781 ordered that all dispatched mail should be cancelled with a postal handstamp. In addition to the handstamp showing the name of the post office where it was posted another handstamp with the word *Franco* was in use for letters where the postage had been paid in advance.

In every country handstamps had their own special evolution. There are handstamps of every possible shape; mute handstamps without any text, elaborate handstamps, handstamps giving just the name of the town, other handstamps with the date and many additional facts and figures.

72 Sir Rowland Hill (1795—1879), the father of postal reform in England.

FRIEND OF LOVERS AND INSTRUMENT OF INFORMERS

There is one more postal innovation that should not be forgotten — the letter-box. It is not known where they were first introduced, but the first reliable documents referring to their existence come from Paris in 1653. It is related that these letter-boxes were an idea of the Marchioness of Longueville, the mistress of the Minister

73 William Dockwra's handstamp of 1680, used by the London City Post.

74 Handstamp of the London local post, 1683–1794. The letters inside the triangle mean: 'T' — the Temple post office, 'TH' — Thursday.

75 Letter with the handstamp 'Kremsier', dating back to the period before the invention of stamps.

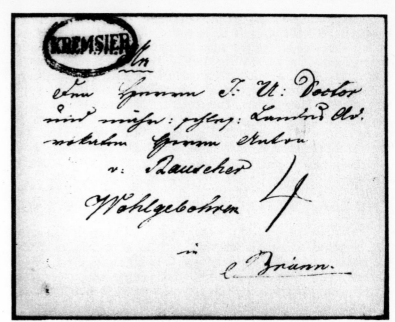

76 An attractive cover — Jamaica to Paris via London — with the appropriate handstamps.

Fouquet, the Postmaster General. In those days a decree was in force requiring that everyone who wanted to send a letter had to hand it in personally at the collection point in the rue St Jacques. The post officials had the right to verify that every letter contained only one sheet of paper. This, however, was not the real reason for their interest. A system of censorship existed, which served the purposes of the all-powerful Cardinal Mazarin, and which was unpleasant for many people, and not only for political reasons. In this way the censors could poke their noses into every love affair, and undoubtedly this was why the Marchioness of Longueville came up with her new idea and invented boxes into which the writer could throw a letter signed even with a false name.

In actual fact, it was not the Marchioness who invented the letter-box. She only copied an invention that had already existed in the sixteenth century in Florence and perhaps in other Italian towns. Boxes with slots for letters hung at the main entrance of all the large churches. They were called *tamburi*. Not only letters were posted here, but also anonymous denunciations addressed to the police.

When Frederic II, King of Prussia, invited French specialists to Berlin towards the end of the eighteenth century to assist him in the reorganization of the postal service, letter-boxes were put up in the streets of Berlin. They did not last for long. In Germany letter-boxes did not become a permanent fixture for another hundred years.

Letter-boxes were at first very simple, wooden boxes, later covered with metal plate. They were improved all the time. Inscriptions and all sorts of information about postal services appeared on them; they were painted and decorated, coats of arms were added, and so on. At the Cape of Good Hope, hollow trees served as letter-boxes. In the Wild West, the letter-boxes were sometimes put on high posts to enable the cowboy to post his letter comfortably without dismounting.

But even letter-boxes could become apples of discord in political struggles. When Elizabeth II ascended the throne in 1952, her initials appeared on the red pillar-boxes in the streets of the cities and villages of the United Kingdom — the letters E and R and the figure II. The Scottish Nationalists protested vehemently. Elizabeth I had not been Queen of Scotland; Scotland at that time was ruled by Mary Stuart. Therefore, the Nationalists contended, the present queen is Elizabeth I in Scotland, not Elizabeth II. More than one pillar-box fell victim to this controversy. The Scottish Nationalists blew them up with high explosives.

THE CLAPPER POST

The ever-widening postal network took better and better care of the carriage of mail from one town to another, from country to country. But there was one important sector which remained almost completely forgotten — the mail service inside the cities. The need for such a local service became more and more urgent in the large towns. A local post was therefore established in 1653 in Paris, in 1680 in London, and similarly in other large towns.

In Vienna the so-called Little Post was founded on 1 April 1772 by Josef Hardy. It took care of the delivery of mail within the city and within a three-mile radius of the capital. The postmen walking through the streets announced their approach with the help of a clapper, and this postal service came to be called the *Clapper Post*. Letters were collected and delivered up to six times a day. The postman printed on the letter handed to him a handstamp showing the date and the hour, and delivered it to the branch post office, which took care of its further delivery. Covers with the mark of the Clapper Post are very much in demand. They can be recognized by the interesting handstamps of the postmen and of the post offices.

Following the example of Vienna a 'Little Post' was established by the Belgian François Carcier in Prague, and later also in Graz. But these local posts did not prove very profitable for their private owners and, furthermore, their activities were interfering with the services of the State post, which eventually took over the private enterprises.

THE PREDECESSORS OF THE STAMP

In this connection it is worthwhile dealing in more detail with the local post of Paris. In 1653 King Louis XIV granted Renouard de Villayer the privilege to establish a local post on the territory of Paris. This postal service was remarkable not only for its letter-boxes; de Villayer introduced another novelty — the so-called *Billets de Port Payé* (Receipts of Postage Paid). They were a sort of sticker sold to the public. The sender of the letter covered the letter with the Billet de Port Payé, or affixed it in some other way. He himself marked the day, month and year of posting on the Billet. At the post office these covers were torn off so that they could not be used again. This cover was actually a predecessor of the postage stamp. It was not stuck to the letter itself, but was

77 Post box in use at the end of the seventeenth century.

78 Richly decorated post box of the nineteenth century.

79 Post box of about 1900.

80 Post box of the German post in Tangier before the First World War.

81 Post box of the Austro-Hungarian post.

a certificate of prepayment of the postage, which made it unnecessary for the sender to take the letter to the post office. It was quite sufficient to post a properly equipped letter in the nearest letter-box. Unfortunately not one of these Billets de Port Payé has survived. They disappeared in the same way as the letter-boxes, as soon as de Villayer's local post ceased to function. The letter-boxes reappeared in Paris much later, but this time they came to stay.

The predecessor of the adhesive stamp was the handstamp, of course. It was Dockwra, who had introduced handstamps in London in 1680, whose inscription stated that the postage of one penny had been paid. Later, special handstamps came into use in England, France and other countries, testifying that the postage had been paid. The handstamp either read *Franco* or P. P. (postage paid), or gave the sum of the postage paid. This handstamp was struck on the letter in addition to the handstamp with the name of the place of posting.

In Sardinia the postal monopoly was, in the last century, a very profitable monopoly and the King took great care to keep it like that. To make sure of an income, even from letters carried by private persons, special letter sheets were issued in 1819 on paper with a watermark showing an eagle with the Cross of Savoy. On the margin of the sheet was the text: '*Direzione Generale Delle Regie Poste. Corrispondenza autorizzata in corso particolare per pedoni ed altri occasioni.*' (General Management of the Postal Regalia. Correspondence permitted by private means through messengers or any other way.) In addition, on every sheet a special handstamp was struck giving the value of the charge —fifteen, twenty-five or fifty *centesimi*. These were not adhesives, of course, and in fact they were intended for letters not carried by the post.

In Germany, too, an interesting forerunner of stamps was in use. When, on 1 December 1827, the local post in Berlin resumed its functions, special postal receipt stamps were introduced. They were printed in sheets and numbered from one to a thousand. When a letter was posted they received the same handstamp as the letter. They represented a receipt for the posting of the letter and the payment of postage and were given to the sender. These receipts were not affixed to the letter. In actual fact they are forerunners of the certificates of posting for registered letters as we know them today.

The Greek charity stamps of 1831 and the Petrograd stamps for the acknowledgement of payment of the postage of 1839 also belong to this early category.

Philatelists call the period before the invention and use of postage stamps the *prephilatelic period*. This period lasted different lengths of time in different countries. It must be borne in mind that stamps were introduced gradually and not at once throughout the world. Letters from this period have a special charm and attraction. The older they are the more valuable they usually are, but even an inconspicuous letter might have a rare handstamp. Every collector of classical stamps is very proud of his stampless letters dating from the prephilatelic period, which he has succeeded in acquiring to enrich his collection. There are many specialists who devote their philatelic interest only to this most difficult sector.

82 Urban post box in Victorian London . . .

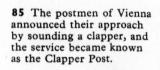

3 . . . and rural American ersion.

85 The postmen of Vienna announced their approach by sounding a clapper, and the service became known as the Clapper Post.

84 The Little Post, for local deliveries, founded in Vienna in 1772.

HOW THE FIRST STAMP WAS BORN

'The father of the postage stamp' — as the reformer of the British postal service, Sir Rowland Hill, is called — certainly deserves great credit for the issue of the first postage stamps, but the adhesive postage stamp was not his idea.

88 Letter with the handstamp of the post office (in Poland) and the handstamp 'Franco'.

89 'Franco' handstamps.

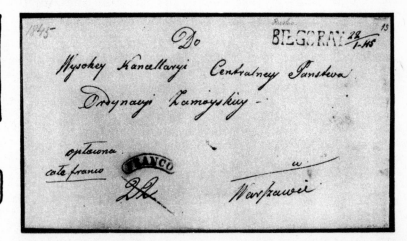

90 Cover with the handstamp 'Milano', where it was posted, and the handstamp 'P.P.'.

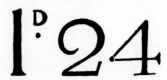

91 London handstamps (1840–9) stating the amount of postage paid.

92 French cover with the handstamp '25' stating the amount of postage paid.

First, let us look at England on the eve of the postal reform of 1840. The amount of postage was high; many people tried to bypass the State post, and postage rates were most complicated. The service lagged behind the general development of the economy. Voices were raised demanding a thorough reform of the post, and the introduction of a uniform letter rate of one penny. As far back as 1824, 1829, and 1836 Samuel Roberts, Member of Parliament for Conway, published documents recommending the introduction of a penny postage for letters. In 1834, the newspaper publisher Charles Knight suggested that the post should deliver newspapers for a common rate of one penny in wrappers with printed postage. He probably based his suggestion on the Sardinian letter sheets with the handstamp giving the value, which were in use from 1819 to 1836.

Postal reform became so urgent that in 1835 a special parliamentary commission was formed to deal with the problem. Although the commission published a number of papers the matter did not make any progress. In 1837 Rowland Hill published his famous paper *Post Office Reform, Its Importance and Practicability*. He suggested the introduction of a uniform postage rate of one penny for a letter weighing up to half an ounce for the whole of the United Kingdom. The postage was to be paid in advance.

Hill's paper caused a sensation. The parliamentary commission was enlarged and Hill's proposal was accepted as a basis for discussions. Finally, in 1839, the proposal of a postal reform was accepted and presented to Queen Victoria for her signature. The reform should have come into force on 1 January 1840.

Rowland Hill's original idea was that letters would be posted in special covers which showed an imprint of the value. William Mulready was commissioned to design these covers. In the meantime James Chalmers (1782—1853), a printer from Dundee, and owner of a book-shop suggested the use of adhesive stamps. This idea was later incorporated by Rowland Hill in his postal reform.

It is worth mentioning that Chalmers was not the first to have had the idea of using adhesive stamps. In 1836 the Slovenian L. Kosir, assistant State accountant at Ljubljana, proposed to the government of Austria a simplification of the postal rates and the introduction of adhesive postage stamps for franking letters. The Vienna government rejected his proposal. Therefore Austria, which could well have been the first, introduced its first postage stamps as late as 1850, ten years after Great Britain.

Nobody had any idea how these adhesive stamps should look. For that reason the British Treasury announced in 1839 a public competition for the design of postage stamps. Some 2,600 entries were handed in and the Treasury awarded four first prizes of one hundred pounds each, but not one of the designs was fit for use; and so Rowland Hill himself had to set about the task. As his model he chose the beautiful commemorative medal by William Wyon with the portrait of Queen Victoria. He painted two rough designs of the stamps in watercolours and these were handed to Charles and Frederic Heath (father and son) for engraving. The stamps were printed by Perkins, Bacon and Co.

Thus the world's first stamps were born. Due to the delay with the design the stamps could not be issued on 1 January 1840 as intended, but both the Penny Black and Twopenny Blue came into use on 6 May 1840.

Naturally letters with the first stamps used on the first day of

93 Sardinian handstamp of 1819 giving the amount of postage.

94 Postal receipt stamp of the Berlin local post.

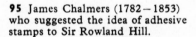

95 James Chalmers (1782—1853) who suggested the idea of adhesive stamps to Sir Rowland Hill.

96 The commemorative medal by William Wyon with the portrait of Queen Victoria, used by Hill for the first postage stamps.

97 Sir Rowland Hill's own rough designs for the stamps.

98 The first postage stamps were printed on this printing press.

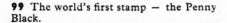

99 The world's first stamp — the Penny Black.

issue are rare, and the first *first day covers* are a gem of every collection for which high prices are paid. In 1967 a unique first day cover was offered for auction. It was a letter posted on 6 May, franked with a block of ten Penny Blacks. The most amazing thing about this letter is that it had been discovered only shortly before it went on sale. It had been forgotten for 127 years. It is little wonder the sale at Harmer's in London became a sensation; bidding was very keen and the cover fetched £4,700 although some of the stamps were creased.

Wednesday, 6 May 1840 was the birthday of postage stamps but it was not the first day of their use. About three letters are known with Penny Blacks cancelled on 2 May 1840, at Bath. How could this happen? The first day of use was 6 May, but since the stamps went on sale on that day all over the country they had to be sent to the post offices earlier. In some places the postmasters sold a few stamps before 6 May and it so happened that stamps were used four days before the fixed date. It is interesting that no covers exist with stamps posted on 3, 4 or 5 May.

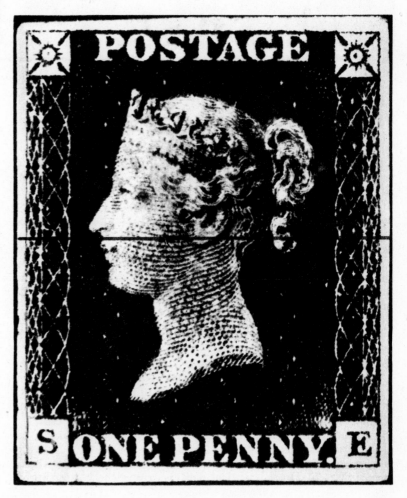

100 Block of eight Twopenny Blues.

WHAT DO THEY LOOK LIKE?

The first stamps were imperforate, of course. The perforating machine was invented much later, in 1847. They were printed in sheets of 240. This number is quite logical, there being 240 pence to a pound. A complete sheet of Penny Blacks, therefore, cost exactly one pound, and a sheet of Twopenny stamps two pounds. The stamps had no text showing the country of origin; it was not necessary, as these were the first stamps in the world. Besides, they were at first intended only for the prepayment of postage on British territory. Great Britain has kept this tradition of not giving the country's name and showing only the ruler's portrait up till the present day. This is the privilege of the country which gave the world, and philately, the first stamps. Above the profile of Queen Victoria is the text 'Postage' and on the bottom of the stamps is the value — 'One Penny' or 'Two Pence'.

The bottom corners of the stamp are interesting. In each horizontal row of twelve stamps the same letters are always in the bottom left-hand corner — in the first row of the sheet the letter A, in the second row the letter B, and so on through the alphabet; twenty different letters for twenty rows of twelve stamps each. In the bottom right-hand corner we find from left to right one letter of the alphabet after the other — A, B, C, D and so on. A horizontal pair, or strip of three, must have the same letter in the left-hand corner of each stamp, a vertical pair or strip in the bottom right-

101 One of the first First-Day covers — a Penny Black cancelled at Bath on 2 May 1840.

hand corner. It is thus possible to identify exactly the position of each individual stamp in the sheet. This fact led to specialists trying to reconstruct the original sheets. This is a very difficult task and it is not easy to find all the existing letter combinations from AA to TL; and with the growing interest in the oldest stamps it has become rather expensive, although the number of existing stamps of 1840 is fairly large.

THE FIND IN THE SHED

Neither the postmen nor the public using stamps in those days were particularly careful when cutting the stamps off the sheet. The space between the stamps was rather small and so it easily happened that the scissors cut a little into the stamps. Therefore all copies untouched by scissors are valued considerably more than carelessly cut stamps. That a stamp should not be damaged in any other way either is obvious. The larger the copy, including the margins, the higher its value. A horizontal or vertical pair has a higher value than two individual stamps. And the value of larger blocks goes up almost in a geometrical line.

Whole sheets have survived only in the National Postal Museum in London, where the original designs and trial prints are also kept. How valuable larger blocks are can be seen from this episode. In 1931 Major R. W. M. St Maur of Storer Park, Newton Abbot, found an envelope with a block of forty-three Penny Blacks in the carriage box of an old coach. In 1959 this outstanding philatelic item of 1840 was put up for sale in an auction in London. It fetched £4,400. More valuable than stamps removed from the envelopes are envelopes complete with stamps. In such cases not only the quality of the stamp and the preservation of the letter is important, but also the cancellations and other details.

Specialists distinguish eleven printing plates of the Penny Black and two plates of the Twopenny Blue. A number of very interesting plate defects and retouches are known. In some cases the print of the Twopenny Blue shines strongly through, so that the portrait of the Queen can be seen more or less distinctly on the reverse of the stamp. This is called an *ivory head*.

Special handstamps in the shape of a Maltese Cross were produced for the first stamps. According to instructions every stamp had to be cancelled individually. At first the colour used for the cancellations was red, but when it was discovered that the red handstamp could be removed and the stamps re-used, black cancellations were experimentally introduced in September 1840 in London, and from February 1841 black ink was used for cancellations everywhere. Nevertheless entirely different colours of the handstamp can be found. The postmasters had to do something when they ran out of ink for their pads, and so cancellations in blue, brown and other colours exist. The rarest is a yellow handstamp.

As a safeguard against forgeries, of which the postal authorities were very much afraid, the first stamps of the world were printed on paper with a watermark. It is a simple design of the small Royal Crown and one watermark always fits each stamp in the sheet.

102 A rare block of forty-three Penny Blacks which came to light in 1931.

THE MULREADY ENVELOPE

Rowland Hill had envisaged that the principal means of prepaying the postage would be by using Mulready's envelopes, but the general public was of quite a different opinion. Although the stamps were immediately accepted both because they proved useful and also because they were most attractive, the Mulready envelopes with their symbolic design proved a failure. Not only did people only use them to a limited extent, but they made fun of them. Very soon cartoons of the envelopes were in circulation. If by chance you should find such a cartoon, do not throw it away; it is very much sought after. In other words, even Mulready's envelopes experienced a rehabilitation of some sort as time passed. They are very popular with collectors of the classical period of stamp printing in Great Britain, postal history, and so on. The envelopes exist in two denominations — in black print with the imprinted value of one penny at the bottom (for a letter up to half an ounce) and in blue print for twopence (for letters up to one ounce).

Despite this setback Rowland Hill entered history as the man who laid the foundations of the tremendous development of modern postal services by introducing his proposal for a postal reform. For this he was greatly honoured. The Queen knighted him, and after his death he was buried in Westminster Abbey, side by side with the most famous men of England.

One of Rowland Hill's most important arguments in his proposal for a postal reform was that the introduction of cheap postage would lead to a great rise in the number of letters posted, and that the postal administration would thus benefit in the long run. At first his predictions did not come true. Whereas the General Post Office had, in 1839, a net profit of £1,634,000 this profit decreased in the first year after the introduction of the postal reform to £501,000. Not until 1874 did the GPO show a higher profit than in 1839. Nevertheless, the new system remained. The British public was satisfied, and nobody was permitted to touch it, for this reason: in 1839, the last year before the postal reform, the GPO forwarded altogether 75,9 million letters, but during the first year after the reform the number of letters rose to 168,7 million — more than twice as many! And so the postal reform, enforced by the evolution of Society, became a very important factor in the future of mankind.

Even so it took a long time for old customs and conservatism to be overcome, before people got used to prepaying all their mail with stamps. As late as 1850, ten years after the introduction of stamps, only about fifty per cent of all mail in England was posted

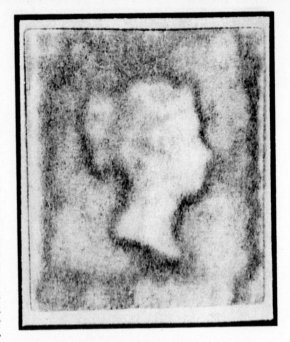

103 A so-called 'ivory head', in which the Queen's head shines through to the reverse side of the stamp.

104 Maltese Cross handstamp.

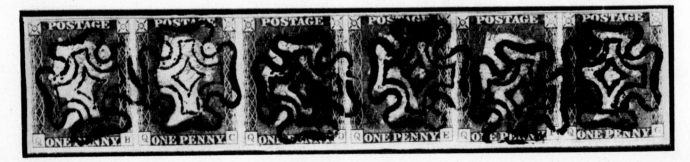

46

with stamps, forty-six per cent of all the mail was prepaid in cash at a post office counter, and the remaining four per cent was sent without payment in advance.

In this connection it should be pointed out that even in the period before the introduction of the postal reform and of stamps, it was also possible to send a letter prepaid. Many people, though, especially the upper classes, felt it was indecent to send a prepaid letter, as if the sender thought that the addressee could not afford to pay the postage. And consequently they refused to accept prepaid letters.

105 Watermark of the first stamps.

106 A Mulready cover.

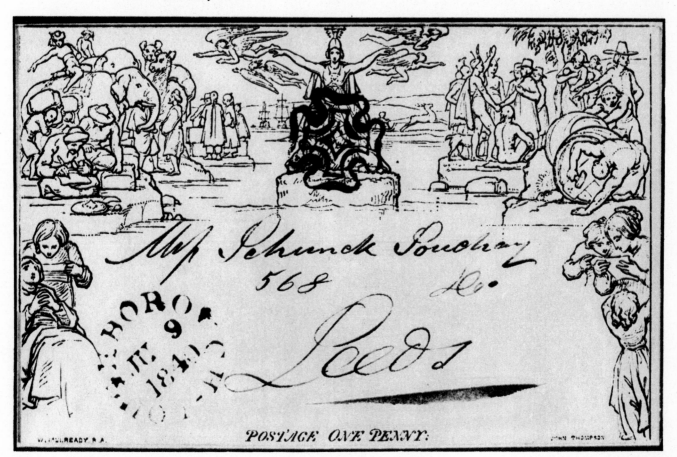

The year 1840 was a turning point in the development of postal services all over the world. The British postal reform showed the way which all the other postal administrations were to take, sooner or later. But all of them changed over in the end to the system of prepaid mail and to the use of adhesive certificates of paid postage — postage stamps.

At first progress was slow. Everybody was curious to see how the postal reform in Britain would work. Therefore the first countries to join Great Britain in the printing of stamps did not do so until three years later. In 1843 stamps were issued by the Swiss cantons of Zurich and Geneva, and by Brazil. In 1845 these countries were joined by Basle (Switzerland), and in 1847 by the United States and Mauritius. But after that there was not a single year when the philatelic family was not enlarged by a new member.

Today their number is in the region of two hundred; in actual fact there are more philatelic countries than there are states, the reason being that political developments the world over have had a decisive influence on stamp issues. As time passed the number of *philatelically terminated countries* grew. This means countries which do not exist any more and have naturally ceased to issue stamps. Such countries are, for instance, the Swiss cantons and Canadian provinces, the German and Italian states (where now stamp issues valid for the whole country are used) and many others. The geography of philately is growing all the time. In the past years

107 Bergedorf stamps, 1861.

108 Hannover, 1863.

1, 2–4

5–6, 7–8

9–11

12, 13

▼ Brazil issued her first stamps in 1843 (1). The Swiss cantons also issued stamps for the first time in the same year; (2–4) and (5–6) are examples of stamps issued for the whole country in the 1850s and 1860s. Belgium issued her first stamps in 1849 (7–8) and the Netherlands in 1852 (9–11). A stamp of the Roman States of 1852 (12) and a French stamp used at the post office in Constantinople, now Istanbul, Turkey (13).

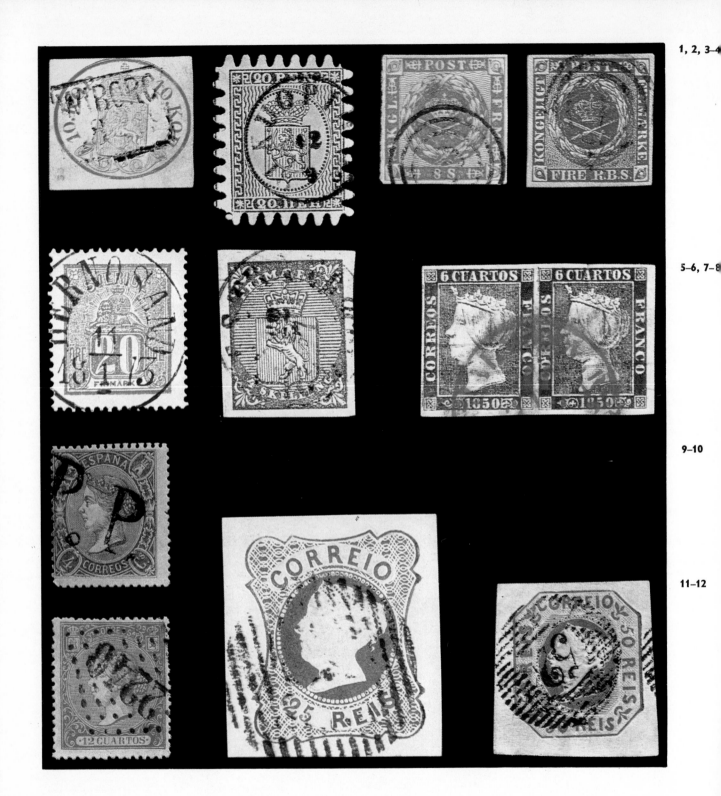

1, 2, 3–4

5–6, 7–8

9–10

11–12

VI The first Finnish stamps issued in 1856 are very much sought after (1); in the case of later issues, the value of the stamp depends upon the condition of the large tooth-like pattern formed by the roulette (2). However, the first Scandinavian country to issue stamps was Denmark, in 1851 (3–4), and Sweden and Norway then followed suit in 1855 (5–6). Spain joined the stamp-issuing countries earlier still, in 1850. This example of one of her first stamps (7–8), like all the early issues, bears the year to prevent forgery; it is followed by two more Spanish stamps, issued in the 1860s (9–10). The wide margins of the two early Portuguese stamps of 1853 shown here (11–12) make these copies outstanding.

109 Mecklenburg-Schwerin, 1856.

110 Brunswick cover of 1863.

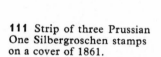

111 Strip of three Prussian One Silbergroschen stamps on a cover of 1861.

112 Cover of the Prussian post in Berlin, 1866.

new nations have emerged, mainly in Africa, but also tiny little countries, as for instance the sheikdoms of the Arab Peninsula and on the shores of the Persian Gulf.

The number of stamps issued grew, due, first of all, to the fact that new countries issued stamps, and also because new issues replaced the old ones. Also, stamps began to serve more purposes, and commemorative stamps were invented.

The first period of stamp printing is known among philatelists as the *classical period*. The reason is that in those days stamps were issued exclusively for postal needs and their printing was in no

way influenced by stamp collecting. Of course, this period is not strictly limited by years but among philatelists it has become common to consider classical stamps as those issued up to 1870 or even 1875, when the agreement about the founding of the Universal Postal Union came into being. The end of the classical period naturally varies from country to country.

The designs of the first stamps were rather simple. The stamp usually depicted the ruler, the coat of arms, a large numeral or some symbol.

But do not think that classical stamps are of no interest to thematic collectors. It is true that the primitive printing techniques did not permit such colourful designs and combinations as is possible today with modern machinery. But although there were no such aesthetic demands on stamps, and although they were not required to fulfil a political service, a great number of these classic stamps are of great beauty and their themes are most attractive; for example, the beautiful sailing boats on the stamps of British Guiana, the llamas of Peru or the Canadian beaver.

These grandfathers of philately can look back on a hundred years or more of life. Every country is proud to celebrate the centenary of its stamps. This is usually an occasion for the issue of a special, commemorative set. Very often the new stamps reproduce the *jubilants* — stamps that have been with us for exactly one hundred years. Such stamps, incidentally, also form a special line of collecting and philatelists form collections both of one hundred-year-old stamps and of *stamps on stamps*.

115 Tuscany 1851.

116–117 Two early Indian: Bhopal and Bhore.

WHEN DOES 'STATIONERY' BECOME AN 'ENTIRE'?

Firstly, these philatelic terms need to be explained. *Stationery* is every postal cover, postcard, aerogram or other item on which the stamp or postage value is imprinted rather than stuck on. On the other hand, *entires* are letters, postcards, covers and aerograms with

118 India, King George VI.

119 King Ferdinand of Rumania.

120 James Monroe, President of the United States.

121 J.J. Dessalines, the founder of Haiti.

122 The President of Tunisia, Habib Bourguiba.

123 The Belgian royal couple, Baudouin and Fabiola.

124 When Juan Peron was President of the Argentine he had stamps printed with the portrait of his wife, Eva Peron.

125–126 Brazil, 1843, and the centenary stamp.

one or more adhesive. That means that stationery with an adhesive stamp in addition to the imprinted stamp becomes an entire.

a) Covers. The first stationery was the Sardinian letter sheet with the handstamp showing a horse and rider and also the value. These have already been mentioned. But they were not real postal stationery, for they were intended for letters not going through the post.

The Mulready covers, although no stamp was printed on them, are genuine postal stationery in the full meaning of the term. But two years before the Mulready covers came into use the postal administration of Sydney issued covers with a stamp printed on them.

Mulready's picturesque covers were rejected by the general public of Britain, but as soon as the British GPO issued covers with an impressed stamp, they were readily accepted.

Such covers started to appear in practically all countries issuing stamps, either simultaneously with the stamps or shortly before or after their issue. They are still used in different forms today. The stamp is normally printed in the top right-hand corner, in the place where stamps are generally affixed.

127 Centenary of the Spanish Isabella, 1850—1950.

128 The Canadian beaver's centenary commemorated as a stamp on a stamp.

129 Centenary of the stamps of Sicily commemorated on an Italian stamp of 1959.

130 Turkey celebrated the centenary of its stamps in 1963.

This rule, though, was not kept everywhere. In Russia, as early as 1848, ten years before the first stamps were issued, covers came into use. A circular fiscal stamp was printed on their flap with a twin-headed tsarist eagle in embossed print in the centre. On top was a text giving the postage for a certain weight of the letter and on the bottom the text '1 Kopek for the cover'.

In 1869 Turkey issued covers with the stamp printed on the reverse as well. But this time the stamp was not printed on the flap but in the centre of the cover. The top part of the stamp is therefore on the flap, whereas the bottom part is on the lower parts of the cover and, when the unused cover is opened, the stamp comes apart. Sometimes the sender did not close the cover properly, and the parts of the stamp did not fit together.

131 From the Soviet Union — a stamp on a stamp.

132 Three Turkish stamps of similar design.

133 Czechoslovakia, 1960: a stamp on a stamp on a stamp!

134 Canadian postal stationery from the end of the nineteenth century.

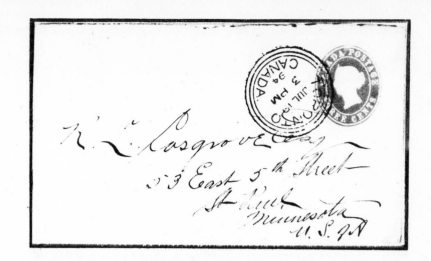

135 Old Austrian postal stationery. Note the interesting registration label.

136 Japanese postal stationery, 1878.

137 Russian postal stationery.

138 Back of a Turkish postal stationery cover.

139 Heinrich von Stephan portrayed on a Cuban stamp.

140 The world's first postcard.

141 Bavarian postcard.

142 French postcard with separately affixed stamp.

b) Postcards and picture postcards. It was the Secret Councillor of the Prussian Post, Heinrich von Stephan, who had the idea of printing postcards. His proposal was not accepted by the Prussian post nor by the Fifth German Postal Conference held in October 1865 in Karlsruhe. This idea, though, was taken up by Professor Dr Emmanuel Herman of Vienna. On 26 January 1869 he published an article in the daily paper *Neue Freie Presse* recommending the introduction of postcards. The Austrian postal administration accepted his proposal, and on 1 October 1869 the first postcards appeared with a yellow stamp of two kreuzer printed on them. In Germany postcards were introduced in 1870, shortly after Heinrich von Stephan became Postmaster General of the North German Confederation.

During the hundred-odd years of their existence postcards have hardly changed at all. In addition to the normal postcards, double postcards were issued soon afterwards, their second half being intended for the reply. On the basis of international agreements these reply postcards could be used anywhere in the world.

54

British reply postcards, for instance, could be found used and cancelled in Germany, France or other countries and sent back to Britain. Another development of the postcard was the letter-card. More recently postcards were printed with drawings or photographs on the front next to the address, the whole of the reverse of the postcard being reserved for the message.

Postcards had an important task in times of war; they were used as early as the Franco-Prussian war of 1870—1, but mainly during the First and Second World Wars. The reasons for this were that they made it possible to write a short message quickly, and also because the censors preferred them. The control of postcards was much easier; letters had to be opened. For security reasons in wartime, printed texts on postcards were used frequently. Only a few words had to be added to the printed text and the inapplicable passages deleted. Pre-printed postcards were also used for the mail from prisoner-of-war camps handled by the Red Cross.

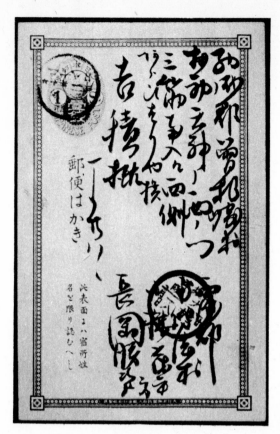

143 Japanese postcard.

144 Letter card from France.

145 Postcard with a propaganda cartoon on the address side.

The British post, for instance, used during the Second World War pre-printed forms for cables with a certain number of standard messages. The sender just deleted the text he did not want and so it was sufficient to telegraph only the address, the numbers of the sentences and the signature. It was a great relief for the telegraph and wireless network over-burdened by a flood of cables from soldiers and their families. After all, the cables and wireless had first of all to serve military and government needs.

The picture postcard is the sister of the postcard. Here only half of the address side is reserved for the message, whereas the other side is taken up by a drawing or a photograph. Sometimes picture postcards were printed with political drawings and cartoons. Picture postcards are not usually issued by the GPO and therefore stamps have to be affixed to them.

c) Pneumatic mail. When a system of pneumatic mail was invented some postal administrations issued special stationery — pneumatic covers and postcards. The mail is put into metal containers which are transported to their destination by compressed air. As soon as they arrive they are handled like special delivery. Special stamps were issued in some countries for pneumatic mail.

d) Wrappers. In the nineteenth century some countries introduced postal wrappers with a printed stamp to be used mainly for the delivery of newspapers.

e) Airletters and airgraphs. The rapid development of air transport soon made the printing of special stationery necessary. In aerial transport it is most important to keep the weight of the mail down in order to increase the plane's payload. Furthermore the postage for airmail was at first very expensive, and airmail covers and letters soon came into use. The paper used is very thin so as to keep the weight and the postage as low as possible.

A number of postal administrations have introduced special letter sheets which are folded and stuck down. There is no need

148 Cover for the Paris pneumatic mail.

149 Airletter from Palestine which travelled a complicated route during the Second World War.

for a cover. These are the popular *airletters*. They are considerably
lighter than letters and the postage is much cheaper. The stamp
is either printed on the airletter or can be affixed. No second sheet
of paper or anything else may be enclosed in airletters.

The burden of the post was especially heavy during the Second
World War. The British GPO had to cope with the enormous
task of delivering mail over great distances throughout the world,
which is why the use of airletters has become so popular in the
United Kingdom.

In addition another novelty was introduced — *airgraphs*. The
sender obtained a form of the size of a normal letter sheet. Into
a reserved frame on top he wrote the address and used the rest of
the front of the sheet for writing his message. This service was
free of charge for soldiers, so that on their airgraphs only the
handstamp of the field post office is found. The rest of the population had either to buy prepaid forms or use a stamp. The airgraph
forms were photographed at the post office by microfilm and the
film was flown to the destination. After arrival diminished copies
were made, size $4\frac{1}{8}'' \times 5\frac{1}{4}''$. The copy was folded, put into a special
envelope with a cut-out for the address, and delivered.

POSTAL ADMINISTRATIONS JOIN HANDS

As postal services developed and widened, frontiers between
countries became more and more of an obstacle. Soon it became
necessary to solve these problems by concluding written agreements. One of the first was the agreement signed by the Postmaster
General of Spain, Juan Taxis, and the superintendent of the
French Post, G. Fouquet de la Verne. Under this treaty the
French post took care of the transportation of mail from Rome
and the Netherlands to and from Spain. Many such agreements
were signed as time passed. For instance in 1873 Germany had
seventeen valid bilateral postal agreements with other countries,
France had sixteen agreements, Belgium fifteen and England
twelve.

These bilateral agreements were rather unsatisfactory as they
were concluded on the basis of different conditions and circumstances, and as a result produced a most complicated system of
postal rates. The time had come to replace all these bilateral
agreements by a wider international system. At about the same
time that world progress led to postal reform in England, the
first plans for the signing of multilateral world agreements started
to be put forward.

The first international postal organization was the German-
Austrian Postal Union founded in 1850, but this was an organization of limited territorial range.

One of the pioneers of a world-wide postal organization was the
Postmaster General of the United States, Montgomery Blair. In
1862 he handed the US Secretary of State such a proposal. On
his initiative an international conference was convened on 11 May
1863 in Paris, and fifteen nations from Europe and the USA
participated. On the agenda of the conference was the standardization of the weight of the mail and of postal rates. An international
postal organization was not founded in Paris, but the recommenda-
tions of the conference had a considerable influence on the later
international agreement. A further influence on development was

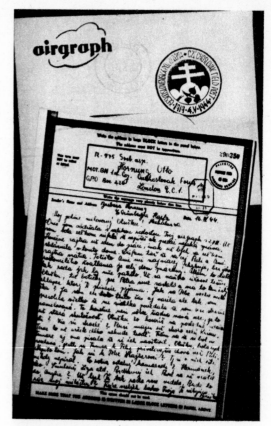

150 Second World War airgraph
with the censor's handstamp on
the form. On the airgraph cover
is an arrival postmark, a
commemorative handstamp of
the Czechoslovak Fieldpost in
England and a double-circle
handstamp of the British post.

151 The development of postal
services is depicted on this
Turkish stamp.

152 Montgomery Blair portrayed on a US stamp issued for the centenary of the International Postal Conference of 1863.

153 US stamp commemorating the centenary of the telegraph, 1944.

the founding of the International Telegraphic Union in 1865 in Paris.

The initiative in the forming of an international postal organization was later taken by the Postmaster General of Germany, Dr Heinrich von Stephan. In October 1874 the first Postal Congress met in Berne, where twenty-two nations were represented, and the Universal Postal Union was founded. The agreement including a unified rate for letters (twenty-five centimes for fifteen grammes), the principle that the postage is paid by the sender, that for mail posted unfranked double the postage is collected, the standardization of transit rates, etc., came into force on 1 July 1875.

The number of members of the Universal Postal Union was growing rapidly. As far back as 1897 the UPU had sixty-two members, in 1939 there were eighty-eight and in 1961 the number had reached 124. So far sixteen World Postal Congresses have been held and each of them has brought a widening of the activity of the UPU and of its services benefiting the general public. The sixteenth World Postal Congress was held in Tokyo in 1969.

In addition to the UPU, there exist further international postal organizations. In 1911 the South American Postal Association was founded. At the Buenos Aires Congress of 1921 its name was changed to Panamerican Postal Union and its headquarters are in Montevideo. In 1954 an Arab Postal Union was also founded. These organizations have a regional authority and their member countries are also members of the Universal Postal Union.

It is natural that scenes depicting the operations of the post in the past and present appear on postage stamps. A perfect occasion for such themes occurred in 1949 when the Universal Postal Union celebrated its seventy-fifth anniversary. Many commemorative stamps and sets were issued. On a number of these stamps there is the memorial of the UPU in Berne where the headquarters of the UPU are. This monument shows the shape of a globe with people of all nations handing each other letters all around the world.

154 The building in Berne where the first World Postal Congress was held in 1874.

Very soon, in 1974, the Universal Postal Union will be celebrating its centenary. No doubt a number of commemorative stamps will mark this important anniversary.

'SPECIMEN' AND 'CANCELLED' STAMPS

One of the obligations of countries who are members of the Universal Postal Union is to inform all other members about new stamp issues. For this purpose samples of new stamps are sent to the other postal administrations, free of charge. Some postal administrations overprinted these sample stamps with the word *specimen* to make their use for the franking of mail impossible. Texts and markings vary according to the country.

But stamps with the overprint 'specimen' were also presented to important personalities and institutions, which is how some of these overprinted stamps reached philatelists. Although they are not really postage stamps, since they cannot be used for franking, specialists are very much interested in them.

In France and other countries it is customary for officials, the Minister, etc., to receive free of charge imperforate copies of newly issued stamps. Much criticism has been voiced against this abuse, but in vain. Such imperforate copies are obviously interesting items and high prices are paid for them. Of a similar character are the so-called *ministerial miniature sheets*. These are newly issued stamps, imperforate, not printed in normal-sized sheets but in the form of miniature sheets. These ministerial miniature sheets are also presented to officials and other personalities. They have no franking value but specialists are nevertheless on the look-out for them.

It often happens that new stamps are issued at a time when large supplies of the valid stamps are still available. In some countries, the very earliest stamps issued are still valid. But elsewhere old stamps have been declared invalid for postage. There are serious reasons for such steps, for instance a change of régime, incorporation of the country by some other nation, currency reform, and so on.

What happens to stamp remainders? This problem is solved in several ways. In some places sales of stamps continue at special counters to philatelists until the supply is exhausted. In other countries the remainders are burned under official supervision or taken to a paper mill. It has frequently happened that, for some reason, for instance during a war, there has been a stamp shortage. In such cases old supplies of stamps have been brought out and used again, usually with an appropriate overprint.

Another way to make stamps invalid was for the stamps withdrawn from circulation to be overprinted with the word cancelled, or with an overprint of black lines or something similar across the design, and this, of course, made them useless for postage. Obviously specialists are interested in such invalidated stamps as well.

155 Austrian stamp issued for the fifteenth World Postal Congress in Vienna, 1964.

156 Czechoslovak stamp showing postal transport of past and present.

157 Stamp from Ceylon symbolizing the postal services of the world.

158 Universal Postal
Union symbol on
a Turkish stamp.

159 'Specimen'
overprint on a British
stamp.

160 Nova Scotia
stamp overprinted
'Specimen'.

HOW STAMPS HELPED TRUE LOVE

Nobody knows who was the first stamp collector. Very soon, though, after the first stamps were issued, when more and more countries were adopting this useful novelty and the number of stamps available started to grow, the first stamp collectors made their appearance.

In the beginning stamp 'collecting' sometimes had a rather peculiar character. In the middle of the last century, for example, the London *Times* published an advertisement in which the advertiser offered to 'buy a large quantity of used Penny stamps for the papering of my bedroom walls'. A lady in England was looking for stamps to decorate her lampshade. Unfortunately her lampshade did not survive — it would be a marvellous find for any collector of classics. There was even a case when an angry father gave his daughter, who wished to marry her true love instead of the young man he had chosen for her, the task of collecting an astronomical number of stamps. But the general public found out about it and came to the assistance of the lovers. The stamps were collected and Mary could marry her John.

As time passed, the family of stamp collectors started to grow. Our grandfathers did not have the problems over what country or philatelic theme to pick for their collection that we have nowadays. In the middle of the last century everybody naturally collected the whole world. Up to 1850 altogether only 154 stamps had been issued, and by 1860 their number was up to a mere 913. But shortly afterwards their number started to grow rapidly. In 1880 there existed 4,848 stamps, in 1900 there were 15,428 and in 1920, after the First World War, almost 38,000. The flood of new stamps reached large proportions after the Second World War and in the fifties, and is swelling all the time. In 1950 their number had passed the 100,000 mark and today there are well over 150,000 different stamps. This figure, of course, covers only normal stamps, not varieties, errors or different perforations.

The first advertisement offering to exchange and buy stamps was by Mr. T.H.S. Smith, the owner of a book shop, and it was published on 22 March 1851 in the London *Family Herald*. There were more and more advertisements, and stamp collectors made their first international contacts and the first philatelic clubs were formed. Soon the first stamp albums were printed and philatelic magazines appeared.

The term *philately* itself is of quite an early date. In the beginning there were all sorts of names for the stamp collecting hobby, some of them derisive. One of them was *timbromanie*, meaning stamp mania. Such names did not please stamp collectors at all. The term philately, which is generally accepted for stamp collecting, was invented by the French stamp collector Herpin. He used it for the first time in an article published on 3 November 1864 in the French magazine *Collectionneur de Timbre-Poste*. And this term became so popular that it remained in common use.

The origin of the expression is Greek. It is composed of the word *philo* (I love) and *atelos* (exempt from tax). In other words this expression means 'love of something exempted from tax', i.e., a love of things exempt from the payment of postage, a hobby dealing with stamps.

Some time ago there was a great discussion concerning this expression. Some people were of the opinion that the correct thing would be to use the term *philotely*. They contended that the name for the hobby was composed of the Greek words *philo* and *teli* (taxes) and its explanation would be 'love of taxes', or love of stamps used for the payment of postage. But the expression formed by Herpin has become so common that it is used all over the world with the exception of Greece and Cyprus, where they say *philotely*.

HUNDRED-YEAR-OLD SOCIETIES

The first philatelic club was founded in 1856 in the United States, and its name was The Omnibus Club. In 1866 The Excelsior Stamp-Association was formed in St John's, Canada. Towards the end of the 1860s the Süddeutscher Philatelisten-Verein was founded in Heidelberg. Most of these old philatelic organizations did not exist for long and were eventually superseded by other bodies.

The oldest and most famous philatelic organization in the world has its headquarters in London. The Philatelic Society, London, was founded in April 1869. In 1906 King Edward VII gave permission for the society to use the prefix 'Royal'. In 1896 HRH Duke of York (later King George V) became President of the Royal Philatelic Society, London, an office which he continued to hold until his accession to the throne in 1910, when he was pleased to announce that he would act as its patron. This royal patronage has continued, and today the society is honoured by the patronage of Her Majesty Queen Elizabeth II.

It was the philatelic societies who organized contacts between stamp collectors and provided them with the necessary conditions for their hobby. First of all, meetings of members were held. There they could buy, sell and exchange stamps. The first approval booklets appeared and the societies undertook their circulation. In many cases societies sponsored the publishing of stamp magazines and assisted in the publication of stamp albums and catalogues. Later, stamp exhibitions were held and the societies appointed experts to assist their members. Philatelic clubs and organizations became a permanent institution.

The place of philatelic clubs which were dissolved or gave up their activities for various reasons was taken by new ones, and today there is hardly any large city in the civilized world where some organization of stamp collectors does not exist. The need for closer contacts, the exchange of stamps and also the exchange of experience brought philatelists closer together and led eventually to the formation of larger bodies and national federations. These federations have in some countries a membership of hundreds of thousands.

One of the great tasks of philatelic clubs and societies is the education of the next generation of stamp collectors, of boys and girls interested in philately.

161 The Czechoslovak stamp issued for the 'Day of FIP' (Fédération Internationale de Philatélie), 1962.

162 Turkish miniature sheet issued for the 'Day of FIP', 1963.

INTERNATIONAL PHILATELY

Long ago proposals were put forward to establish a world-wide organization of philatelists. These suggestions materialized in 1926 when a conference of representatives of national philatelic societies was held and the Fédération Internationale de Philatélie (International Federation of Philately—FIP) was founded. At present FIP counts among its members over forty national philatelic societies from countries in Europe, America, Asia and Africa. The headquarters of FIP are in Geneva.

FIP looks after international contacts between philatelic organizations of different countries, co-ordinates international philatelic activities, for instance, international stamp exhibitions, organizes an international fight against stamp forgers and their products, propagates philately, etc. FIP is trying to ensure that the number of newly issued stamps is limited as much as possible and blacklists unnecessary stamp issues. Furthermore, FIP is doing its best to facilitate the international exchange of stamps, takes interest in the education of young philatelists and takes care of philatelic documentation.

The FIP Congress in Budapest held in 1961 accepted a decision to celebrate a *Day of FIP*, always in the city where the FIP Congress is held. The first Day of FIP was celebrated on 1 September 1962 during the First World Stamp Exhibition PRAGA 1962 in Czechoslovakia.

In 1962 a conference of representatives of the world philatelic press was held in Prague and their international organization was founded then and there, the Association Internationale de Journalistes Philatéliques (The International Association of Philatelic Journalists — AIJP).

163 'Day of FIP' handstamp, Istanbul, 1963.

164 'Day of FIP' handstamp used at the WIPA 1965 International Stamp Exhibition in Vienna.

165 During the WIPA 1965 Exhibition the Congress of AIJP (Association Internationale de Journalistes Philatéliques) was held, and the event recorded by this commemorative handstamp.

III. LEARNING ABOUT PHILATELY

166–171 Subject collecting. Emblems and heraldic shields depicted on stamps are one of many possible fields for the collector.

There are very few people who have not at some time or another in their youth collected stamps. Not only boys collect stamps; there are quite a number of girls, too, who are keen philatelists. No wonder the modern stamps, with their multicoloured and interesting pictures, attract everybody's attention. Usually it starts with a few stamps taken off letters and postcards, then perhaps a stamp packet given as a Christmas present is added, and so it grows. The young collector studies the colourful designs of his treasures, tries to decipher the inscriptions and starts looking for more. Boys swap stamps picturing cosmonauts and ships for those with locomotives and aeroplanes. A collection slowly grows.

But a heap of stamps, even if it goes into thousands, is not yet a collection. I once met an elderly gentleman who set himself the task of accumulating a million stamps. He collects and keeps everything he can lay his hands on. He carefully bundles the stamps into packets of a hundred each, puts them away in boxes and goes on collecting. I do not know how many stamps he has managed to accumulate during the thirty or forty years he has been doing this. Perhaps he already has his million, maybe even more. I don't suppose he knows either. But it is not a stamp collection in the true meaning of the word and it never will be.

This, of course, is an exceptional case. Young collectors do not set themselves such targets. In many cases their interest starts to wane after some time and they give up collecting. Every philatelist experiences such a crisis, and not only once. After some time he usually returns to his stamps, scrutinizes them again, and this time he sees them in a different light. He starts to collect anew but on a higher level, with a clearer conception and more knowledge. That is how a real collection is born, and also a real philatelist.

For the making of a philatelist out of a collector one thing is necessary above all else — a clear idea of how to arrange the collection and what to concentrate on. The idyllic times are long gone when it was possible to collect the stamps of the whole world. Every philatelist has to limit his field of collecting. Usually he starts to build up a general collection of his own country. That means that he collects all issued stamps in the order of their appearance. Another possibility is to start a thematic collection.

First of all, though, he must realize that it is impossible to form a collection just from stamps which happen to come his way. If a stamp collector really wants to become a philatelist he must devote his time not only to stamps but to enlarging his knowledge, too. That includes the study of the appropriate catalogues, getting acquainted with the principles of handling stamps, reading philatelic magazines, studying specialized philatelic literature, and learning from other philatelists who have a wider range and more knowledge. In philately, exactly the same as in any other field of human

167

169

168

64

1, 2

3

4

VII Most sheets of the first Turkish stamps were printed in *tête-bêche* rows, as in the pair illustrated (1); larger blocks (2) and covers (3) of these stamps are in great demand. These second issue Turkish stamps on cover (4) were cancelled at Sarajevo, which is now in Yugoslavia; for historical reasons such an envelope would be interesting to collectors of Bosnia and Yugoslavia.

VIII Three envelopes showing early stamps and postmarks of different German states.

170

171

activity, it is imperative to build on the experience and knowledge of older generations. As soon as a philatelist has absorbed a sufficient knowledge from the experience of others, he can begin work on the forming of a perfect collection, at the same time watching out for new discoveries and results of study. In the case of a thematic collector a well-founded knowledge of the chosen theme is just as important. This is the only way he can form a valuable collection.

The first step for a beginner, therefore, will be to give the philatelic material he has obtained so far careful thought, and to decide what to do next. He must work out a plan of collecting. There is no need to compose a long, written paper. It is quite sufficient to choose France, for example, or cosmic flights. It would be a great mistake to embark upon a task surpassing the collector's capabilities. It would be wrong if a beginner immediately started a highly specialized collection including all sorts of varieties and specialities, or if he chose a complicated theme requiring detailed special knowledge which he did not possess. There is time enough for such a task. An easy target is quite sufficient to begin with and

172–173 Maps on stamps.   173

174–176 National flags.

177

178

179

180

181

182

183

180-183 Fruit and
vegetable subjects.

184

185

184-190
Agriculture.

66

186

187

188

189

190

191 Rocks and minerals: here an emerald crystal is shown on a Soviet stamp.

194

192–195 Plant life.

193

195

196

197

198 How the peoples of the world live: this stamp portrays an Indian village in Canada.

196–197 Natural phenomena.

199

200

201

202

199–202 Animal subjects: here a selection of mammals is shown.

203–205 Birds on stamps.

204

205

68

206

207

208

209

206–209 Fishes of sea and river.

later, when there is more experience, more material and greater knowledge, it is always possible to expand and define the aim of the collection.

CHOOSING A COLLECTION

Philatelic collections can be divided into two large, basic groups. These are collections formed in the *original, classical way*, sometimes called *catalogue collections*, and *thematic collections*. Let us have a short look at these two groups.

1. Catalogue collections

This is the oldest category of collections, and can be divided into three basic groups:

a) The most simple example is a **general collection.** In such a collection the stamps are arranged according to the date of issue, in chronological order, without any regard to varieties or specialities. Such a collection can comprise one or more countries or just certain periods, for instance Great Britain up to 1900 or Germany after the Second World War. The advantage of forming a general collection is that the stamp collector can obtain, for every country he has chosen and for every period, an album with printed space for the stamps, and that he can collect with the help of a catalogue. There is a great disadvantage, too. Such a collection naturally includes the rarest stamps which are very expensive and difficult to obtain. And so it happens that the collector finds himself with empty, irritating spaces on his album pages.

b) Forming a **specialized collection** requires a different approach. The specialized collector is no longer satisfied with the arrangement of his stamps in a chronological order on the basis of the catalogue, although he respects it to a certain extent. He concentrates on different perforations, types of stamps, printing errors, deficiencies, etc. In other words he is interested in all circumstances of the production and use of stamps. Such a collection should also include entires and stationery, postmarks and even stamp forgeries. It is naturally up to the philatelist which sector he chooses for his specialized collection. He is quite free to specialize in a whole country or just in a certain period. A specialized collection requires very thorough philatelic knowledge and it is necessary to study literature continuously. A normal catalogue is insufficient for a specialist.

c) The most demanding of this type is the **study collection.** For such a collection, in addition to all the requirements listed under the heading Specialized Collection, further thorough research into other material and documents and postal archives etc. is necessary. For a study collection, endless patience and effort is needed, for instance the minute study of several thousand copies of the same stamp to discover typical marks. It is the philatelists who have formed study collections who explain unknown facts concerning the printing and the use of stamps. For the forming of a study collection very varied and rich philatelic material is essential. From the ranks of study collectors come the philatelic experts who can confirm whether stamps are genuine or forgeries. The owners of study collections usually provide the

210

213

211

214

212

210–214 A sample collection of insects.

most valuable exhibits for stamp exhibitions, and pass on their experience to other philatelists by means of articles for the philatelic press, books and lectures.

2. Thematic collections

This is actually the youngest branch of philately, based nowadays on a wealth of stamps with all sorts of *motifs*, issued all over the world. The first thematic collections were formed prior to the Second World War, but the great development of thematic philately did not come till after the war. That is the reason why so far not all the principles of this young branch of philately have been clarified. Thematic philately is still developing. First of all it must be understood that thematic philately differs from original philately in one basic point. Whereas for the philatelist forming a catalogue collection the design and *motif* of the stamp is only of inferior importance, for the thematic collector it is the most important thing. The classical collector (particularly the specialist) is interested in technical details of the stamp, in its perforation, paper, details of design, and so on. On the other hand, the thematic collector concentrates on the picture on the stamp. He is interested in its meaning, acquires thereby knowledge in all sorts of fields, pursues variants of the factual and artistic expression of certain *motifs*, notes objective connections. He considers how he can

215 Famous authors: below is J.A. Comenius.

216 Jean-Jacques Rousseau.   217 Friedrich Schiller.   218 Alexander Puṣhkin.

219 Jules Verne.

220 Walt Whitman.

221 Leo Tolstoy.

222 Sholem Aleichem.   223 Vladimir Mayakovsky.   224 Henry Longfellow.   225 Karel Čapek.

apply the pictures to the basic theme, and how he can illustrate the theme with the help of philatelic material. All through this work the theme and its elaboration on the one hand, and the use and application of the philatelic material on the other, are of equal importance.

In thematic collecting, too, two main groups are distinguished: **a)** The lowest level of this field of philately is formed by **subject collections.** Such a collection is based either exclusively on the design pictured on the stamps (collecting ships on stamps, flowers, etc.) or on the purpose of issue (Red Cross, Europa, World Refugee Year, etc.). These collections are prepared in a very simple way without any libretto or guide-line and without a detailed explanatory text. Usually whole sets of stamps are included. Take, for example, a collection of flowers on stamps. The simplest way of organizing such a collection is to arrange the individual stamps and sets showing flowers according to the country of issue in alphabetical order, and within each country in chronological order based upon the catalogue. A slightly more ambitious way would be to arrange the flower *motifs* on the basis of a botanical key. Here it is absolutely necessary to discard the chronological sequence and the issuing countries. Individual sets have to be split. For the forming of such a collection a minimum of basic botanical knowledge is required. The same applies to other subject collec-

226

227

228

226–231
Cultural relics of early civilizations.

231

229

230

232 The famous painter Rembrandt.

233 Reproduction of a painting by the American artist Frederic Remington.

234 The fragile beauty of Meissen china.

tions. A minimal amount of text is needed for each page of the collection. In the first case it is sufficient to give the name of the country of issue and perhaps the date of issue. If such a collection is arranged according to a botanical key it will be necessary to add the appropriate technical terms.

b) A higher and much more demanding level of this type of philately is represented by **thematic collections.** For such a collection a libretto is prepared, the collection provided with explanatory texts, and the stamp sets split up and distributed according to the requirements of the libretto. A thematic collection expresses with the help of stamps and philatelic material a certain chosen theme. To form a good thematic collection the philatelist must acquire a great deal of knowledge in the field of this theme. Otherwise he could not work it properly into a libretto, he could not correctly evaluate suitable stamps and philatelic material, and he would not be able to arrange everything in the best way to illustrate the individual sections of his theme. The collection as a whole must show the amount of creative work invested in the preparation and study of the theme, as well as in the styling of the texts and the whole arrangement of the collection. Profound philatelic knowledge, though, is an absolute requirement. A proper way of working with catalogues and the ability to select the right stamps is also most important. Obviously it is very important to choose the right theme and, by carefully wording the title of the collection, to limit the scope so that it remains within the limitations of the collector. Every thematic collection, if it is a really good one represents a genuine, original achievement.

3. Other collections

Every philatelic collection can be placed according to its basic characteristics into one of the main groups previously mentioned, original (catalogue) collections or thematic collections. Nevertheless there are some other types of collections which have been chosen by specialists and sometimes by large groups of collectors.

235 Masters of music:
Ludwig van Beethoven.
238 Franz Liszt and Hector
Berlioz.

236 Peter Tchaikovsky.

237 Frederic Chopin.

239 Bedřich Smetana.

240 Antonín Dvořák.

---

a) Collections of postmarks. Such a collection contains mainly cancellations; stamps are only of secondary importance, although they are not, of course, ignored. Try to obtain a perfect strike of a handstamp on a perfect copy of a stamp, if possible. But if this is unobtainable a clear postmark on a damaged stamp is also acceptable. Philatelic knowledge is a must, and so are detailed studies of the postal history in the country or countries concerned.
b) Collections of postal stationery. This collection is not one of stamps but of postcards, wrappers with the stamp printed on them, covers with printed stamp, letter-cards, airletters, etc.
c) Collections of entires. Such a collection deals with covers as a whole, with affixed stamps, categorized either by period or country.
d) Postal history collections. This is a very popular type of collection. It can combine everything, i. e. stamps, entires, postal stationery and to some extent even non-philatelic material. Philatelic knowledge is essential, as is a very wide knowledge of the postal history of the country and period in question. In addition a good basic education is necessary, as are studies of political developments in the period under consideration, geographical knowledge and sometimes also linguistic knowledge. Such a collection can deal with the development of postal services in the home town of the collector going as far back as possible to pre-philatelic days. It is possible to form a collection of censored mail from the First

241–244 Another area for the collector includes: concert halls and theatres, music and musical instruments.

242

243

244

World War, for instance, or a collection of postal services on a railway line, collections of maritime mail, and so on.

e) Aerophilatelic collections. Collections of airmail items can be formed as catalogue collections, or as thematic collections. A collection of airmail stamps arranged according to countries of issue and date of issue, or a specialized or study collection in this field (to which airmail letters and similar material also obviously belong), would basically be a catalogue-type collection. But it is quite possible to form aerophilatelic collections on a thematic basis. The field of aerophilately includes, for example, collections of balloon mail, Zeppelin mail, pigeon post, and first flights.

f) Further types of collections. As examples of random items, mention should be made here of collections of polar mail, local mail, private stamps, collections of crash mail, collections of registration labels and many more.

For all collections listed, and all the other types in existence, the same principles apply: every philatelic collection is to a certain extent an image of the philatelist, of his interests, knowledge and ability.

THE WIDE WORLD OF STAMPS

Before we take a closer look at all the different sorts of stamps it is necessary to state which are the main attributes a stamp must have to be considered a postage stamp at all.

A postage stamp must be issued by the postal administration of a State, or by the postal authorities of a part of this State, or by other authorities who are entitled to do so. That means a postage stamp must be issued officially and must prepay the cost of conveying an item of mail from the place of posting to the addressee in any part of the world by the regular services of any of the world's post offices.

Postage stamps do not have to be issued for the whole territory of a State (viz. the cantonal stamps of Switzerland, the stamps of the Canadian provinces), and do not have to be valid for the whole territory of a State (for example, the Czechoslovak 'service' stamps issued after 1945 which were valid only on the territory of Slovakia).

The issuing office must have postal sovereignity over the territory and also the means to transport mail. Therefore stamps issued by governments in exile cannot be considered to be postage stamps.

Although the overwhelming majority of postage stamps bear the name of the issuing State or country this is not absolutely necessary. British stamps, for instance, have no text giving the name of the country; they just feature the portrait of the King or Queen. After all, Great Britain was the first country to issue stamps and it is certainly entitled to this privilege.

Postage stamps usually have a text giving the franking value, but this is not absolutely necessary. Take for example the Austrian newspaper stamps with the head of Mercury of 1851. There are no value figures on the stamps; this was denoted by colour.

In addition to officially issued postage stamps there are other stamps worth attention. In various places during different periods postal services were established which supplemented and enlarged the postal network of the State. For these purposes the executive authorities, for instance the regional or local authorities or private companies and persons charged to supply these postal services, issued their own stamps. Although in such cases there is no actual

245

246

247

245–253 Famous buildings

248

249

250

251

252

253

State postal service, such stamps are interesting for collectors. It is important to decide whether such issues are postage stamps or not, whether their issue really did serve a need, whether it was necessary and whether they really were used as payment for the delivery of mail. If these conditions are met, then such issues achieve the character of stamps and become items of philatelic interest.

Such semi-official and private issues can be found used on their own on mail or in combination with official stamps in places where such a local or private postal service was connected to the official network of postal services. Such mixed frankings are of great interest and are very much sought after.

PHILATELISTS WILL PAY

Those who issue stamps are obviously well aware of the fact that there are tens of millions of philatelists all over the world, and that it is possible to get considerable sums of money out of their pockets. Some postal administrations take advantage of this fact and print unlimited quantities of new stamp issues.

These issues practically always have all the attributes of postage stamps and serve postal needs as well. There have been cases, though, when sets of stamps were printed but were never used postally. Later these sets appeared on the market and became good

254–262 Religious themes.

255

256

257

258

259

260

261

262

263–276
Scientists and
scientific
achievements
offer a vast
number of
motifs.

263

264

265

266

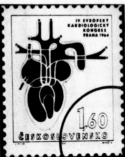

267

268

269

270

271

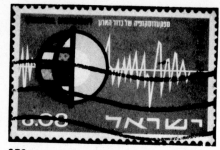

272

273

274

275

276

277

277–281 The history of transport.

279

278

280

281

282

283

282–284 Radio and
television.

284

285

287

286

285–287 Modern industry
and its products.

Early Austrian covers a piece showing the 9 kreuzer stamp in a block of six and a strip of five and underneath a 6 kreuzer stamp with traces of a St Andrew's Cross (1); cover showing the mute postmark of Tabor, which is now in Czechoslovakia (2); and another bearing a 3 kreuzer stamp with exceptionally wide margins and the red postmark of Tannwald (3).

1

2

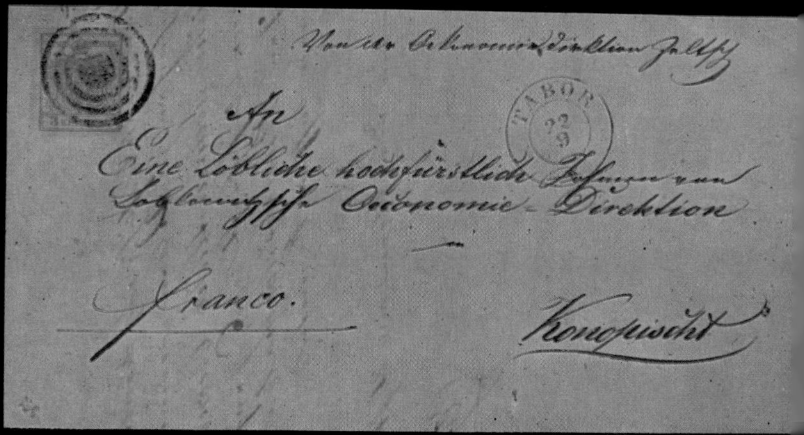

3

✕ More early Austrian envelopes: one bearing a 9 kreuzer stamp with
a complete St Andrew's Cross, a great rarity (1), and the other dating back
to the pre-stamp period and showing the red postmark of Prague and two
strikes of the postmark 'Grenze', which means 'frontier' (2).

289

business items. Such things happened in many countries. Here it is always necessary to study all the facts, If such stamps were genuinely intended for use and issued by the appropriate authorities, they are considered as unissued stamps, listed in some catalogues and collected by specialists.

Much worse are the stamp issues which appeared after a State ceased to exist, or were issued while it still existed but were never used for postal service. Take, for example, the last stamps of Montenegro, issued after this State ceased to exist. They were never in postal circulation but they are frequently found in collections. The same applies to some sets issued by White Russians after their defeat and expulsion from the territory of Soviet Russia. These 'stamps' have no philatelic value and do not belong in a collection. Only specialists, perhaps, are interested in these issues as curiosities.

Some time after the Second World War, for instance, a so-called 'royal government of Bulgaria' issued 'stamps' which were marketed from Spain. Obviously they are labels without any philatelic value. In fact, after both World Wars all sorts of issues appeared which had been ordered by private businessmen. In some cases 'stamps' were printed, but more often they were overprints on official stamp issues. None of these issues are stamps in the true sense of the word as they were not issued officially, were not required by actual needs, and did not serve any postal use. Therefore, do not collect them unless you are forming a specialized collection of such 'cinderella' material.

In the past, philatelists were confronted with another dangerous problem. The owners of little islands along the British coast and

290–300 Important political events, anniversaries and personalities depicted on stamps.

291

292

293

294

295

in other parts of the world had a brilliant idea. They had so-called private, local issues printed for their islands which were on sale to visitors, but the bulk, of course, went to stamp dealers. It was stated that these private, local issues served for the payment of the transport of visitors' mail to the mainland or nearest post office, from whence they were sent on to the addressees after payment of the full normal postage. In some cases there was hardly anybody living on these islands, and at close scrutiny no postal need for these private, local issues. They are not postage stamps, as they do not have all the attributes of postage stamps. If people like their designs and want to pay money for them, that is their own affair. Educated philatelists can distinguish between real postage stamps and private, local issues. The danger arises when someone is not well enough informed, and mistakes these issues for postage stamps.

296

297

MARIA I, RULER OF SEDANG

The history of philately knows of many attempts to defraud stamp collectors. A group of enterprising dealers in West Germany bought large quantities of official stamp sets issued for the eighteenth

299

298

300

301–314 The Olympic movement and the world of sport.

302

303

304

305

306

307

308

Olympic Games in Tokyo. They had them perforated with the text 'TOKIO 1964' and they even managed to find some post officials at the Bonn post office who cancelled them large numbers of first-day covers with these forgeries. They also obtained some declaration from an official of the German Olympic Committee authorizing them to issue this set of perforated stamps. And then they started to sell their 'stamps' from Liechtenstein, at a handsome profit. According to private estimates the organizers made a profit of about 400,000 Deutschmarks (over £ 40,000).

Swindlers in the field of philately never suffered from a lack of imagination. In 1905 a distinguished young man with his private secretary took quarters in one of the most elegant hotels in Paris. Through 'indiscretion' it soon leaked out that the incognito concealed King Maria I, ruler of Sedang, said to be a small country somewhere on the borders of China on the plains of Ryu-kyu. The hotel personnel were instructed not to give away the secret of the visitor, especially not to representatives of the Press. His Highness did not want to be disturbed. After a few days a chambermaid found a cover with exotic stamps of Sedang discarded in a waste-

309

310

311

312

313

paper-basket. During the following days more such covers were found. Eventually they came into the hands of some Paris stamp dealers who became most interested in the attractive stamps.

In the end some of the dealers succeeded in getting to His Highness and, in strictest secrecy, they bought a considerable quantity of Sedang stamps from the young king. They paid about 800,000 francs for the 'stamps' of Sedang, and that was a considerable sum in 1905.

The most interesting point is that not one of the stamp dealers, who were so interested in this seemingly most profitable business venture, thought of looking at a map or of making enquiries through the French authorities. By the time they realized that they had been cheated, the young 'king' and his secretary were gone and out of their reach.

314

THE STAMP WAR

Faked stamps were printed not only by speculators. Forging was even undertaken by governments. It is well known that the Nazis established large counterfeit workshops, during the Second World War, mainly in concentration camps. They used the inmates of the camps for their purposes, because prisoners were completely isolated and that made it much easier to keep it a secret. But there were other reasons, too. Among the thousands of prisoners it was no problem to find experts; their labour was very cheap and, if necessary, it was always possible to liquidate the forgers and destroy all evidence. In these workshops large quantities of forged sterling banknotes were produced, mostly five-pound notes, but also American dollars, Swiss francs and other currencies. Hitler's economic specialists contemplated undermining the economies of their enemies with the help of forged money. The fake banknotes were very good reproductions. The Nazis did not have enough time to accomplish their plans and so they destroyed or hid their products. Large wooden crates full of forged banknotes were recovered not so long ago from the bottom of Lake Töplitz in Austria.

In their workshops for forged banknotes the Nazis produced some forged stamps, too. These were mostly stamps which at first sight looked like the real stamps of their enemies, but some parts of the design and the portraits on the stamps were changed and propaganda texts included.

This idea was taken up by Hitler's enemies, too. In England, for instance, stamps were printed closely resembling the German stamps of 1943, issued to commemorate the twentieth anniversary of the Munich rising and the fallen members of the SA. Even the text 'Und ihr habt doch gesiegt' (You have been victorious after all) was left on the stamps. Only instead of the portrait of a member of the SA carrying a flag there was a portrait of General von Witzleben, one of the organizers of the unsuccessful attempt on Hitler's life on 20 July 1944. The date commemorating the anniversary of the SA fights was replaced by the date of von Witzleben's execution.

The United States also took up this activity. At that time the

315 Parody of the stamp issued for Hitler's fifty-first birthday in 1940. The child is spitting in Hitler's face.

most common stamp in Germany was a red twelve pfennig stamp with the portrait of Hitler. The stamp printed in the USA had the same appearance, but Hitler's portrait was changed in such a way that it looked like a skull. The text 'Deutsches Reich' on the stamp was changed to 'Futsches Reich' — meaning Lost Reich.

After the war there was a great demand for these interesting documents of the stamp war. As the supply of these 'official forgeries' was rather limited and it was impossible to satisfy the demand, keen entrepreneurs had this forgery reprinted; and so a forgery of a forged stamp started to circulate among philatelists.

UNDESIRABLE STAMP ISSUES

Stamps became not only an important postal attribute and a means for official propaganda, but also a source of large profits. Some postal administrations misuse their authority to such an extent that it becomes unbearable.

In 1889 Nicholas Frederic Seebeck, a representative of the New York printers Hamilton Banknote Company, signed an agreement with the Central American republic El Salvador for a period of ten years. He undertook to supply every year, free of charge, a set of stamps under the following conditions: that 1. the stamps became invalid after one year; 2. the unsold postage stamps would be returned to Seebeck; 3. Seebeck would be entitled to use the printing plates of the stamps withdrawn from circulation for the production of reprints. Similar agreements with Seebeck were later also signed by Nicaragua, Honduras and Ecuador. Seebeck sold the remainder of the stamps to philatelists under their face value, and these stamps flooded the whole world. After his death some of the sets were reprinted, but mostly on different paper.

Shortly after the signing of these contracts there was an outcry of protest from philatelists against this sort of business. Some of the countries which had originally signed contracts with Seebeck cancelled their agreements or did not turn over their remainders of postage stamps. A heated discussion started amongst philatelists as to whether these sets could be considered as stamps at all, and whether they were worth collecting. Now that so many years have passed it can be said that the Seebeck issues are postage stamps but their reprints do not have the characteristics of real postage stamps.

After all, today some postal administrations issue long sets of stamps every year (the sets issued by Seebeck comprised only nine to eleven stamps!). Even worse, these sets are directly supplied to certain firms for sale, or directly printed by these firms. In some cases these stamps have not been available at post office counters at all.

Very popular among thematic collectors are, for instance, postage stamps with sports themes, especially Olympic stamps. Large numbers of Olympic stamps are issued, not only in the course of the Olympic year, but long before or after the Olympic Games. In addition, some countries issue a set of normal stamps, another set of airmail stamps, miniature sheets, and, on top of all this, sets of perforated and imperforate stamps and miniature sheets. What is there to be said about the fact that a small country like Burundi, on the frontiers of the Congo, issued for the ninth Winter Olympic Games at Innsbruck in 1964 a set of very attractive stamps dedicated, naturally, to winter sports? But not one sportsman from

316 The skull shines through the portrait and the text reads 'Futsches Reich' (the Reich is lost).

317 Stamp issued by Burundi to mark the Winter Olympic Games.

Burundi participated in the Games at Innsbruck, and it is most doubtful that, in a country where there is never any snow, there is anybody who can do a slalom.

Similar cases, though, can be met with in Europe. Famous for their long sets of stamps are such dwarf States as San Marino and Monaco. Some time ago Albania, though not belonging to the organization of western European countries, issued a Europa set. The four stamps were issued perforate, in different colours imperforate, and in addition there were two miniature sheets.

Some States trying to prove their originality and to attract the interest of philatelists in their stamps are no longer satisfied with the traditional shapes of postage stamps. Thus there are not only stamps of extraordinary size, and of triangular and other geometrical shapes, but also the most fantastic, irregular shapes. The Tonga Islands in the Pacific Ocean surprised the world with a set of stamps resembling gold coins. The stamps are circular and printed on gold foil. But the record is probably held by Sierra Leone, with stamps in the shape of the country's frontiers, looking as if mice had nibbled at them. These stamps were later issued for a second time, but with an overprint. It seems the first attempt at this novelty was not such a success after all.

The latest 'invention' comes from Bhutan, a country situated between India and China. The Bhutan postal administration, or rather their agents, conceived the idea of printing the world's first three-dimensional stamps.

Many philatelists are naturally disgusted with such unnecessary stamp issues, and protest against them. The International Federation of Philately formed a special commission to fight such stamp issues, which were called 'abusive'. The task of this commission is to persuade postal administrations to abandon the issuing of *undesirable and abusive stamps*. Under this heading come not only unnecessarily long sets, stamps printed perforated and imperforate, but also stamps and miniature sheets issued with a very high surcharge, stamps printed on purpose in small quantities and not available at post offices but supplied only to certain agents, blocked stamps — i.e. stamps not on sale at post offices but supplied only to philatelists or dealers together with the rest of the set in limited numbers, and other stamps or miniature sheets where an intention to abuse philately is evident.

318 Sierra Leone stamp designed in the shape of the country.

319 Postage stamps of
St Vincent bearing a portrait
of Queen Victoria.

320 Canadian stamp with
a portrait of Queen
Elizabeth II.

The efforts of the FIP Commission have had some results. In some cases postal administrations revised their issuing policy to comply with FIP rules.

Stamps blacklisted by the FIP Commission are excluded from international stamp exhibitions held under the auspices of FIP. The FIP Commission has issued a list of unnecessary, undesirable and abusive stamps and supplements of this list are published from time to time.

Some of the largest catalogue printers have joined the fight. Stanley Gibbons (United Kingdom and USA), and Yvert & Tellier (France) have decided not to list these dubious stamp issues with other stamps of the countries in question. They are shown in a special appendix at the end of the catalogue, without illustrations and without a price. The American Philatelic Society lists such issues in their magazine with a 'black blot'.

This, of course, is just a beginning. To overcome the danger of abusive stamp issues the concerted effort of the whole world of philately will be necessary, including philatelists, the serious stamp trade and the philatelic press.

THE DIFFERENT TYPES OF STAMPS

As time passed, postage stamps acquired functions in addition to their original task, i.e. to serve for the prepayment of postage for letters and other mail. This is how a whole gamut of stamps was introduced. It should be pointed out right at the beginning that not all the types of stamps are to be found in all stamp-issuing countries. Furthermore, circumstances often made it necessary to use stamps issued for a specific use for a quite different purpose. In some cases their functions coincide.

The first large group is formed by postage stamps. A closer look at the most important representatives of this group, giving some details about the place and time of their first use, will be useful.

I. POSTAGE STAMPS

1. Normal postage stamps

This is the most common type of stamp. You see them every day. They are usually used for the prepayment of postage for letters, postcards and other mail. In some countries, or in some periods, the validity of certain normal postage stamps was limited to do-

321 Postage stamp of the
Netherlands Antilles bearing
a portrait of Queen Juliana.

322 Southern Poland, 1919 — 20 heller.

323 Northern Poland, 1919 — 25 pfennig.

324 Commemorative stamp from Peru, 1870. The bottom left corner is damaged.

325 Just three years later (1873) this fine Peruvian stamp showing a llama was issued.

mestic use only (Hanover 1850, Turkey 1876), or, on the other hand, to mail going abroad (Turkey 1876, Peru 1880). Other stamps could be used only in a part of the country's territory. For instance, in 1852 the postal administration of Thurn and Taxis issued stamps in two currencies then used in the regions of Germany where this postal service functioned, in silbergroschen and kreuzer. Stamps with the printed currency were always used in that part of Germany where the particular currency was in circulation. Something similar later occurred in Poland. After the establishment of the Polish State in 1918, stamps were printed for the southern part of the country with values in heller and kronen, and stamps of the same design for the northern part of Poland in pfennigs and marks. As late as 1924 a common new currency of groszy and zloty was introduced in a currency reform, and stamps were issued for the whole country.

a) The majority of normal postage stamps are common stamps, usually issued in long sets which remain in circulation for a long time, sometimes dozens of years. These sets of definitives include all values necessary for all types of frankings. They are mostly smaller in size, less elaborate and are printed in huge quantities. It is these common definitives which provide a promising field for the activity of specialists. During the long years of use the printing plates naturally become worn. They have to be repaired or replaced by new plates, the colours are changed and many colour shades appear. It therefore becomes possible to form, from these stamps, interesting specialized and study collections.

b) The postal administrations found out very soon that there are philatelists all over the world who prefer colourful stamps with interesting *motifs*. But first of all they realized what tremendous propaganda importance stamps have. They know no borders and reach even the remotest corner of the world. That is how the first *special and commemorative stamps* came into existence. The first stamps of this kind were issued by Peru in 1870 to commemorate the twentieth anniversary of railway service on the Lima-Callao

326–327 Two Czechoslovak commemorative stamps: publicity for the spa at Piestany, and the twenty-sixth meeting of the Council of Governors of Red Cross Societies in Prague, 1961.

line. These special and commemorative stamps have become the hoard from which thematic collectors draw material for their collections.

c) Long ago government offices and postal administrations found out that it was possible to obtain large sums of money for all sorts of welfare and other purposes. In some cases a part of the face value of the stamps is given to welfare bodies, for example the Red Cross; in other cases a special surcharge is collected. The first stamps with a surcharge were issued in 1897 by Victoria (Australia) on the occasion of the sixtieth anniversary of Queen Victoria's rule. The franking value printed on the stamps was 1d and 2½d, but they were sold for 1s and 2s 6d, twelve times their face value. In 1905 Russia issued stamps with a surcharge for the benefit of orphans of soldiers killed during the Russo-Japanese War.

In this connection it is necessary to explain the terms 'face value' and 'surcharge'. The franking value is always (with a few rare exceptions dating back to the earliest times of stamp use) printed on the stamp. It represents the amount accepted by the post when using the stamp for the franking of mail. The surcharge (which does not have to be printed on the stamp) is paid in addition to the face value and it is this amount which is used for welfare purposes. In most cases, stamps with a surcharge show both figures, for instance 30+10 and in this case the second figure is the

328

329

330

331

328 USA — Christmas stamps, 1964.

329 Rumanian stamps issued to commemorate the World Congress of Mothers in Lausanne, 1955.

330–331 Two anti-malaria stamps issued by Israel and Brazil.

332 Soviet stamps issued in aid of starving people in the Volga region, 1921.

333 From France — aid for polio victims.

334 Chile — World Refugee Year.

335 Monaco — blood donors.

336 Surcharge stamps issued in Victoria (Australia) in 1897.

337–338 Czechoslovak surcharge stamps issued in aid of the Red Cross and for children.

surcharge. Because some postal administrations started to misuse this profitable source of income according to the rules laid down by the FIP Commission, stamps with too high a surcharge, representing more than fifty per cent of the franking value of the stamp, are considered to be abusive.

d) It often happened, especially in wartime, that post offices and whole countries ran out of postage stamps. The postal administration had to take emergency measures. Either the use of other types of stamps (newspaper stamps, official stamps, etc.) was permitted for the posting of mail, or provisional issues were made available by overprinting stamps, fiscal stamps or private labels. To this group belong provisional stamps issued after the forming of new States. Very often the still-valid stamps of the preceding State were issued with an appropriate overprint. This was common practice after the First World War. When an army occupied enemy territory either its own stamps with or without an overprint were used, or captured stamps were overprinted. Here are some examples:

Other types of stamps used as normal postage stamps without overprint or any other change

Austria 1854 — fiscal stamps
Spain 1879 — telegraph stamps

339 France — surcharge stamp to help in the fight against cancer.

340

340–341 Turkish surcharge stamps supporting the fight against malaria, and the Red Crescent.

342 Emergency issue of the Russian post in Rethymnon (Crete), 1899. The stamp was produced by handstamping.

343 Colombian fiscal stamp with an overprint, used in 1903 as a postage stamp.

344 Turkish stamp with the overprint 'Cilicie', used by the French when they occupied Asia Minor after the First World War.

345 French stamp with overprint for the occupied area of Memel.

346 Hungarian stamp converted by means of the overprint into a Czechoslovak stamp.

347 When Cyprus became independent the colonial stamps were overprinted.

Ivory Coast 1903 — parcel stamps
Spain 1916 — stamps of the Postal Savings Bank
Denmark 1919 — ferry service parcel post stamps
Soviet Union 1921 — control stamps
Germany 1923 — tax stamps
Ethiopia 1931 — official stamps
Spain 1931 — delivery stamps
Brazil 1953 — obligatory surcharge stamps

348 Dutch postcard with the
original denomination
overprinted by an ornament
bearing the new value.

349 Polish stamp with
a German propaganda
overprint.

350 Czechoslovak postage-
due stamp perforated and
overprinted 'Overall Food
Tax 2 Crowns'.

*Other types of stamps used as normal postage stamps with overprint
or other indication*

British Guiana 1878 — official stamps
Dominica 1879 — fiscal stamps
Gabon 1889 — postage due stamps
Italy 1891 — parcel stamps
Brazil 1898 — newspaper stamps
Costa Rica 1911 — telegraph stamps
Denmark 1918 — accountancy stamps
Spanish Morocco 1920 — postal order stamps
Turkey 1921 — Navy League labels
Ecuador 1924 — tobacco tax stamps
Peru 1930 — airmail stamps

It is obvious that in the same way as all sorts of labels and non-
postal adhesives were used in times of need as postage stamps,
the latter were sometimes used for non-postal purposes, with and
without overprint.

2. Airmail stamps

When airmail services started, the postage for an airmail letter was high, much higher than for surface mail. Shortly after the introduction of airmail services, special airmail stamps, or stamps for the additional airmail surcharge, were printed. In some countries it is permitted to use airmail stamps also for surface mail and normal postage stamps for airmail. In other countries different regulations apply. There exist stamps issued for just one flight of a certain aeroplane (Germany 1912, aeroplane *Gelber Hund*), airmail stamps for mail going abroad only (Guatemala 1931), stamps for domestic use only and valid only for certain routes (Italy 1917), stamps for Zeppelin mail (Germany 1928), for helicopter mail (Belgium 1950). The first airmail stamps were produced by overprinting other stamps:

Italy 1917 — express letter stamps
Austria 1918 — normal postage stamps
Sweden 1920 — official stamps
Chile 1927 — unissued commemorative stamps
Persia 1928 — fiscal stamps
Costa Rica 1930 — telegraph stamps
Greece 1938 — postage due stamps
Ecuador 1938 — surcharge stamps
Spanish Morocco 1939 — consular stamps
Bulgaria 1945 — parcel stamps

351 Czechoslovak airmail stamp produced by overprinting a normal postage stamp with an aircraft design and the new value.

352 Airmail stamp of the Argentine with the overprint 'Aereo' and the new value.

353

354 Lebanon.

355 Ceylon.

353 Most airmail stamps contain an aircraft motif. Here are some examples: firstly from Chile.

356 Yugoslavia.

358 Czechoslovakia.

357 Iraq.

359 USA.

360 Argentina.

Airmail stamps, like normal postage stamps, can have an additional function. There are stamps for registered airmail, official airmail stamps (Soviet Union 1922), airmail express stamps (Brazil 1929), obligatory airmail surcharge stamps (Turkey 1929), airmail fieldpost stamps and express airmail fieldpost stamps (Italy 1943). And there are also a large number of airmail stamps with a surcharge for welfare purposes.

In this connection mention should be made of another attribute belonging to airmail. In Europe the transportation of mail by air has become commonplace and no extra charge is made for airmail. Such letters bear no mark of distinction. The practice was quite different in the past as far as airmail in Europe was concerned, and still is for overseas airmail. At first airmail was marked as such in handwriting. Very soon, though, the postal administrations printed special labels with texts like 'Air Mail', 'Par Avion', 'Flugpost', etc. To save weight, special, light notepaper and covers are used for airmail and on such covers the label is already printed. An airmail label belongs to an airmail letter. It is not an absolute necessity, especially in the case of letters and postcards dating back to pioneer days, but it adds to the appearance of an airmail cover and is an integral part of it. There exist many different labels. Although they are not postal adhesives proper, some specialists collect them.

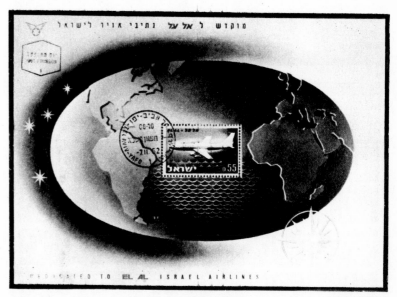

361 Israeli miniature airmail sheet.

362 Registered airmail cover dated 1965 and bearing all the required attributes including the airmail label.

364

365

363–366 A selection of airmail labels.

366

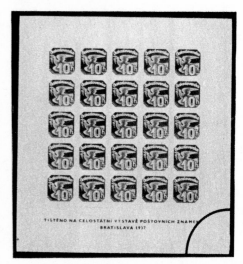

367 Block of eighty blue Mercury (Austria, 1851), the largest multiple in existence. In March 1970 it was stolen from the Postal Museum, Prague.

368 Miniature sheet of twenty-five newspaper stamps.

XI Covers from France and Italy: a rare French example with a great deal of franking, including a 5 franc stamp (1); a cover from one of the Italian States with Modena stamps (2); and one showing fan-shaped mixed franking the green 5 centesimi stamp is Sardinian, whereas the blue fifteen centesimi stamps come from the Kingdom of Italy (3).

XII The Cape of Good Hope issued the world's first triangular stamps in 1853 (1). Envelopes dating back a hundred years or more have not always retained their freshness, as this American example dated 1858 demonstrates (2). The Canadian halfpenny stamp is no rarity but a cover with twenty copies of this stamp is certainly a showpiece for any collection of Canadian stamps (3).

1

2

3

369–370 Two provisional newspaper stamps issued after the First World War in Czechoslovakia.

371 Newspaper stamp produced by overprinting an express stamp.

372 Austrian Imperial Journal Stamp of 1890.

3. Newspaper stamps

These have won a very prominent place in classical philately. The first newspaper stamps were issued by Austria as far back as 1851, just one year after Austria's first postage stamps came into use. These are the famous stamps with the effigy of Mercury. No value was printed on these stamps — it was denoted by their colour. More will be said about them in a later chapter. Of great interest are the stamps introduced in 1865 in the USA for the franking of postbags and newspaper parcels. They were the largest stamps of the nineteenth century and their dimensions have only recently been exceeded by certain commemorative stamps. The first miniature sheet of newspaper stamps was printed in 1937 during a stamp exhibition in Bratislava (Czechoslovakia). The miniature sheet was composed of twenty-five newspaper stamps of ten heller. Newspaper stamps were in many cases produced by overprinting other types of stamps:

Italy 1878 — official stamps
Turkey 1879 — normal postage stamps
Persia 1909 — registration labels
Belgium 1922 — parcel stamps
Czechoslovakia 1926 — express stamps

In some cases newspaper stamps have additional functions, as for instance:

USA 1875 — accountancy stamps for newspaper parcels
Denmark 1907 — accountancy stamps for newspaper taxes
Austria 1916 — fieldpost newspaper stamps
Belgium 1928 — stamps for newspaper parcels

Journal fiscal stamps were used in many countries, the first being issued by Austria in 1853. With their help the tax for the printing of newspapers was collected and also the tax for newspapers imported from abroad. In actual fact they are not postage stamps at all but, since they were (especially in the case of imported newspapers) cancelled with normal postal handstamps, these journal fiscal stamps are being collected.

When fiscals were introduced they had to be stuck on to every single copy of a newspaper and had to be cancelled by hand, which was a painstaking business. The problem was solved in a clever way by affixing them to the newsprint before the printing and the adhesives were automatically cancelled by printing across them. This system was used in France, Turkey and in other countries. Fiscal stamps are normally of no interest to philatelists. Sometimes though, it happened that there was a shortage of fiscal stamps. In such a case the lowest values of normal postage stamps were used instead. Postage stamps showing part of the newspaper printing are rare and specialists are on the look-out for them. More interesting than just a stamp with newspaper print is, of course, a complete copy of an old newspaper with a postage stamp instead of a fiscal stamp.

4. Official stamps

These belong to the group of stamps which are not normally on sale at post office counters. Their function is exactly the same as the function of normal postage stamps, with the sole difference that they can be used only by government bodies and official institutions, and also by international organizations. In some countries official stamps could be used by all official bodies; in other countries there are special issues of official stamps for some ministries or offices. Most official stamps have a value printed, but there are some official stamps without a value given. Here are some types of official stamps:

Spain 1854 — official stamps for ministries
Würtemberg 1875 — for communal offices
New Zealand 1891 — for the Life Insurance Department
Austria 1897 — court delivery stamps for Galizia
Transvaal 1902 — for railway offices
Denmark 1902 — for police offices
Sudan 1905 — for military offices
Bulgaria 1905 — for the telegraph administration
USA 1910 — for the Post Office Savings Bank
Netherlands 1913 — for social welfare offices

Different sorts of official stamps were issued for international authorities:

Schleswig   1920 — for the Inter-allied Commission
Switzerland 1922 — for the League of Nations

373 Austrian Imperial Journal Stamp affixed to blank newsprint and automatically cancelled when the newspaper is printed.

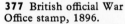

374 The title of a Constantinople newspaper of 1895 with a Turkish fiscal affixed before printing, together with a postage stamp of the Austrian post in Turkey and the handstamp 'Constantinople', and an Austrian Imperial Journal Stamp affixed at the destination cancelled with the handstamp 'Cattaro'.

375 French fiscal cancelled by newsprint.

377 British official War Office stamp, 1896.

376 Turkish stamp used instead of a fiscal and cancelled by newsprint.

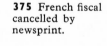

378 Swiss postal label with handstamp for official mail. In practice this label is virtually equal to an official stamp. Such labels were used until 1934.

379 From 1935 onwards the Swiss used postage stamps with a perforation, and later with an overprint.

380 An overprint converted this Turkish postage stamp into an official stamp.

381 Argentinian official stamp.

382 Italian official stamp.

383 Czechoslovak official stamp.

384 Official stamp from Ecuador.

385 Official stamp from North Korea.

386 Court Delivery stamp of Austria-Hungary issued for Galicia (Poland).

387 Swiss official stamp for the European office of the United Nations.

Switzerland 1923 — for the International Labour Office
Netherlands 1934 — for the Court of International Justice
Switzerland 1944 — for the International Education Office
Switzerland 1948 — for the World Health Organization
Switzerland 1950 — for the European Office of the United Nations
Switzerland 1950 — for the International Refugees Organization
Switzerland 1956 — for the World Meteorological Organization
Switzerland 1957 — for the Universal Postal Union
Switzerland 1958 — for the International Telecommunication Union

5. Express stamps

These serve for the payment of special delivery of mail. On arrival at the post office of destination express mail is immediately delivered by a special messenger and arrives sooner than mail carried by the postman on his usual rounds. This extra service has to be paid for. In most countries the express surcharge is paid by normal stamps, but some countries have issued special stamps for this purpose. The first express stamps were issued in 1885 by the United States. Some express stamps include the functions of other types of stamps, too:

Belgium 1874 — telegraph stamps used as express stamps
Aegean Islands 1904 — express surcharge stamps
Austria 1916 — express stamps for printed matter
Bosnia and Hercegovina 1916 — express stamps of the military post
Italy 1943 — express stamps of the fieldpost
Italy 1943 — express airmail stamps of the fieldpost

Express mail and special delivery are not a modern invention. In the past, express letters were often inscribed 'cito' — meaning fast, urgent, even 'citissimo' — most urgent. Later other signs were used. In some countries a little feather was stuck into the seal on the back of the cover marking such letters as express. Such *feather letters* were used in Sweden, for instance, in the last century and earlier. Nowadays post offices use special labels, usually with the French word 'Exprès' or, in England, 'Special Delivery'. The reason why French expressions are so often used in postal services and on postal documents is that French has been adopted as the international postal language. Unlike airmail labels, express labels are practically always issued by the post. They are an integral part of an express letter. Some specialists collect express labels.

388 Italian express stamp.

389 Czechoslovak express stamp.

390-391 Express labels from all over the world.

392 Picture postcard with text in shorthand, mailed express.

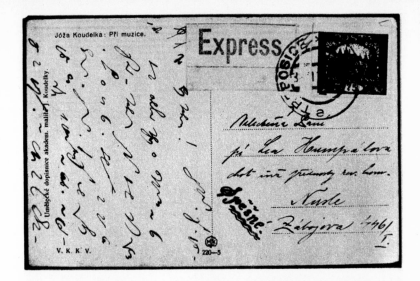

393 Registered letter with the registration label of the British post office in Constantinople.

394 Registered letter from Jerusalem, 1900, bearing the registration handstamp 'Jerusalem Palestin R'; the registration number is handwritten.

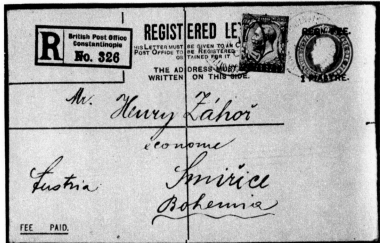

6. Stamps for registered mail

In most countries the extra charge for registered mail is paid with postage stamps of all kinds. In addition a special registration label with a number is stuck on the letter, or the letter is stamped with a registration handstamp and the number written into it. Some countries, though, especially in Latin America, have printed special stamps for registered mail. They are very similar to registration labels. A large 'R' is printed on them and the number of the mail item is entered by hand. The first stamps of this type were issued by Colombia in 1865.

Registration labels are also issued only by the post offices. On their own they have no franking value at all. They are a most important attribute of a registered letter (instead of a label a handstamp is sometimes used) and, because they are issued by the postal administration and are very interesting, they have attracted a number of specialized collectors. The first predecessors of the registration labels are probably the postage receipt stamps of the Berlin post of 1827, which have already been mentioned. Registration labels are varied in appearance and collectors distinguish different issues and types.

Sometimes when a shortage of stamps occurred, registration labels with an overprint were used as postage stamps (e.g. New Guinea, taken by the British in 1914. When supplies of overprinted German colonial stamps were exhausted, registration labels were overprinted.) The German Democratic Republic introduced, in 1967, self-service machines selling registration labels with the value '50 Pf.' printed on them. In actual fact these are stamps for registered mail. The machine issues them in pairs with the same number, one to be used on the registered letter, the other to be kept by the sender as a certificate of posting.

395 Colombian stamp for registered mail.

7. Stamps for money-letters

Again it was Colombia where the first stamps of this type were issued in 1865. Most interesting are the semi-official money-letter stamps issued in 1916 in Germany. The shipping company Deutsche Ozean-Reederei, whose commercial submarines *Deutsch-*

396 Colombia: registration stamp for the province of Antioquia.

397

398

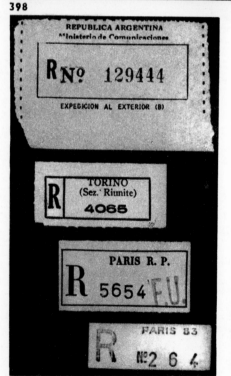

397–398 Registration labels from all over the world.

399 Reverse sides of two Czechoslovak registration labels with the town's name set off after printing from the sheet underneath.

400 Stamp for money letters carried by German submarines in 1916.

land and *Bremen* were breaking the allied blockade to bring vital raw-material from the USA, issued, with the consent of the government, special stamps for money-letters. Up to 1917, when the USA entered the war against Germany, the submarine *Deutschland* made the trip to America only twice. The submarine *Bremen* made only one trip and was sunk on the return voyage. The Netherlands introduced in 1921—3 a special service for money-letters sent overseas. On the deck of the steamers, mainly the boats sailing to the Netherlands Antilles, fireproof and unsinkable safes were installed. In the event of shipwreck the safe would float on the surface and, with the help of a system of light signals, would attract the attention of other passing ships. The mail locked in these safes had to be franked with special stamps bearing the inscription 'Drijvende Brandkast'.

8. Stamps for receipt on delivery

In a number of countries, mainly in Latin America, it became customary to use specially issued stamps for the payment of the charge for mail sent for receipt on delivery. They are recognized by the large letters 'AR', which is the abbreviation for the international term used in postal service 'Avis de réception' — receipt on delivery. In 1898 a stamp was issued in Chile with the text 'Avis de paiement' — receipt of payment. This stamp paid for a receipt confirming that the addressee had properly received a sum of money sent to him and the receipt was then sent to the sender of the money.

9. Stamps for printed matter

The first stamps of this type were issued by Turkey in 1879 (stamps with the overprint 'Imprimé'). They were also used as newspaper stamps. Austria issued in 1916 express stamps for printed matter. In 1934 three newspaper stamps were overprinted in Czechoslovakia with the letters 'OT'. They were intended for business printed matter.

10. Parcel stamps

401–403 Dutch marine insurance stamps.

There are quite a number of postal administrations that have issued special stamps for the posting of parcels. The first appeared

402   403

404 Colombian stamp for receipt on delivery issued for the province of Antioquia.

405 Czechoslovak stamp for commercial printed matter.

406 Peruvian parcel stamp.

408 Danish parcel freight stamp for Greenland.

407 Italian parcel-post stamp designed in two parts.

409 Danish stamp for parcels carried by postal ferry boats.

410 Stamp for pneumatic mail, Italy.

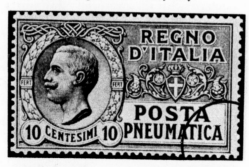

in Italy in 1884. Nowadays Italian parcel stamps consist of two parts — the left half is affixed to the part of the packet-card remaining as a document at the post office and the right half is stuck on the receipt. Up to 1927 parcel stamps were sometimes used as a whole, which is why some catalogues give two prices for cancelled parcel stamps, the higher price being for the unsevered double stamp. According to Stanley Gibbons, unsevered stamps in used condition are from cancelled-to-order material. The following types of parcel stamps are in existence:

Denmark 1905 — parcel freight stamps for Greenland
USA 1912 — express parcel stamps
Denmark 1919 — stamps for parcels carried by postal ferry boats
Belgium 1928 — railway parcel stamps
Belgium 1928 — newspaper parcel stamps

411 Venezuelan stamp for sea mail.

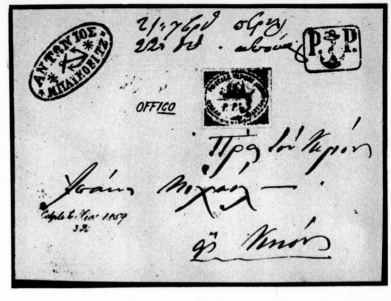

412 Cover with stamp of the Turkish Admiralty, 1859.

414 Italian fieldpost, 1943.

415 Stamp authorizing submarine mail. It was issued in March 1945 to German troops cut off on the Hela peninsula.

413 Finnish fieldpost stamp, 1941.

Belgium 1939 — stamps for soldiers' parcels
Finland 1949 — parcel stamps for the automobile post

11. Stamps for money-orders

The Netherlands issued in 1884 special stamps for money-orders. Similar stamps were introduced in 1895 in San Salvador and in 1915 in Spain.

12. Stamps for pneumatic mail

The first stamps for pneumatic mail were issued in 1913 by Italy. There are not many stamps for pneumatic mail in existence, but there is a fair amount of stationery for pneumatic mail, such as postcards, covers, etc.

13. Sea-mail stamps

Right from the beginning, shortly after the first stamps came into use, special stamps were printed for mail carried by boats.

The most famous stamp of this type is probably the 'Lady McLeod' of Trinidad. It is a blue stamp with the initials 'L.McL' and a drawing of a steamer on it. It was issued in 1847 by David Bryce, the owner of the vessel, and sold for five cents, the charge for mail carried between Port of Spain and San Fernando. This stamp, especially on a cover, is a gem in any collection.

In 1865 Colombia issued stamps with the text 'Sobre porte' (above postage), which means an extra payment for the higher postage usually charged by foreign navigation companies. There are official issues of sea-mail stamps, semi-official issues and private issues of shipping companies. (In the twentieth century some airlines issued their own stamps, too.)

In 1859 the Turkish Admiralty issued a stamp which was used for the franking of letters carried by the ships of the Admiralty. Actually it was the first Turkish stamp, as postage stamps of Turkey were not issued until 1863. It is an interesting, rare specimen. In the centre of the dark red stamp is the silhouette of an old steamer and around it a text in Italian, not in Turkish, as Italian was the most used language in the Levant. No value is printed on the stamp, just the letters 'P.P.' — postage paid. The amount of postage had to be entered into the stamp.

The Austrian steamship company DDSG (Donau-Dampfschiffahrtsgesellschaft) operating on the Danube, issued their own stamps in 1866. All these semi-official and private stamps are of philatelic interest due to the fact that they were used for mail.

In 1938, during the Spanish Civil War, the Spanish Republic, encircled by a blockade of General Franco's warships, issued stamps for use on mail carried by submarines breaking the enemy blockade.

14. Fieldpost stamps

These stamps are issued to soldiers or their families free of charge (in which case there is usually no value printed on the stamps), or at a price lower than the normal postage. They are either normal postage stamps with an overprint denoting their purpose, or specially issued stamps. The first stamps for soldiers

416 Colombian stamp for delayed mail.

417 Czechoslovak personal delivery stamp.

418 French telegraph stamp of 1868.

419 Austrian telegraph stamp.

420 Cover with Austrian fiscal used instead of a stamp. Use of fiscals was against regulations and such covers are rare.

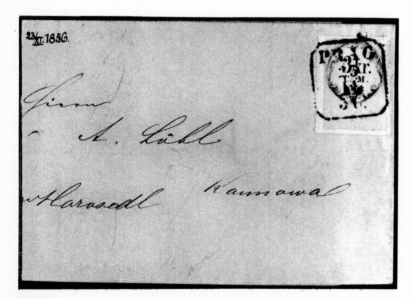

421 Classical French postage-due stamp.

422 Postage-due stamp from the USA.

423 Postage-due stamp from Chile, 1895.

424 British postage-due stamp.

were printed in 1901 in France. The common fifteen centime stamp was overprinted with the letters 'F.M.', the abbreviation for 'franchise militaire' — free of charge, military. In some countries, soldiers using the fieldpost did not have to affix stamps at all. Such mail can be distinguished by the fieldpost handstamps. This, too, is a special branch of collecting which has found many specialists. There are also military and fieldpost stamps with a special designation, as for instance:

Austria 1918 — fieldpost newspaper stamps
Belgium 1939 — parcel stamps for military mail
Italy 1943 — fieldpost express stamps
Italy 1943 — fieldpost airmail stamps
Italy 1943 — fieldpost express airmail stamps

15. Telegraph stamps

In some countries separate stamps were printed for the payment of telegrams. One of the reasons, probably, was that in a number of States the telegraph service had its own administration not linked with the post. The first telegraph stamps were introduced by Prussia in 1864. Sometimes provisional telegraph stamps were used; these were normal postage stamps with an overprint, as, for instance, in 1943 in Algeria. In 1891 telegraph stamps were used in Chile without any overprint for normal postage, as there was a shortage of stamps. Telegraph stamps are not philatelic items, unless they were used as postage stamps.

16. Telephone stamps

These exist in a limited number of countries and were used for the payment of telephone calls made at a post office. They are not philatelic items.

17. Other types of postage stamps

A great variety of stamps exist. Here are some examples:

Victoria 1854 — the stamp 'Too-Late', i.e. for mail handed in after post office business hours
Hungary 1916 — savings bank stamp
Spain 1931 — delivery stamps

425 Modern French postage-due stamp.

426 Dutch postage stamp changed by an overprint into a postage-due stamp.

427 Czechoslovakia: a postage stamp used as postage-due and marked as such with a rubber handstamp 'Doplatne' (postage due).

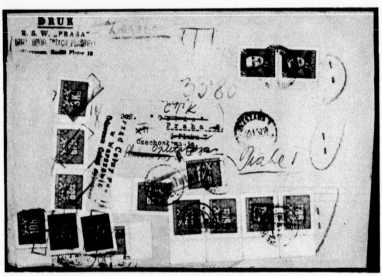

428 Cover from Poland, 1952. The Czechoslovak post affixed by mistake a great number of postage-due stamps. They were cancelled with a rubber handstamp 'Neplatne' (invalid) and the postage due was not collected.

Mexico 1935 — insured letter stamps
Dominican Republic 1935 — surcharge stamps for obligatory use on mail addressed to the president or ministers
Czechoslovakia 1937 — personal delivery stamps

429 Turkish postage-due stamp of 1865.

II. POSTAGE-DUE STAMPS

These serve for the collection of postage on mail posted without stamps or with insufficient franking. The first postage-due stamps were introduced in 1859 by France. There were cases, though, when postage-due stamps were used as normal postage stamps. There are quite a number of normal postage stamps changed by an overprint into postage-due stamps, and vice versa.

430 Rumanian surcharge stamp for social relief.

431 West German surcharge stamp in aid of Berlin.

432 Canadian stamp with overprint 'War Tax'.

433 Obligatory Turkish surcharge stamp for airmail.

A very special role was given to the first issues of postage-due stamps in Turkey. Simultaneously with the first set of postage stamps, a set of postage-due stamps was issued in 1863. The postage-due stamps are of exactly the same design as the postage stamps, but all values are printed in black on reddish-brown paper. The network of the Turkish post was at first rather small. Therefore, in places where there were no post offices and no stamps available, letters were collected together with the postage; later the brown stamps, instead of the normal postage stamps, were affixed at the nearest post office. Whereas normally an amount equal to double the normal postage is collected for the missing franking on a letter, in this case stamps equal to the normal value of the postage were used.

As time passed many special sorts of postage-due stamps came into use:

Baden 1862 — rural postage-due stamps
Rumania 1895 — parcel postage-due stamps
France 1908 — postage-due stamps for official mail where the addressee had to pay the postage
USA 1912 — parcel postage-due stamps
Rumania 1915 — postage-due stamps used for the collection of a war tax
Rumania 1932 — postage-due stamps used for the collection of a tax on picture postcards
Yugoslavia 1933 — postage-due surcharge stamps
Czechoslovakia 1937 — surcharge postage-due stamp for personal delivery of mail

III. FURTHER CATEGORIES OF STAMPS

1. Stamps exempting payment of postage

In a number of countries many official bodies, societies or individual persons were exempt from the payment of postage. For this purpose special stamps, printed without any indication of value, confirmed the exemption from postage. The catalogues do not always list these stamps in the same manner. In the sections dealing with some countries they are listed according to the year of issue together with other postage stamps; in other cases they are listed at the end of the country amongst stamps issued for special purposes. There are also differences between catalogues. Some of them do not list these stamps at all, although they are postage stamps of a philatelic nature and value. Such stamps were issued for such purposes as the following:

Spain 1869 — for the authors of works on postal history, to enable them to distribute the book free of charge
Switzerland 1871 — for interned French soldiers who crossed the Swiss frontier during the Franco-Prussian war
Afghanistan 1882 — for postal offices
Spain 1895 — for Members of Parliament and later also for Senators
Portugal 1899 — for all sorts of societies
Italy 1924 — for public institutions
Spain 1938 — for the official philatelic office
France 1939 — for Spanish refugees

434 Turkish registered letter with normal postage stamps and additional surcharge stamp for the Red Crescent.

435 Czechoslovak sealing label.

2. Surcharge stamps

These stamps do not have a franking value, but they are on sale at post office counters and the income from their sale is usually destined for welfare purposes. The sender can affix them to his mail in addition to the normal postage, and they are generally cancelled with the normal handstamps. In some cases their use is obligatory. If the sender did not use obligatory surcharge stamps during the period when he should have done so, the post collected the surcharge from the addressee with the help of a postage due surcharge stamp. The following types of surcharge stamps are known:

Portugal 1911 — charity tax stamps
Turkey 1911 — surcharge stamps for the Red Crescent and Child Welfare; their use was obligatory on twenty-three State and religious holidays during the year, and they could be used voluntarily on other days
Greece 1914 — surcharge stamps for the Red Cross
Guatemala 1919 — surcharge stamps for the building of new post offices
Portugal 1925 — surcharge stamps for the collection of funds for the building of war memorials
France 1927 — surcharge for the amortization of the State debt. No surcharge stamps were used, but the surcharge was collected by means of an overprint on normal postage stamps
Portugal 1928 — surcharge stamps for the collection of funds to enable Portugal to participate in the Olympic Games at Amsterdam
Greece 1939 — surcharge stamps for the benefit of postal employees suffering from tuberculosis

These stamps are not always listed in catalogues in the usual manner. With some countries they are listed amongst normal postage stamps, and in other cases they are mentioned at the end under the heading 'Surcharge stamps'.

436 Mexican return label.

437 US return stamp.

438 Theresienstadt stamp.

439 German census stamp.

440 US Christmas seal.

441 Stamp of the cantonal administration of Zurich (Switzerland), 1843.

3. Labels and stamps without franking value

A number of stamps and adhesive labels were produced which had no franking value. They are of interest to specialized collectors as part of entires. Here are a few examples:

a) Official adhesive labels. Sometimes the post office has to open undeliverable mail if the sender's name is not on the cover. In the United Kingdom such mail is returned to the sender in an official envelope, but in other countries a postal adhesive label is used to close the letter again and to show that it had been officially opened. The first stamps for the closing of letters were introduced in 1857 in Württemberg. These labels are not usually listed in catalogues. They had no franking value and are therefore not real stamps. They are of interest only to specialized collectors.

b) Return labels. Mail refused by the addressee was returned to the sender. In some cases this was marked on the letter by a handstamp, in other cases a special label was used. The first labels of this sort were introduced by the post of Thurn and Taxis in 1852.

c) Licensing stamps. Such stamps were introduced during the Second World War by the Nazi rulers for the concentration camp of Theresienstadt in occupied Czechoslovakia. The prisoners of this camp were issued with a limited number of such stamps and could send them to their relatives and friends. This stamp was the licence to send a parcel (mostly food) to the prisoner, and had to be affixed to the parcel or, in exceptional cases, to the packet card.

From 1 May to 15 October 1948 in West Germany only mail which was marked by a licence stamp was carried by airmail. Only a limited number of persons were issued with such stamps. The remaining supplies were later used as airmail labels.

d) Census stamps. In the years 1903 and 1905 the German authorities wanted to discontinue the use of stamps by some government offices. To find out the overall sum of this postage, a special type of stamp was issued marked with the text 'Frei durch Ablösung' or 'Frei laut Avers'. The amount of use of these stamps during one year enabled the post to judge the lump sum to be paid by these offices for the carriage of their mail.

e) Accountancy stamps. These were used only for the internal accountancy of the official authorities. In 1923 and 1924 such stamps were used in the Netherlands. Austria issued them in 1948, and they served for the accounting of the internal delivery charges for money orders. Up to the beginning of 1956 they were used for the accounting of pensions paid to employees of the post.

f) Christmas seals. In 1904 Denmark was the first to issue special seals at Christmas. From the proceeds of their sale at post office counters, the fight against tuberculosis was to be supported. They were called *Jul* stamps, because of the inscription Jul, meaning Christmas. Similar seals, which are not cancelled on covers, have been subsequently issued by other countries, too. In the United States they are called *Christmas Seals*.

g) Duty stamps. In Italy a special extra franking exists for all mail delivered by private post. This custom reminds one of the Sardinian lettersheets with a handstamp of 1819. For the collecting of this duty special stamps with the inscription 'Recapito autorizzato' were issued in 1928.

IV. LOCAL STAMPS

In some countries of the world the local authorities started to issue stamps sooner than the national authorities. In Switzerland, for instance, the first stamps were issued in 1843 by the canton Zurich, and later in 1843 by the canton Geneva, and in 1845 by Basle. The federal post of Switzerland undertook this task as late as 1848. Something similar happened in the USA, where the first local stamps were issued in 1846. They are called postmasters' stamps and are very rare. The first general issues of stamps came into use in 1847. Postmasters' stamps made their appearance again in 1861, after the beginning of the Civil War in the Confederate States, but they were soon replaced by general issues for the whole territory of the Confederate States.

In many cases local stamps were issued later in other countries if for some reason there was a shortage of stamps. Quickly printed provisional stamps, substitutes, fiscal stamps and overprints were used; stamps were bisected, quartered, and so on.

By a decree of the Russian Minister of Home Affairs, issued in 1860, local administrative offices were established, the so-called *zemstvos*. These offices had the right to print stamps for their own use. Although these stamps are not listed in normal catalogues (with the exception of Wenden stamps listed by Stanley Gibbons

442 Argentine stamp for Corrientes.

443 City post of Bogota (Colombia).

444 Chinese local post.

445 Cover with a stamp of the zemstvo (provincial council) of Borovich in Russia.

446 Used stamp of the zemstvo Dmitrov.

447 Stamp for the local post of Luboml (Poland) with text in four languages.

445

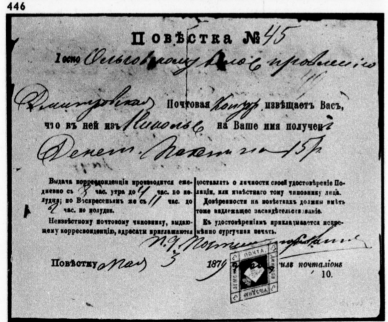

446

447

XIII The beautiful colours of modern stamps are apparent in these examples illustrating flowers and fruit or commemorating United Nations' activities.

448 Private post, New York.

449 German private post.

450 Private hotel post, Austria.

451 Cover delivered by the Lianos private post of Istanbul, 1866.

and in German catalogues, mainly because the first issues had German inscriptions), they are official postage stamps with franking value. They are collected by a great number of specialists. During the First World War, local stamps were issued in many Polish towns.

Similar examples of stamps issued by local postal authorities could be listed from all over the world. The approach of different stamp catalogues is not always the same. Some local posts are listed normally, while others can only be found in a specialized catalogue and in philatelic literature.

V. PRIVATE STAMPS

As mentioned earlier, the State postal service was often unable to cover the whole territory of the country, or could not cope with the amount of mail in large cities. This gap was filled by private posts. They took care of the delivery of mail, collected charges for their services and printed their own stamps. Private posts existed in many countries and in some places they still exist. Between 1861 and 1900 many private postal establishments were, for instance, functioning in Germany. In 1865 a private post of the firm 'Lianos & Cie' was opened in Istanbul. All these private posts used their own stamps. Stamps of private posts are to be found in Norway and Denmark, where they are called *Bypost*, and elsewhere.

The stamps of these private posts are frequently and undeservedly ignored by stamp collectors. They are stamps which really served postal needs and have all the attributes of stamps. There

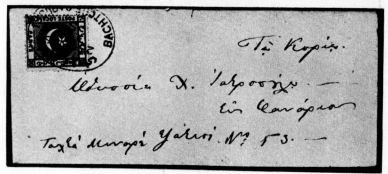

is only one difference, and that is that they were not issued by the official postal authorities. The organizers of the private posts, though, had the consent of the authorities to run their posts and issue stamps. The stamps of private posts, therefore, do belong to philatelic collections, in particular to specialized and study collections. Entires with these stamps are very often rather expensive and rare, and there are not many of them in existence. The most interesting specimens are entires with mixed franking, i.e. a combination of private post stamps and stamps of the official post. They originate from places where these two networks met.

VI. PRIVATE LOCAL ISSUES

The owners of certain islands round the British coast produce adhesives for the prepayment of the ferrying of letters and parcels to the nearest point on the mainland. They are not valid for national or international postage and the British Post Office does not recognise them as postage stamps. Some islands like Herm and Lundy have been producing locals for over thirty years and they appear to have been of interest to visitors mostly as souvenirs.

In 1966 the Stamp Trade Standing Committee was jointly established by the Philatelic Traders' Society and the British Philatelic Association to inquire into the status of stamps and other philatelic material and to ensure that items offered for sale are sold with a fair and just description. The Committee has considered these island issues and has described their character. They are called 'British Private Local Issues'.

Similar issues resembling postage stamps have appeared in other countries as well, for instance in the United States. Some of these Private Local Issues are rather attractive, other issues are more primitive. Collectors must not mistake them for postage stamps, although there is a limited number of philatelists who collect such items.

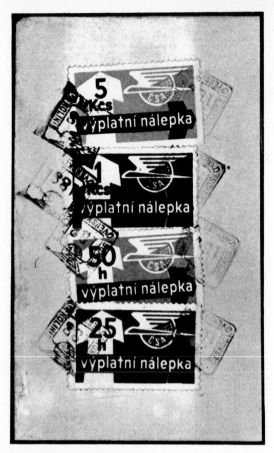

452 Labels of the Czechoslovak airline CSA.

453 Private stamp of the Hamburg American Packet Company.

454–456 The smallest stamps in the world: Mecklenburg-Schwerin, Brunswick and Colombia.

457 Stamp from Victoria (Australia), also one of the smallest stamps issued.

FROM THE SMALLEST TO THE LARGEST

458

The British stamps of 1840 are classical, not only because they were the first stamps of the world, nor because they showed good taste and their production was perfect. They are also classical because of their size and shape. They were neither too small nor too large and were ideally suited to their purpose. Their size and shape therefore became a yardstick for other stamps. The overwhelming majority of all stamps have the shape of a vertical or horizontal rectangle. But as far back as the classical period stamps of different shapes are to be found. The first step was from a rectangle to a square. A novelty was introduced in 1853 by the Cape of Good Hope when the first triangular stamps were issued.

As time passed, stamps appeared in a greater variety of shapes. In some cases the postal administrations had special reasons for a different shape. They wanted to distinguish special types of stamps from other issues by their appearance, to make their handling easier. Thus Austria printed express stamps in triangular shape and Belgium issued hexagonal telegraph stamps.

The smallest stamps of the world were also issued during the classical period by Mecklenburg-Schwerin in 1856. In actual fact they are quarters of a shilling stamp, but they could be used separately. The size of these tiny stamps is 9×9 millimetres (less than $\frac{3}{8}''$ square). Just a fraction larger are the quarter stamps of Brunswick of 1857—$11\frac{1}{2} \times 11\frac{1}{2}$ millimetres (a little over $\frac{7}{32}''$ square). Soon it became apparent, though, that such tiny stamp sizes were not practical, and they were discarded.

458–459 Two giant stamps from the USA.

460 The record for width was formerly held by this Polish stamp.

The record as far as size is concerned was held for many years by the USA newspaper stamps of 1865. The design is 97.3 millimetres (over $3\frac{3}{4}''$) high and 53.3 millimetres (just under $2\frac{1}{8}''$) wide. Not very much smaller were the United States stamps for registered letters of 1872. In 1960 Polland issued an imperforate ten zloty stamp with a reproduction of the altar in the Maria Church of Krakow. The design measures 96×76 millimetres ($3\frac{3}{4}'' \times 3''$). A year later Poland issued a 5,60 zloty stamp, showing a tanker, which is 107 millimetres (about $4\frac{1}{4}''$) wide and 26 millimetres ($1''$) high. These record sizes have recently been matched and even surpassed by other stamps.

In later years, and especially after the Second World War, the stamp market was flooded by a great number of different shapes of stamps — octagonals, rhomboids, trapezoids, etc. These shapes are not necessitated by any postal needs. They are designed for one purpose — to make the stamps more attractive to stamp collectors, and therefore more saleable. The most unusual are the circular stamps of Tonga and the irregular shapes of Sierra Leone stamps.

461 Octagonal Turkish stamp for Thessaly, 1898.

THE STAMP MATERIAL

Let us now consider a young philatelist. He has accumulated his first stamps from letters and postcards; he has been given, as a present, a stamp packet or even an old collection. Here it should be pointed out that it is not advisable to entrust a beginner immediately with a stamp collection, however large or small, unless it too is a beginner's collection. For as long as the young philatelist has no basic experience and has not learned how to handle stamps, he can do great harm. By unprofessional handling he could damage valuable stamps or break up a collection which has already reached a certain level. It is later very difficult to undo such mistakes, and it is much safer to give beginners, especially children, whole collections only at a later stage.

462 Triangular stamp from Nigeria.

463 Rumanian rhombic stamp.

We can hardly assume that the beginner knows right from the start which road to choose in his collecting. That does not matter, though. Whilst working with his philatelic material he will get used to stamps and he will hit upon the basic theme of his collection — the target he is aiming at.

On the table in front of the future philatelist there are heaps of stamps and other philatelic material. The first and most important philatelic task begins now — the sorting. This is the task that a philatelist meets with most frequently. Whenever he acquires new stamps, whenever he reorganizes his collection, whatever he does, he always has to sort and group his stamps. Philately requires a perfect organization, arrangement and system. The more his stamps pass through his hands the better he will learn to know them.

At first the beginner should distribute the stamps on the table before him into three heaps: cancelled stamps, mint stamps, and entires and stationery. If there is a great quantity of material it is advisable to sort it out first according to countries, or on the basis of stamp designs.

But let us now return to the three basic heaps of material.

MINT AND USED

Uncancelled stamps are called *unused*. Unused stamps with untouched gum on their back, not even touched by a stamp hinge, are called *mint*. Some stamp collectors refuse all stamps whose gum is not completely untouched and look only for mint copies. This, of course, is not a purely philatelic requirement. It is to a great extent influenced by business or investment considerations due to the fact that it is easier to sell a mint stamp and in many cases, for a higher price. From a philatelic point of view, though, traces of a hinge (especially in the case of old stamps) are not a deficiency, as long as the reverse is not all covered by old hinges. It can be best expressed by the motto: collect stamps, not their gum!

Although the backs of stamps stuck into an album or put into a stock book cannot be seen, they should not be forgotten. A stamp collector who, without further thought, affixes a new stamp hinge on top of the remains of an old one will never be a good philatelist. A stamp should have only one hinge. It is quite easy to remove the rest of an old hinge, as will be seen later.

Gum is an attribute of a mint stamp, but there are exceptions. In some tropical countries stamps are issued without gum to make sure they do not get stuck together in the humid climate.

Beware: mint stamps should not be left lying around! Not only could they be carried away by a gust of wind, but very often they start curling up and can easily be damaged. Therefore it is advisable to weigh them down during sorting on the table, and to put them away as soon as possible into a stock book, album or at least into a transparent or normal envelope.

Nothing should be written on stamps. If you have to note some details or the price, write them down on the cover or on a piece of paper which you put together with the stamp into the envelope, or stick behind the stamp in the stock book. If there is no other way and you have to write on the stamp, use a normal, soft pencil and write lightly on the reverse. Never use an ink pencil or a pen. This applies to cancelled stamps, too.

Whilst sorting unused stamps from used ones, eliminate all damaged copies at the same time.

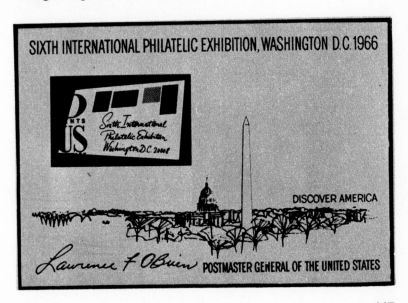

464 US miniature sheet.

465 Classical Rumanian cover.

466 Hungarian cover with 15 krajcár stamp, 1871.

467 Registered letter from Colombia.

468 Cover from Mexico.

469 Highly attractive cover from the USSR.

470 This cover travelled from Austria to Liverpool, and a British stamp was added in transit and cancelled.

471 Interesting modern cover returned from Colombia as not deliverable.
In Prague the cover was officially opened to find the sender. The post collected a delivery fee of 0.40 crowns as recorded by a special handstamp.

472 Another non-deliverable cover which travelled from one Berlin post office to the other.

473 Advice for the collector: stamps should be cut out carefully from covers and postcards.

Used stamps are sorted in a similar way to mint stamps. Just as gum is an attribute of mint stamps, so, in the case of used stamps, a cancellation is a necessity. You will sometimes come across stamps cancelled by pencil or pen.

LARGER UNITS

474 Everything which might colour stamps in water must be removed.

Among great numbers of single stamps you are also bound to find larger units of stamps: *pairs*, *strips*, *blocks* and *part sheets*, *miniature sheets*, *entires* and *stationery*.

First of all, do not tear apart pairs, strips and blocks of stamps. In the case of modern stamps this probably would not be a great disaster, but with old stamps you could do a great deal of damage. The best thing to do in such a case is to ask an experienced philatelist for his advice. The stamps of a miniature sheet should never be separated, whether it is a modern miniature sheet or an older one. Miniature sheets are sorted in a similar way to stamps.

In the end you are left with the third heap — covers, postcards, cut-outs, entires and stationery. First sort out postal stationery, i.e. covers and postcards with a stamp printed on them. They must remain as they are; never cut out the imprinted stamp with the cancellation.

The letters and postcards with affixed stamps must be inspected very carefully, every single item separately. Old covers dating back to the classical period, even if the stamp on such a cover is

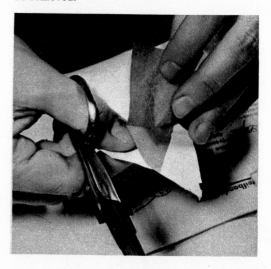

475 Immerse a batch of stamps in warm water.

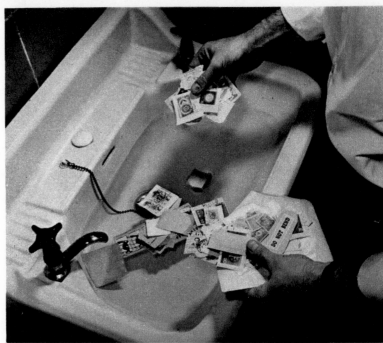

476 Remove soaked-off pieces of paper from the water.

477 Carefully take the stamps one by one out of the water.

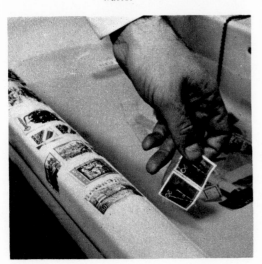

a very cheap one, should always be left untouched. Modern letters must be inspected, too. Have a look at the cancellation and other postal markings. As soon as you find anything special on such a letter or postcard, keep it untouched. Whenever you are not sure, seek advice.

Take care of the remaining letters, postcards and pieces. With a pair of scissors carefully cut out the stamp, but with a wider paper-margin all around to make sure that the perforations are not damaged. Everything that could colour the stamps must be carefully removed — parts of the cover with remarks or lines in indelible pencil, coloured paperlining of the envelopes and also the coloured printing on the sides of some airmail covers which could dissolve in water.

THE SOAKING AND DRYING OF STAMPS

Put all cancelled stamps with remains of paper and gum on their reverse, and also stamps cut out from letters and postcards, in a large cover or box until you find time to soak them off.

Pour clean water into a washbasin or a large bowl. The gum of stamps does not dissolve very well in cold water, but if the water is too hot it is not good either. Pleasantly warm water is ideal, and the best thermometer is your own hand.

Some philatelists like to add chemicals to the water to remove all traces of dirt from the stamps and to add to the freshness of their colours. But a word of warning here. The chemicals or washing powder should not contain ingredients, such as soda, which could damage the stamps. If some of your stamps are very dirty it is best to leave them till last and soak them separately.

On individual stamps you can use a little toilet soap, but in every case where you have used soap you must rinse the stamps in clean water afterwards, and also stamps soaked in water with chemicals must be rinsed afterwards in clean, lukewarm water. Rinsing is a necessity also if salt has been added to the water, or some hydrogen peroxide to achieve fresher and more stable colours. The beginner, though, will be safest if he just uses clean water without any chemicals.

Then put a batch of not more than one hundred stamps into the water. Carefully immerse them and let them soak. The remains of paper and bits of envelope will come off after two to three minutes. Usually there is no need to pull them off. Always bear in mind that the wet paper of the stamps is very delicate and can be easily damaged in the water by rash handling.

First extract from the water the soaked-off pieces of paper and the old hinges. Then start to take out the stamps, carefully, one by one. If all the gum has not yet been dissolved you can feel it by the slippery reverse of the stamps. If you rub such a stamp with great caution in the water you should usually be able to remove the gum. Stamps with obstinate gum are best left right to the end. The stamps fished out of the water are left on the rim of the basin for a short while to let the surplus water drip off.

For the drying of stamps prepare sheets of strong, good quality white blotting paper, which must be absolutely clean. It is also advisable to have two pieces of cardboard ready. Now take the stamps from the rim of the basin and place them one by one on the first sheet of blotting paper, completing one row after the other. For safety reasons, leave a small margin at the top and bottom of the sheet and on both sides. When the first sheet of blotting paper is full of stamps cover them with the next sheet and continue until you have dealt with the lot.

Now it's the turn of the stamps with obstinate gum. Place them carefully on a clean glass plate or tile and with a blunt knife carefully scrape off the wet gum. Once more the stamps are rinsed in lukewarm water, and only after this procedure can you put them between blotting paper. It is best to use separate sheets of blotting paper and leave plenty of space between the stamps because, even after these precautions, they tend to get stuck.

When you have finished your batch of stamps cover the last blotting paper with cardboard and let the stamps dry. The best way is to put books or flat, heavy objects on top of the cardboard, and leave the stamps between the blotting paper and under pressure for at least twenty-four hours.

Stamps with embossed print must not be pressed; the embossing would disappear. Such stamps are also placed between sheets of blotting paper but let them dry covered but not weighed down.

The colour of some stamps is sensitive to water and tends to come off (for instance, the colour of English stamps printed in green from the period 1883-1920). In some catalogues there is a footnote warning the collectors that the stamps have to be soaked in such a way that they lie on the water and only their reverse gets wet. Another way is carefully to wet their reverse by hand. Even so, great caution and patience is needed, and the soaking must not last long. Stamps printed on some types of coated paper must be dealt with in a similar way, otherwise they might lose their lustre.

When delicate or expensive stamps are to be soaked, it is better to keep them separate and soak them only a few, or just one, at a time so as to be able to watch them constantly and to take care of them. It always pays in the end to take every possible precaution.

Some philatelists use their tweezers to fish the soaked stamps

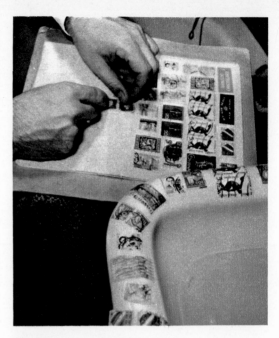

478 Place the wet stamps in rows on blotting paper.

479 With tweezers remove them from the blotting paper and sort them.

480 Stamp with a tear.

481 Badly damaged stamp with a large hole.

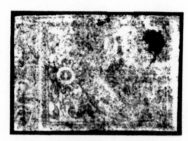

482 Corner torn off and clumsily affixed.

483 Perforations clipped on the left.

out of the water. This is not wrong, of course, but it should be borne in mind that the tweezers are made of metal, and wet paper can be easily damaged. The safest and most sensitive method is to use one's own fingers.

It is true that soaking diminishes the resistance of the paper. But so far no better way of removing paper remainders from stamps has been found. Besides, gum can sometimes do greater harm than water. It may contain chemicals which can damage the paper of the stamps and their colour. Furthermore, on certain old stamps the gum gets wrinkled and breaks. To make sure that such a stamp does not tear and get damaged, there is no other way but to soak the gum off, even though the stamp is mint.

It is frequently necessary to remove old hinges or bits of paper from mint stamps without destroying the gum. One method is to wet the paper remainders or hinges on the reverse with the help of a thin, fine brush. The wet paper or hinge can be easily removed by pulling it off with tweezers. A sweat box is a great help. In the damp atmosphere the gum of the stamp softens, and after a certain time it is possible to peel off the paper or hinge without damaging the gum. Care has to be taken, afterwards, though, when the stamp dries. It is bound to start curling and should therefore be carefully held down. If it does curl up sometimes, it helps to breathe on it, and then it is possible to straighten it. A sweat box also helps to get mint stamps apart that have stuck together, unless this has happened to whole sheets. Sometimes it is possible to put sheets over steam and save them.

Nowadays modern cancelled stamps are often found with complete, untouched gum. These are stamps cancelled to order. Some governments sell whole sheets of these stamps, cancelled in large quantities, at reduced prices to stamp wholesalers who use them for stamp packets. It is advisable to soak such stamps, too, as the gum is unnecessary on used stamps. It is much easier to handle a stamp without gum; it cannot get stuck and does not curl up.

484 One perforation missing on bottom and some short perforations.

DAMAGED STAMPS

The next day take the pad of blotting paper with the stamps, which are in the meantime dry and nicely pressed. It is possible to deal with the stamps after a few hours, but it is better to wait until they are completely dry. If they are still wet they are liable to curl up and could be damaged. Again the sorting starts. Cautiously lift the stamps one by one off the blotting paper with tweezers and sort them into little heaps according to countries, themes, sets, etc. While doing this scrutinize every single stamp and eliminate all damaged copies. What are the most important defects, and what is a damaged stamp?

a) **Stamps with a tear.** If a stamp has a tear, be it ever so small, it is damaged. Put such copies aside and eliminate them. They do not belong in your collection and it is not honest to offer them for sale or in exchange to other philatelists who might overlook the fault at first glance.

b) **Damaged perforation.** If a few perforations are missing or just one perforation is pulled off, or if a stamp has a so-called *blunt corner*, it is also damaged.

485 Blunt bottom left corner.

c) **Thinned stamps.** Beginners and laymen very often simply tear stamps off covers and postcards. In most cases bits of paper from the reverse of the stamp remain on the cover. When you look at such a stamp against the light you can easily see a lighter area in the place where the paper is thinner. Philatelists call such a stamp *thin*. Sometimes unused stamps are thin, too. This happens when somebody carelessly tears off an old hinge. Some unscrupulous collectors try to hide this fault by covering the thin spot with a new hinge. Caution is advisable, therefore, when you buy or exchange stamps. The best thing to do is to have a look at the reverse of the stamp and hold it against the light.

486 Stamp with pen mark.

d) **Traces of indelible pencil.** It sometimes happens that the post office misses a letter and does not stamp it. In such a case the postmen are instructed to cancel the unstamped stamps with a stroke of an indelible pencil or biro. Such a stamp is of no use for a collection. When you soak such a stamp to get it off the paper the indelible pencil dissolves in the water and a wide, violet line spreads across the stamp. It is better not to soak such stamps at all as some other good stamps might be discoloured. Sometimes it cannot be helped. Some postal clerks mark the postage with an indelible pencil on covers and later stick a stamp across their mark. This is discovered when the stamps are soaked. Such a stamp is damaged, too, although there is no violet mark on the obverse.

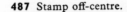

487 Stamp off-centre.

If the copies thus discoloured are stamps much needed for your collection you can try to put them into spirit and leave them submerged for ten to twenty minutes. Sometimes this succeeds in removing the violet traces or at least making them less conspicuous. It is a good idea to pour pure spirit into a small bowl and after a while to repeat the treatment with a new measure of spirit. This treatment, of course, could affect the colour and thus damage the

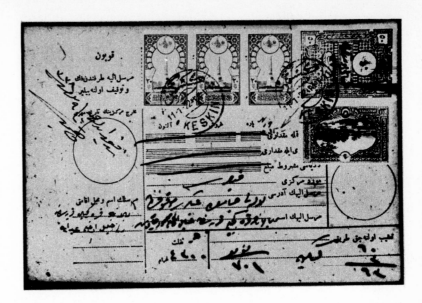

stamp even more. There are other chemicals that can also be used for the removal of indelible pencil stains.

e) Off-centre stamps. Sometimes the perforation is displaced, so that the design of the stamp is not in the centre of the surface. Such a stamp is called off-centre, although it would be more correct to say that the perforation is displaced. It should be your aim to find perfectly centred copies for your collection. Although off-centre copies are of less value than well-centred stamps they are by no means worthless, and you can put them among your exchange material. Some collectors, especially if it applies to a stamp which is hard to come by, do not mind so much if the copy is not well centred. There have been, of course, occasions when almost the whole run of a stamp issue was carelessly perforated, and in such a case an off-centre stamp is quite admissible. The catalogues usually have a footnote stating that the stamps are mostly off-centre and that the value of perfectly centred copies is higher. Every stamp-printing workshop, especially nowadays, exercises a very strict control and all imperfect stamp sheets, including sheets with displaced perforations, are eliminated on the spot and do not reach the post office counters. If it still happens that such a sheet of off-centre stamps escapes the vigilance of the controllers then it becomes a rarity of great interest to specialists. Sometimes the perforation is displaced to such an extent that it touches the stamp design or even cuts across its centre. Such copies are most welcome finds for specialists.

f) Cut-into stamps. With imperforate stamps, especially old stamps, the postal clerks, and the public, were often not very careful with their scissors and cut into the edge of the design or even deep into the stamp. The value of such stamps is much lower than the value of perfect copies; sometimes they have hardly any value at all. There were, of course, some classical stamps printed in such a way that the space between stamps was extremely narrow, perhaps just half a millimetre. In such cases you cannot expect stamps to have large margins, and should be quite satisfied when the design is nowhere touched, or even just touched.

Many a perforated stamp was hopelessly damaged when it was carelessly cut out from a cover or a postcard. Not only is a stamp

practically worthless when cut into; in many cases the damage is done if the scissors cut away or shorten a few perforations. An exception are Turkish stamps of the period 1913–26. Here an instruction was in force according to which stamps on packet cards and other documents kept by the post office had to be cut into with scissors or a knife in addition to the normal cancellation by handstamp. The reason was to make their re-use after removal of the handstamp impossible. Such stamps came on to the stamp market when old postal remainders were sold after a certain number of years had passed. These stamps, although cut into, are of philatelic value since they were cut officially by the postal authorities. Their value, though, represents only about one-tenth of the value of normal, used stamps. Some catalogues list the higher values with scissor cuts separately. The lower values are not listed, as they are practically worthless.

g) Creased stamps. When stamps are not handled properly they can become bent and folded. Such stamps are called *creased*. This fault can be discovered easily when looking at a stamp from the reverse and against a light. The crease can be seen as a dark line going across the stamp. This is a serious fault. Sometimes a stamp is just bent and no dark line can be seen. If it is a used stamp it can be soaked and pressed. If it is unused you can try to iron out the crease. The stamp must be slightly moistened on top, put between two layers of blotting paper, and carefully ironed with not too hot an iron. One more piece of advice: sometimes a cover comes with the stamp not properly affixed and the corners sticking up. Do not try to straighten it out! Leave the stamp as it is and soak it. In water the stamp will straighten itself and sometimes can be saved. By straightening the dry stamp you could break it.

h) Stamp colour. A stamp of good quality should have its original colour and the colour should be even and fresh. The influence of sunlight and of various chemicals causes changes of colour or spots on the stamp. It is obvious that such a stamp depreciates in value. Great caution is advisable, though. Many classical stamps, and some modern stamps, too, which have been in circulation for a long time, have had to be reprinted. The printers could not always achieve exactly the same colour shades as in the first printing and sometimes they did not bother; there is therefore a great variety of shades with a remarkably wide range of colouring. Furthermore, stamps were sometimes printed in the wrong colour by mistake. Catalogues usually mention these facts. If you are in doubt, you had better ask an experienced collector. Specialists are most interested in clear colour shades, and especially in errors of colour.

i) Damaged gum. One often finds unused stamps without gum. If the stamps have not been issued without gum on purpose, as for instance in tropical countries, this is a deficiency. Such a stamp is not worthless but its value is diminished. In most cases philatelists value such an unused stamp as a used stamp unless, of course, the used stamp has a higher catalogue price than the mint stamp. The general stamp collector will not object to an unused stamp with traces of hinge. It is worse if the gum is badly damaged, is missing on parts of the surface, or if the whole reverse of the stamp is covered by old hinges. Such an appearance greatly reduces the value of an unused stamp and it will be practically on a level with a cheaper, used copy.

j) Cancellations. If you have made the decision to include cancelled stamps in your collection, look for copies with a light, legible cancellation which does not disfigure the stamp. Stamps with heavy

490 Heavily smudged cancellation.

491 Heavy cancellation is sometimes visible on the back.

492 Cancellation too heavy in centre of stamp. Such a stamp is not suitable for a thematic collection.

smudged cancellations which sometimes show even on the reverse of the stamp should be eliminated. Philatelists who are forming thematic collections (unless they decide to include in their collection only unused stamps, which is preferable), must see to it that the cancellation of the stamp is as small as possible and does not touch the thematic design of the stamp.

These general rules for cancellations do not always apply. Many stamp collectors prefer to have stamps with a large part, or the whole of the handstamp, legible. Even then the cancellation should be light and not smudged. Philatelists forming postal history collections, or collections of postmarks, favour having in their collection stamps with possibly the whole cancellation, so as to be able to read when and where the stamp was cancelled.

k) Stains. These can originate from many different causes. Indelible pencil stains have already been mentioned. It is even more difficult to remove ink stains. When chemicals are used, not only the stain is removed, but frequently the colour of the stamp, too. Grease can be removed with the help of clean petroleum spirit. Sometimes it is advisable to place the stamp, soaked in petroleum spirit, between two pieces of blotting paper and to iron it. So far no remedy has been found for the brown stains caused by humidity and for the grey-black stains of mildew.

After the First World War a new type of stamp hinge was brought on to the market, especially in Germany, the so-called *Schonfalze*. It could be easily pulled off a mint stamp without damaging the gum. After a certain time, though, it appeared that these hinges left ugly grease stains on the stamps. The longer such a hinge was affixed to a stamp, the larger and more obstinate the stain became. Philatelists experimented for many years, and finally a solution to this problem was found. It is a combination of 90% ether, 7% acid of vinegar, and 3% acetone. This solution is very volatile and inflammable, and the utmost caution is necessary when using it. It should be kept in a corked bottle, covered with cellophane. From a bottle with a fitted glass stopper it would evaporate quickly. The stamp is put into a shallow glass bowl, a little of the liquid is poured on to the stamp, and it is left like that for a while. If the stain is large and difficult the whole procedure must be repeated. Since the liquid evaporates very quickly, it is advisable to work with the windows open. This chemical cannot be used on some types of stamps, as their colour comes off.

All stains, whatever their origin, greatly diminish the value of a stamp. Sometimes, though, stains are found on a stamp which have been caused, not by chemicals, but during the process of printing. Their character is quite different. Such flaws are of great interest to specialists.

l) Punched stamps. Some large firms or institutions had the stamps used for their correspondence punched with the initials of the enterprise. This was done to make it impossible for the employees to use such stamps for their private correspondene. As far as normal stamp collectors are concerned such punching makes a stamp undesirable and not fit for a collection. This, of course, cuts the value of a stamp considerably. On the other hand, there are some specialists who collect punched stamps. They are called *perfins*, which is an abbreviation for 'perforated initials'. If this line of collecting develops further it is quite possible that some of the rarer perfins may prove to be quite valuable.

Sometimes stamps were punched officially by the postal authorities. In France, for instance, in 1930 an airmail stamp of 1.50 francs was issued for the international Aero-Philatelic Exhibition and

493–494 Two perforated stamps (from the back).

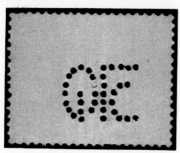

495 Official British perforation. 'B.T.' stands for Board of Trade.

punched with the text 'E.I.P.A. 30'. Spanish stamps of 1865—
1901, and some British colonial stamps punched with a large hole,
were used as telegraph stamps. A star-shaped hole was punched
into Portuguese stamps for the same purpose. Western Australian
stamps used in official correspondence also had a hole. These were
official measures, and such stamps have a philatelic value, although
their value represents in some cases only about one-twentieth of
that of a stamp normally cancelled.

In conclusion it has to be pointed out that most of the things
said about damaged stamps apply first of all to cheap, modern
stamps which are in sufficient supply. Where valuable, and especially classical, stamps are concerned the same rules do not apply.
The above mentioned faults diminish the value of stamps considerably, but rare stamps, even if they are damaged, do retain their
value — and sometimes this is considerable. The rarest and most
famous stamps in the world exist only in a few copies, and a great
number of these are damaged to some extent.

This means that you can include damaged rare stamps in your
collection. It should, though, be the aim of a good philatelist to
replace damaged stamps in his collection, if possible, by perfect
copies. You can, of course, also include a modern damaged stamp,
but only in your private collection. Never try to enter damaged
stamps in an exhibition. This would greatly lower the marks
awarded by the judges for your collection.

Keep even badly damaged, irreparable copies of good classical
stamps. They do not belong in a collection but they can serve very
well as comparative material, for example for ascertaining the
genuineness of another stamp.

Frequently to be found are rare stamps which have been repaired. Some stamp repairers are real artists. They can enlarge narrow margins, cover thinning with paper material, close tears, re-
gum a stamp, etc. Repairs improve the aesthetic appearance of
a stamp but do not add to its value. Unless it is a very valuable
stamp indeed there is not much sense in repairing it. The greatest
danger of repairs is, of course, that unethical persons try to sell
such repaired stamps as perfect copies for a high price.

The Swiss philatelist, Cueni, worked out some time ago a very
detailed and clear table of different types of stamp faults and of
their influence on the value of a stamp. This table deals primarily
with classical stamps and is most useful as a guide. See also the
table on the valuation of stamps, pp. 308—9.

HOW TO LOOK AT A STAMP

When you look at a stamp the first thing to catch your eye is the
design, especially in the case of colourful, modern stamps. Next
you will probably try to find out where the stamp comes from and
what value is printed on it. Not until then should you start to
scrutinize the stamp closely. Judge its colour or colours, look at
the way it was detached (imperforate or perforated), inspect the
paper, watermark, etc.

Therefore consider first the face of the stamp, its design. Its
size is usually measured in millimetres, first the width and then
the height. The proper way to measure it is from one edge of the
design to the other, not from perforations to perforations. This is
necessary mainly because, in the case of a line perforation, the

496 The first English
stamps of 1840 did not
have the name of the
country printed on them
and this privilege is still
kept by Great Britain
today. Some other
countries also omitted the
name of the country on
their first stamps, as can
be seen from this Belgian
example.

XV Stamp designers have found unlimited inspiration in the natural world.

XVI Boats and ships often appear on stamps, and they can be the basis for attractive thematic collections.

497 On the first stamps of the Roman States (Vatican) was an inscription 'Franco Bollo Postale' (postage stamp) but not the name of the country. Instead there was the coat of arms

498 Stamp of Eastern Roumelia with a four-language text.

499 Colour circle showing the main categories of colours used in stamps.

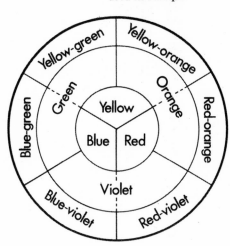

distance between the perforation lines can vary considerably. The size of a stamp is of importance when there were several printings, or if different printing techniques were used. They can very often be distinguished by the different size of the stamp design. That, of course, does not mean you must always measure the size of the design; do so only where necessary, and as far as thematic collectors are concerned, the size of a stamp design is of no importance anyway.

For thematic collectors, on the other hand, it will be sometimes important to decipher the text written in small print underneath the design proper. Frequently you will find there the name of the stamp designer and of the engraver if you are dealing with an engraved stamp. Together with the name of the designer there are sometimes the abbreviations 'del', short for the Latin word 'delineavit' (drew); 'inv', for 'invenit' (designed): or 'pinx' meaning 'pinxit' (painted). In addition to the name of the engraver there might be the abbreviation 'sc' for 'sculpsit' (engraved). Furthermore, underneath some stamps, mostly stamps issued in recent years, there is the year the stamp was issued.

According to the rules of the Universal Postal Union, the name of the country should be given if possible in roman characters and the postage value in arabic figures. This rule, though, is not always respected. There are quite a number of countries where the name of the State is printed on stamps in its native script. There are stamps with the text not only in two, but in three or four, languages. For instance, Turkey issued, as far back as 1881, stamps for Eastern Roumelia (Southern Bulgaria) in four languages: at the top is the country's name in Turkish, at the bottom it appears in Greek, on the left in French and on the right in Bulgarian.

THE COLOUR OF A STAMP

Stamps are printed in numbers running into millions and even hundreds of millions. It is, of course, impossible to print such large numbers in one run. Even nowadays, with the most modern techniques, the printers do not always succeed in mixing exactly the same colour when they start a new printing. From time to time it becomes necessary to clean the machines, or the supply of ink runs out and a new supply has to be used, coming, perhaps, from another factory. All this has its effect on the colour of the stamps. And if such problems still have to be dealt with today, you can imagine how great they were in the classical stamp period when printing techniques were much more primitive.

That is how different *colour shades* are produced. They are of great interest to specialists. Often, for a reprinting, new plates were used or the old plate was repaired. This is the origin of different *types*, as stamps are called which differ, as a result of reprinting, from the original issue.

Philatelists use *colour guides* as an accessory to help them with the most difficult colour problems. Some of the common colour guides list about 160 squares with colour shades. In many cases there is a hole in the centre of each colour to enable the philatelist to put the stamp in question underneath and to compare colours with the printed squares. The name of the colour is printed underneath the square, generally in several languages, using the names of the colours found in the most important world catalogues.

Philatelists will often be at a loss as they may not be able to find the exact shade of their stamp in the colour guide. In such a case they have to use their judgement and decide which colour is nearest to the shade of their stamp. One can distinguish about 200 clear colour tones but when colours are mixed, the number of shades reaches 15,000 or more. Obviously it would be impossible to publish a colour guide listing such a vast number, or to produce in print all the finest shades or even to give them names.

There are three basic colours: yellow, red and blue. If equal quantities of two of these colours are mixed, the results are: green (blue and yellow), orange (yellow and red), and violet (red and blue). Shades are obtained according to the proportion of the individual colour components. If all the basic colours are mixed (yellow, red and blue), the result is black. The mixing of colours is best illustrated in the diagram of a *colour circle*.

For the stamp collector it is of importance to understand the system of listing colours in a catalogue. Whenever a combined name for a colour is given, the last named colour always predominates. For instance, yellowish-green means green with yellow added. On the other hand, greenish-yellow means yellow with green added. In the first case green is predominant, whereas in the second case it is the yellow.

Even the most comprehensive catalogues cannot go into all the details of colours. Therefore everything will depend on the collector: his experience, and most of all on the comparative philatelic material he has for making the right decisions on the colours and shades concerned. This is frequently of great importance; there are many cheap and common stamps which have some colour shades that are rare and very expensive.

500 Stamp from Ecuador with wide margins.

501 Early Chilean stamp with fine margins and good central cancellation.

502 A perfect item: Spain 1855, 4 cuartos, a corner copy.

503–504 Imperforate stamps of the twentieth century: Epirus, 1914, and Czechoslovakia, 1945.

502   503

505 North Korea, 1951.

506 Imperforate Argentine stamp of 1960 from a miniature sheet.

507 Stamp of Bosnia and Herzegovina with a compound perforation.

508–512 Czechoslovak stamp originally issued imperforate and later issued with different perforations.

IMPERFORATE STAMPS

It has already been mentioned that you should try to acquire copies of imperforate stamps with perfect margins, stamps whose design is neither touched nor cut into. The wider the *margins of a stamp*, the higher it is valued by stamp collectors. Extra luxury copies of stamps with margins so wide that traces of the adjoining stamps can be seen, are sometimes called *a miniature block of nine*.

The width of the margins depends, of course, upon the original width of the space between rows of stamps on a sheet, and this width varies to a great extent. Details can be found in some catalogues, but mainly in specialized literature. This is of importance not only for judging the quality of a stamp. It often happened that stamps originally issued as imperforate were later reissued perforated, and the older imperforate issues are frequently much more expensive. This tempted many stamp forgers to produce 'rare' imperforate copies by simply cutting off the perforations. Therefore, you must know the width of the space between stamps to be able to state the minimal width of margins of an imperforate stamp which would exclude the possibility of clipped perforations. It is a rule that the width of the margin of an imperforate stamp should equal or be wider than half the space between the stamps. It would be safest, naturally, to acquire a copy from the sheet margin, a corner copy, or a pair or block. In any case it is advisable to ask for an expert opinion before buying or exchanging.

Sometimes imperforate stamps with obliquely cut or uneven margins come to hand. Do not try to make the margins even. The only thing to do is to cut off carefully the tiny threads protruding from the margins. Do bear in mind that a stamp's value grows with the width of its margins.

508   509

510   511

PERFORATIONS AND PERFORATION GAUGE

The country which issued the first stamps was also the first to
introduce perforated stamps. The perforating machine was invented by Henry Archer who was of Irish origin. He once visited
a friend who was in the midst of a most tiring task — he was
laboriously punching holes with a needle all along the space between stamp rows to make the separation of the stamps easier. That
gave Archer the idea of constructing a perforation machine. His
invention was completed in 1847, but the first perforated stamps
were not issued in England until 1854.

Everybody who examines stamps closely will discover that the
perforation of stamps varies to a great extent. Whereas in some
cases the perforations are small and close together, on other stamps
they are much larger and with wider spaces between them. It is
of great importance to philatelists if they find stamps of the same
design and denomination in different perforations or in all sorts
of perforation combinations. To make the differentiation of perforations possible the dimension of twenty millimetres was introduced as an international philatelic unit. If you read in a catalogue
that a stamp is 'perforated 12', then it does not mean that such
a stamp has on top or on its side 12 perforations, but that exactly
12 perforations fit into twenty millimetres. Perforations are
measured up to a quarter of a perforation. Therefore you will find
in catalogues perforations of $13\frac{1}{4}$, $13\frac{1}{2}$, $13\frac{3}{4}$, 14, etc.

Many stamps are listed in catalogues with two figures for their
perforation, for instance $12 \times 13\frac{1}{4}$. The first figure always gives
the horizontal perforation, the second figure the vertical. This is
a so-called *compound perforation*. Naturally there exist stamps with
all their sides in different perforations.

To measure stamp perforations philatelists use an important

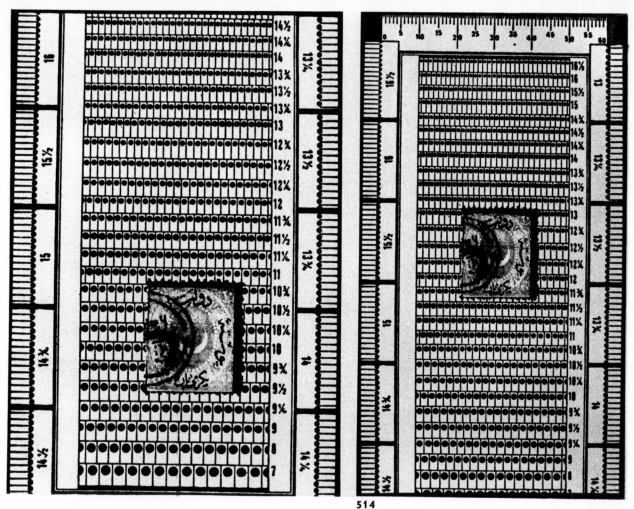

513 The top of this stamp is placed against perforation 11 on a perforation gauge. As you can see, the perforation does not fit – the lines between the dots on the perforation gauge do not pass through all perforations on the top of the stamp.

514 The same stamp placed against perforation 13½. This time the perforation fits.

accessory — a perforation gauge. Every perforation can be ascertained very quickly and easily by putting the stamp on the perforation gauge and moving it upwards and downwards until the printed perforations fit the perforation of the stamp. Some time ago modern transparent perforation gauges were brought on to the market, which enable perforations to be measured very accurately up to fractions of a point. This can be of importance to experts.

Sometimes it is very difficult to measure the perforations of a stamp. For instance, the first stamps of Portuguese India of 1871 were perforated with toothed strips of ivory. Naturally this perforation is so irregular that no figure can be given. In addition the paper of the stamps was either thin and hard or thick, and so the catalogue just states that these stamps are 'perforated'.

The technique of perforation also developed, and different types of perforations can therefore be distinguished.

a) Single-line perforation. The simplest perforating machine is just a long row of regularly spaced needles. A sheet of stamps is put into the machine and by treading on a pedal the first row of holes is punched along the outer margin of the stamps. Then the sheet is moved by one stamp and the next row is punched between two rows of stamps. This goes on until the whole sheet is perfora-

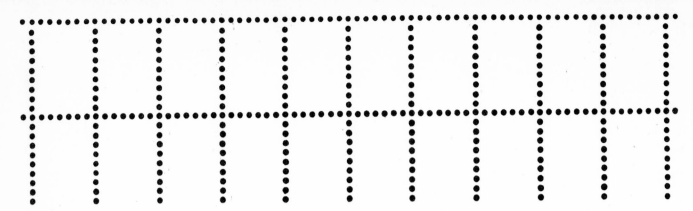

ted. After the first run is finished the sheet is turned ninety degrees and is perforated across the first rows of perforations.

It is obvious that in this perforation system the holes punched
by the needles hardly ever meet in the corners of the stamps. This
results in irregular corners, which are very typical of a single-line
perforation.

Sometimes the production process — for instance the horizontal
perforating — was done on one machine whereas the second
process — the vertical perforations — was done on a second
machine. If these two machines did not have exactly the same size
of perforation needles with the same spacing a compound perforation was the result.

In the classical period of stamp production all these production
processes were done on primitive machines. Sometimes a worker
forgot to punch a line of perforations along the margin of a stamp
sheet or even in the middle of the sheet, and stamps perforated
only on three sides were produced, or pairs of stamps imperforate
on their horizontal or vertical sides. If more lines of perforations
were omitted stamps perforated only on two sides, or one side,
or imperforate altogether, resulted.

Sometimes the worker punched two lines of holes almost in the
same place, or punched the second line just inside the stamp
design, and stamps with double perforation, or stamps perforated
on all four sides and also across the design, were produced. All the
above mentioned perforation varieties are a welcome addition to
a specialist's collection.

When the worker handling the perforating machine was careless
the horizontal or vertical perforation was slightly displaced, and
off-centre stamps were produced.

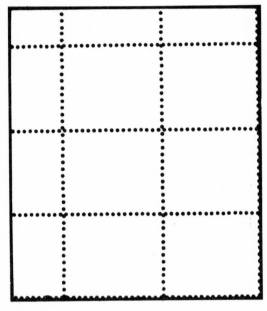

516 Line perforation as seen
from the back of the stamps.

517 A comb perforation.

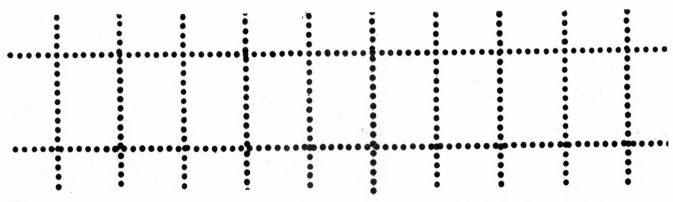

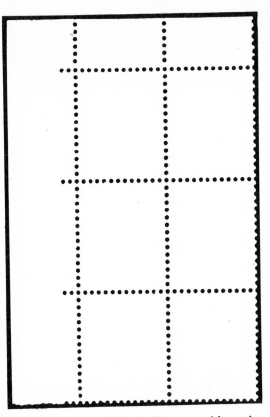

518 Back of stamps with comb perforation.

519 Machine for Harrow perforations.

520 Miniature sheet with a Harrow perforation.

b) Comb perforation. The perforating machines were later improved by adding short, vertical lines of pins to the long horizontal row. In most cases there are eleven of the short, vertical rows. The first stroke of the machine now perforated not only the whole top row of the stamps but also both sides of each stamp in the first row. The sheet was then moved by one stamp and the comb perforator at the next stroke simultaneously perforated the bottom of the first row of stamps and the top and both sides of the second row. The work continued until the whole sheet was perforated and no second process or turning of the sheet was necessary. This method proved much faster. To speed up work even more, double and triple comb perforators have been constructed. At one stroke they perforate two or three rows of stamps.

In most cases comb perforators are of the same size horizontally and vertically, but there are compound perforations produced by comb perforators. This has occurred when the setting of the vertical pins and their spacing has been different from the horizontal row.

Comb perforations can be recognized by the regular appearance of the stamp corners. The comb perforator strikes regularly and one corner looks just like the other.

Some Czechoslovak stamps of 1920 depicting the *Allegory of the Republic* exist in single-line and comb perforation. When a comb perforator was used the sheets were normally perforated from top to bottom, but some sheets were put into the machine sideways. That is the origin of the so-called *lying comb*, which is rarer. This perforation can best be identified by margin copies where the sheet margin on the side is perforated through.

c) Harrow perforation. The next logical development of the perforating machine was a perforator producing at one stroke perforations over the whole sheet. Such a perforator with several rows of pins crossing each other is called a *Harrow perforator* and is mostly used for smaller sheets of stamps. It is obvious that in this type of perforating all stamp corners are absolutely identical as the pin holes could not possibly meet or cross each other.

522 Swedish stamp from a sheet with normal perforation.

523 The same stamp but perforated only on the sides. It comes from a coil machine.

524 Another Swedish stamp with a coil perforation.

d) Coil and stamp booklet perforations. When stamp machines were introduced it was necessary to supply them with stamps in a different arrangement — not in sheets but in coils. The perforation of such coils lengthwise was unnecessary and so only the perforations across the coil were left. Most coil stamps can thus be easily recognized as they are perforated on only two sides.

This was not universal practice, though. In Great Britain and East Germany, for instance, coil stamps were issued perforated on all four sides. If a philatelist wants to enter some of the German coil stamps into his collection and to prove that they do not come from a normal sheet, he has to obtain a coil of at least eleven stamps, as it would be impossible to get a row of eleven stamps from a normal sheet printed in the 10×10 stamps arrangement. A special slip is either printed (also perforated) at the end of the coil or affixed to it. With this slip the coil is fixed into the machine.

In the Netherlands and some other countries a special type of perforation was introduced for coil stamps. To make sure that stamps in the coil do not tear off easily in the machine, several perforating pins were removed and so-called *interrupted perforations* resulted. Some Dutch stamps were issued also in sheet form with interrupted perforations, and these were sometimes called *syncopated perforations*.

Some stamps, for instance Swedish stamps, can be found with

525 Strip of five American stamps from a coil.

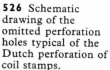

normal perforation (on all four sides), coil perforation (on two sides only), or perforated on three sides. The last mentioned come from *stamp booklets* and this form of perforation for stamp booklets was adopted by several countries.

ROULETTE

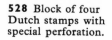

526 Schematic drawing of the omitted perforation holes typical of the Dutch perforation of coil stamps.

Perforating is the most common way of separating stamps but other systems are used as well. The most important of these is the roulette. With this system the machine does not punch holes in the paper but cuts little slits. Many types of roulettes are known, for example:

a) Arc roulette. The cuts are curved and the edges form little hollows or scallops.
b) Diamond or lozenge roulette. Cuts are made in the shape of little crosses, forming diamonds with the outer corners open.
c) Oblique roulette. The cuts are set slanting, parallel to one another.
d) Pin roulette. Instead of cuts, tiny holes are pricked in the paper, without any of it being cut out as in perforating.
e) Rouletted. Straight cuts. Many different lengths and distances of cut exist.

527 Dutch coil stamps.

528 Block of four Dutch stamps with special perforation.

f) Rouletted in colour. Notched rules are set between the clichés forming the printing plate of the stamps. The rules are inked with the plate, and, whilst cutting little slits, they also colour their edges.

g) Saw-tooth roulette. The edges of the separated stamps resemble the edge of a saw.

h) Serpentine roulette. Wavy lines are cut between the rows of stamps.

i) Zigzag roulette. The cuts produce sharp points along the stamp edges.

The separation of rouletted stamps is rather difficult and very often one of the protruding edges is torn off. That is why the old Finnish stamps of 1860, where the teeth produced by the roulette were extremely long, are valued so highly with complete rouletted teeth.

Sometimes, when nothing else was available, even sewing machines were used to produce something resembling a pin roulette.

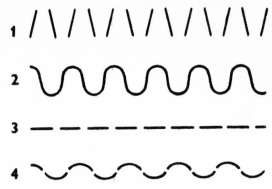

529 Schematic drawing of different roulettes.

WHAT ARE STAMPS PRINTED ON?

The overwhelming majority of stamps are printed on paper, but, of course, paper differs enormously in type and quality. Classical stamps were to a great extent printed on *hand-made paper* which is of the best quality. It is strongest and does not go yellow. It was not always possible to manufacture paper of the same thick-

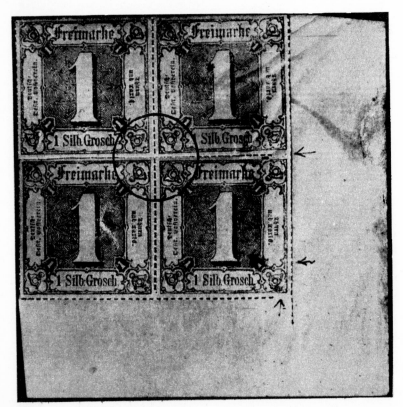

530 Stamps of Thurn and Taxis rouletted in colour.

531 Finnish roulette, a perfect copy with all teeth complete.

ness, and classical stamps can be found on papers of varying texture, from the very thin to the very thick. This, in some cases, enables philatelists to differentiate the periods of printing of some stamp issues. Depending on the method of production, *wove paper* or *laid (vergé) paper* was obtained. Wove paper is of a plain, even texture; laid paper is watermarked by close, parallel lines, crossed at right-angles by widely spaced lines.

Hand-made paper was an excellent raw material, produced mostly from rags, but it was rather expensive. Due to the increasing number of stamps being printed, a cheaper paper had to be found, upholding as far as possible the demand for the highest quality. In some exceptional cases hand-made paper is still used for stamps, but generally *machine-made paper* has taken its place. Good quality paper should not contain wood fibre, but occasionally does so in times of need. The use of poorer paper, of course, has a great influence on the appearance and also the durability of the stamps.

According to the printing technique employed, paper with a lower or higher finish is used. Paper with a high surface finish is used for surface printing and line engraving, whereas paper with a coarser surface is more suitable for offset printing.

Usually white paper is used for the production of stamps, but the white colour is not always permanent. If the paper (and naturally the stamp, too) is exposed for some time to sunlight it becomes yellow. This, of course, is a deficiency that reduces the value of a stamp. In addition, white paper can have different tinges. Very much depends on the water used in the paper mill. In mountain regions, for instance, paper produced in winter with the help of snow water has a slightly bluish tinge. In spring, when the snow is melting and the rapid waters carry particles of clay, the paper has a slightly brownish tinge. There are also greyish shades and other tinges. All this is of great importance to specialists. In the case of stamps which have been in use for a long time the tinge of the paper tells us when they were issued. Take, for instance, the French stamps with the Sower. Prior to the First World War they were printed on white paper. Printing continued during the war, but on greyish granite paper of poor quality, the so-called *grande consommation*.

Sometimes, though, coloured paper was used on purpose for the printing of stamps. As far back as 1851 the stamps of Baden were printed with each value on a paper of different colour. In other countries surface-coloured paper was used for the production of stamps. Sometimes a sheet of surface-coloured paper was put into the printing press upside down, and the surface-colouring can be found on the reverse of the stamp, making it a rarity.

Sometimes there was a great shortage of suitable paper but it was absolutely necessary to print stamps as quickly as possible. Then, use was made of such supplies as were available. When there was a shortage of stamps in British Guiana in 1862 and no other suitable material was available, stamps were printed on sugar bags. In 1918 stamps for the newly established State of Latvia had to be printed. As there was nothing else available, a large supply of maps left behind by the German General Staff in Riga was used. The stamps were printed on the backs of the maps. Turn such a stamp round, and you will find bits of the map on the back. Also Russian unfinished bank-notes, cigarette paper, ration coupons, etc. were used for the printing of stamps. All these types of paper are known under the common name of *makeshift paper*.

The backs of stamps served other purposes, too. Shortly after stamps were first issued, they were used by some firms for

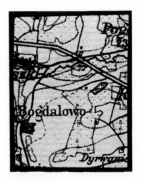

532–533 Backs of two Latvian stamps of 1918.

534 The face of this Latvian stamp is quite normal . . .

535 . . . but on the back you can see that it was printed on an unfinished 10 mark banknote.

536 Back of a British stamp of 1854 with an advertising text.

advertisements, as can be seen on the illustrated British Penny stamp of 1854. Advertisements are found also on French and other stamps. In 1895 Portugal issued a set of stamps for the seven hundredth anniversary of the birth of St Anthony, with a prayer in Latin printed on the back of the stamps. Spain printed control sheet numbers on the back, Greece repeated the value on the back, etc.

Russia issued, in 1915, stamps on card. On their back is a text explaining that they could be used as currency stamps to replace coins which were in short supply. Occasionally these stamps were used for the franking of mail. In 1900, at the time of the Boer War, a shortage of silver in Rhodesia necessitated the use of postage stamps as currency. Stamps were stuck on cards bearing a printed authority for issue. After the First World War there was a great paper shortage in Turkey as the fighting continued in Asia Minor. When stamp supplies ran out in the city of Kilis, cigarette paper with a violet handstamp was used for one-piastre stamps.

In recent years some countries tried to print stamps on material other than paper. The Soviet Union and Hungary issued stamps printed on aluminium foil, Poland issued a miniature sheet printed

537 Russian stamp of 1915 used as a coin — 1 kopek.

538 A 2 kopek stamp on cardboard. The text on the back explains that it serves as a coin.

539 Turkish provisional stamp issued in Kilis (Asia Minor) in 1921 — a violet handstamp on cigarette paper.

140

540 Soviet 1 rouble stamp printed on aluminium foil.

on silk, Tonga printed stamps on gold foil and there were also attempts to print stamps on plastics. So far these experiments have proved unsuccessful.

There are many different types of paper surface finish. Quite common is coated paper with a chalky, glazed or enamelled surface. Such paper is most suitable for lithowork. It also serves as a safeguard against attempts to remove the handstamp with chemicals. If chemicals are used, not only the handstamp disappears but the printing of the stamp also. When handling stamps printed on *coated paper*, great care must be taken, especially when soaking them.

The postal authorities have always been very much afraid of stamp forgers. To make the production of fakes as difficult as possible, they used specially treated paper. Switzerland introduced in 1854 paper with a *coloured silk thread*. It can be clearly seen on the back of the stamp. The Austrian post used a paper mixed with coloured fibres called *granite paper*. In the United States special grilles were embossed into some stamp issues of the nineteenth century. They were formed by a pattern of small, square dots and their purpose was to make the removal of a cancellation difficult.

The postal authorities of Spain had such a fear of stamp forgers that during the first years after the introduction of stamps in 1850, a new set of stamps was issued every year with the year of issue incorporated in the design. A stamp set of 1875 had each stamp overprinted on the back with a rectangle with dots and an uncoloured rectangle in the centre with the number of the stamp. Each stamp had its position numbered, from one to a hundred, and was overprinted in blue on the back. Not satisfied with this arrangement the Spanish post had stamp issues of the period 1901-32 overprinted on the back with the *sheet number* repeated on each stamp of the sheet. The number was printed in blue and was composed of a letter and a six-figure number, for instance 'A 003 186'. Proofs had the number 'A 000 000'. Philatelists found some errors with different numbers on the same sheet.

541 Swiss stamp with silk thread in paper.

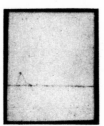

542 Back of a Spanish stamp with sheet number.

WATERMARKS

The most common method, though, that is used as a safeguard against stamp forgers is a *watermark*. Watermarks are still widely employed.

The invention of the watermark is much older than that of the postage stamp. Way back in the past, when paper was hand-made, special metal designs were woven into the wire nets used for taking the pulp out of the vats. In the place where the metal design was, the paper is a little thinner, as can be seen very well if such a sheet is held against the light. Watermarks are still very common on notepaper, too.

Watermarks are also used in the production of machine-paper. The design of the watermark is affixed in the form of a wire design to the dandy-roll. This again causes a thinning of the paper where

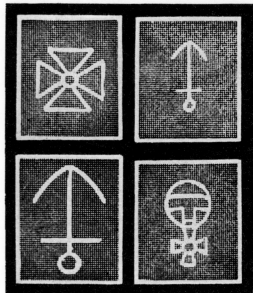

543 Four old British watermarks.

544 The watermark of this gutter pair of Bavarian stamps is so clear that it shines through.

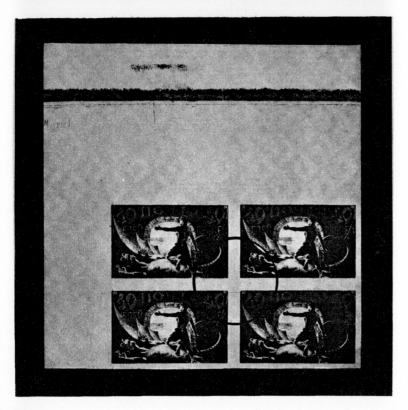

545 Soviet stamps with very distinct watermark.

142

the wire design is impressed into the pulp. Another way is to impress the watermark into the unfinished paper pulp when it still contains about eighty per cent humidity. The special roll used for this purpose is called an *égoutteur*.

The majority of watermarks are a result of paper thinning. These are *negative watermarks*. There exist, though, some watermarks which were produced exactly in the opposite way. Instead of affixing a metal design to the dandy-roll, depressions are made on it and, as a result, the design of the watermark is thicker than the remaining surface of the paper. Such *positive watermarks* were used by Rumania, for instance.

Swiss stamps of 1862 have a watermark representing a cross in a double oval. This watermark was not produced during the manufacture of the paper. It was later impressed into the paper with a die.

The first stamps of the world, the British Penny Black and Twopenny Blue of 1840, already had watermarks.

Watermarks are of great importance to philatelists. The reason is that on apparently identical stamps different watermarks can be found. As time passed, either the types of watermarks were changed or the watermarked paper was fed into the printing press in a different position. That is how inverted watermarks and watermarks printed sideways came into existence. In the case of the Czechoslovak watermark of linden leaves used from 1923 to 1927, eight different positions of the watermark can be distinguished.

There are a very great number of watermark types and shapes, but it would be impossible to list them all here. Every stamp collector has to rely on the details in his catalogue, where he will also find drawings of the watermarks and all facts relating to the types of watermark found on individual stamp issues and their positions.

There is one point of great importance, though. Catalogues

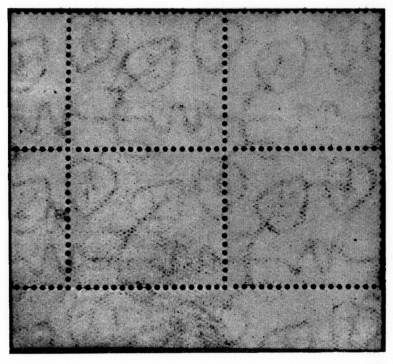

546 Watermark visible on the back of Czechoslovak stamps.

always illustrate watermarks as they look when seen from the front of the stamp. But from the front it is practically impossible to identify watermarks, as the stamp design is in the way, and watermarks are best seen by looking at the back of a stamp. Therefore always bear in mind that the drawing in the catalogue shows the watermark the other way round. The only exception is the already mentioned Czechoslovak watermark of linden leaves. This watermark is in all catalogues illustrated as seen from the back of the stamp.

There are two main groups of watermarks. They can be arranged on a sheet of paper in such a way that one watermark always appears on one stamp, and this is known as a *single watermark*. The other possibility is that the watermark forms a continuous design, repeating itself over and over again on the whole sheet, and these are called *multiple watermarks*. A good example is the watermarked paper used for the printing of British colonial stamps. The stamps were produced by the Crown Agents, and therefore the watermark is a crown and the abbreviation 'CA'. At first a single watermark was used and it appeared on every stamp in the sheet. Later a multiple watermark replaced it.

A watermark applied to the whole sheet does not necessarily have to be an all-over watermark repeating itself. The first stamps of Austria of 1850, for instance, were initially printed on hand-made paper, but from 1854 onwards on machine-paper. The printing sheet was composed of four counter sheets of sixty-four fields each. In the centre of the sheet of hand-made paper was a large watermark formed by the written letters 'KKHM', the abbreviation for Kaiserlich-Königliches Handels-Ministerium (Imperial and Royal Ministry of Commerce). The greater part of these letters appears in the space between counter sheets, but portions of the letters are sometimes found on marginal stamps which, naturally, adds to their value. According to the size of the watermark portion found on the stamp its value is higher by between fifty and three hundred per cent.

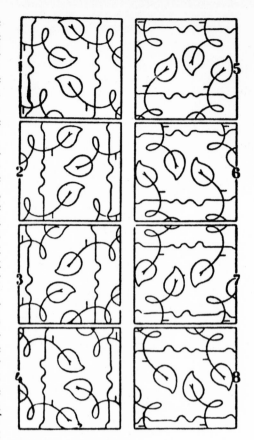

547 The eight existing positions of Czechoslovak watermarks.

548 A small black tray is most commonly used for the detection of watermarks.

XVII A recent trend in stamp design is to use reproductions of famous paintings.

XVIII Many philatelists specialize in stamps with sporting designs, especially stamps issued for the Olympic Games (1). Others are interested in first day covers, such as (2) which shows half the set of stamps issued for the Vienna International Stamp Exhibition (the WIPA) in 1965; this set of stamps illustrated the development of writing.

549 Identification of watermarks on British stamps with the help of petroleum spirit.

THE DETECTION OF WATERMARKS

Sometimes it is sufficient to place a stamp turned upside down on black paper, and the watermark can be seen fairly well. Watermarks can be easily identified on stamps with sheet margins. But such stamps are an exception.

Philatelists therefore use a watermark detector. There are two main systems. The simplest and most commonly used method is with the help of benzine (petroleum spirit). Place the stamp face downwards in a small, black tray made of pottery or plastic, and pour a few drops of benzine on to it. Under the influence of the benzine the stamp becomes more transparent, and where the paper is thinner the black colour of the tray shines through stronger. That means that the watermark will stand out clearly in black from the grey surface of the stamp. Benzine evaporates very quickly and does not hurt the stamp. Only absolutely pure benzine without any additional chemicals should be used so as not to ruin the stamp. A dropper-type bottle is best used for this purpose.

The ink of some stamps dissolves in benzine. There is usually a cautionary footnote in the catalogue. For instance, the Czechoslovak stamps of 1925 cannot be touched by benzine.

Benzine can serve in another way, too. Very often you can discover if a stamp has been repaired, for damaged paper shows as darker spots and lines, and it usually dries unevenly.

Some time ago another type of watermark detector was introduced, based on the principle of strong light shining through the stamp. The main problem is that the print of the stamp design obscures vision. Therefore the more elaborate detectors of this type use transparent filters of different colours to neutralize the colour of the stamp and thus show the watermark clearly as if it were on plain paper.

550 Rumanian stamp showing how the first stamps of Moldavia were printed in 1858.

551 Schematic drawing of surface printing: (1) the printing form (2) the ink (3) the paper (4) pressure.

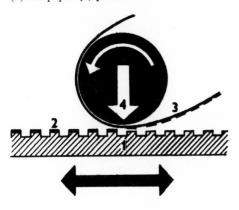

THE PRINTING OF STAMPS

Since 1840, when the first two stamps of the world made their début, practically all known systems of printing have been used in their production. Some methods proved very appropriate, others were not so successful. After all, much depends on what machinery the printer has installed, how experienced his specialists are and, of course, whether the printers have a long-standing reputation. As time passed, practically all stamp-issuing countries established their own methods of production. As a result, although the designs, themes and shapes of stamps differ to a great extent, nevertheless the stamps of many countries have a certain aspect in common and an experienced philatelist can judge at first glance where a stamp comes from.

There are three main groups of printing techniques: surface printing, or letterpress, lithography and intaglio printing.

1. Surface printing

This is the oldest method of printing. It was perfected in 1440 in Mainz by Johann Gutenberg, who used movable letters. For surface printing the ink is normally transferred to the paper by raised type. There is no ink in the hollows and they do not print. These areas appear as white on the paper.

In the printing of stamps, especially to start with, the letterpress method was used. In this technique many faults and mistakes occurred in the process of production and of printing, and the printing plate or cylinder was also often damaged. This resulted in numerous errors and stamp varieties.

Surface printing can be distinguished on stamps by several typical marks. The design usually has sharp contour outlines; it is even and straight, the layer of ink is minimal and sometimes there can be discerned on the back of the stamp a slight embossing of the design into the paper (especially in overprints).

552

2. Lithography

In lithography there are no relief parts or hollows on the printing plate or cylinder. This printing method is based on the fact that areas of the plate which are greasy accept ink but reject water, whereas the rest of the surface absorbs water and rejects ink.

In the old days of stamp production printing stones were mostly used for the production of stamps. At present flat printing is mainly represented by *offset printing*.

Stamps printed by this technique do not have the sharp contour outlines of stamps printed by surface printing. Here again the design is flat and the layer of ink very thin. Obviously the design is not embossed into the paper.

553

3. Intaglio printing

This is in fact the exact opposite of surface printing. In intaglio printing it is the hollows of the surface which contain the ink and print, whereas the relief parts are clean and leave areas without print. First the ink is dabbed on to the whole surface of the plate or cylinder; the ink is removed from the surface and it remains only in the hollows and lines. The ink is then printed on the paper.

The most common methods of intaglio printing used in the production of stamps are *line engraving* and *photogravure*.

In intaglio printing the appearance of the stamps is quite different from the previous two methods. Even with your finger (and certainly with a magnifying glass), you will discover a thicker layer of ink on the stamp, giving it a plastic appearance.

A special type of printing is called *embossing*. With the help of a pair of matched dies a relief design, with or without colour, is impressed into the stamp paper. Usually embossing is combined with another printing method which adds the remainder of the design, including the frame, in colour.

Nowadays many stamps are printed in a number of colours. For every colour a separate plate or cylinder has to be used. How this works depends on the system of machines used. Sometimes the sheet of stamps has to re-enter the machine for every colour printed, sometimes modern machinery prints several colours in one run. There are also printing presses which combine different printing methods, for instance steel engraving and photogravure.

In modern printing shops, rotary presses have superseded the flat plate printing machines, just as the printing machines supplanted the primitive hand presses.

552–554 Two German stamps and a Turkish miniature sheet in embossed print.

555 Schematic drawing of lithography: (1) printing stone (2) water (3) ink (4) paper (5) printing cylinder (6) pressure.

556 Schematic drawing of intaglio printing: (1) copper plate or cylinder (2) ink (3) wiping (4) paper (5) pressure

ČTYŘICET LET
ČESKOSLOVENSKÉ POŠTOVNÍ ZNÁMKY
1918 1958

557 The artist Alfons Mucha (1860—1939) who designed the first Czechoslovak stamp, 1918.

A STAMP IS BORN

In the past, stamps came into existence whenever they were needed. Nowadays this has changed completely. In practically every country the postal administration prepares a *plan of issues*, and sometimes such a basic plan is drawn up for a period of several years. The plan of issues is composed of stamp sets intended for issue by the postal administration. It includes not only stamps actually needed by the postal service, but also stamp issues demanded by the government and all sorts of public, cultural and other organizations.

On the basis of the plan of issues, stamp designs are ordered from experienced designers, or a competition is organized. In most developed countries a commission judges the submitted designs and there are many countries where philatelists and artists are members of such a commission.

Suppose that a new line-engraved stamp printed in two colours by rotary steel engraving is to be issued. The commission has decided upon the design and given its instructions concerning all details.

The final drawing of the designer goes to an engraver. His first task will be to produce, on the basis of the drawing, a line drawing, usually six times the size of the future stamp. In many cases it is necessary to simplify the original drawing, which very often contains unnecessary details difficult to reproduce on the tiny surface of a stamp. This line drawing is then considered jointly by the designer and the engraver, and corrected where necessary.

Not until then can the engraving start. By photography a mirror image of the line drawing is transposed on to a perfectly polished steel plate and the important work of the engraver begins. With the line drawing in front of him he starts to work on the metal. With the help of scorpers of different shape he engraves line after line, point after point. From time to time he makes trial prints to see where he has to deepen the lines and to correct the design. It is a very exacting task. The design is very small, the engraver has to use a magnifying glass all the time and whatever line has been engraved is there to stay. It cannot be removed from the steel.

As soon as the steel engraving is finished it goes to the printers, where it is tempered. Next, the original engraving is mounted on a machine and a ring of soft steel is rolled over it under great pressure (a roller-die). The design of the original recess-engraved die is impressed inverted into the roller-die. Where there were lines on the engraving there are now relief lines on the roller-die.

Then the roller-die is hardened in turn. Under pressures of up to 70,000 pounds per square inch it is pressed into the printing plate or cylinder. The same roller-die transfers the design on to the plate or cylinder as often as there are stamps to a sheet. This process is slow and must be very accurate. The cylinder or plate has to be polished in between impressions and again the roller-die starts its work. Whenever the roller-die is placed upon the first impression it is up to the experience, fingertip feeling and eyes of the workman to put it exactly in the same spot. All impressions on the cylinder or plate must be exactly the same.

As soon as this work is done, the cylinder (or plate) has to be hardened to protect it against wear. Then the cylinder can be mounted on the rotary press. Printing, though, cannot start yet.

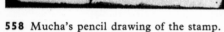

558 Mucha's pencil drawing of the stamp.   **559** Final design of the stamp, as yet without value.

First, trial prints have to be made to ensure that the cylinder is perfect and that all stamp spaces print properly.

Colours have to be tried out next. The designer will have submitted suggested colours together with his drawing of the stamp. Very seldom, though, are the stamps printed in the colour shades originally intended. Many trials are made, and out of the different colour shades the designer and the commission select the most suitable.

This is the moment when the proper printing of the stamp can begin. Very often the stamp designer and the engraver are present when printing starts. They want to make sure that the stamps are really perfect in all respects.

That is how the artist, engraver and the printer give birth to a new stamp — which then, in sheet form, makes its way into the world.

560 Engraver at work.

ESSAY, BLACK PRINT, REPRINT, PRINTER'S WASTE

Just as unseparated sheets of stamps reached the stamp market by legal and illegal means, so that gutter pairs of stamps appeared, so has other material from the printers found its way to philatelists, as for instance unfinished stamps, designs, etc.

Here is one example. The first Russian stamps were issued in 1858. Before the Russian postal administration had the stamps printed, it had a number of designs prepared and sent in for consideration. In 1857 the Prague printing firm of Haase & Son was approached, too. This firm not only prepared a stamp design but also had samples printed. These samples served as a basis for the drawing of the definitive design of Russia's first stamps which resemble the essays of Haase & Son to a great extent. A part of these designs came into the hands of philatelists. The Haase designs are not stamps and they do not have a value printed on them, but they are nevertheless highly valued by specialized

561 The stamp design is transferred onto a cylinder with the help of a roller die.

562 Roller die and cylinder.

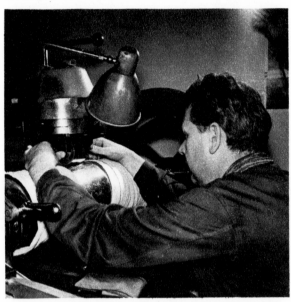

563 Hand feeding a printing press.

564 Roll of paper running through a modern printing press.

collectors of early Russian stamps. Similar things happened with stamp designs of other countries.

During the printing preparations a number of tests are carried out. For instance the stamp design is tested in the actual size of the future stamp to see what it is going to look like reduced. Such prints are very often changed and corrected before the final design is adopted. They are called *essays*. Different types of paper and different colours are tested. All these *trial prints*, although they are in fact unfinished stamps (usually they are imperforate), represent items of great interest to specialized collectors who follow all details of the origin and production of stamps.

The same applies to *black prints*. These are auxiliary control prints taken from the individual blocks. Their purpose is to find out before the printing starts whether there are any mistakes in the

566 Essay of an unissued Belgian stamp.

567 A *tête-bêche* pair from an essay of an unissued Belgian stamp.

568 The essay produced by the firm Haase for the first Russian stamp.

569 The first Russian stamp as issued.

design. In some cases black prints are issued specially for philatelists. The catalogues sold, for instance, at postwar stamp exhibitions in Czechoslovakia contained black prints of some stamps in the form of an imperforate miniature sheet, numbered and ungummed. The value figures on the stamp were defaced to show that these prints were not valid for postage.

The Austrian GPO sends out press releases with detailed descriptions of the new stamps and explanations of what they commemorate. Black prints of the stamps are stuck as samples on these press releases. All black prints are of interest to specialists.

When the printing of a stamp issue is finished the original printing plates are usually taken to the GPO or postal museum. In many instances such printing plates have been defaced by lines or scratches to make their re-use impossible. Sometimes black prints are taken from old printing plates. They are of importance to specialized collectors, even if they are defaced, as they serve as a basis for studies on the occurrence and position of typical faults and marks. Only very small numbers of such black prints are taken from the original plates, and only in very rare cases do they come into the hands of philatelists, but they are accessible in postal museums as study material.

As soon as philately became popular and started spreading, old stamps were in great demand. Soon it became evident that some stamps were in very short supply and that they were rare. The demand of philatelists could not be satisfied on the stamp market. Therefore some postal administrations took the old printing plates and had old stamps reprinted, many years after the original issue. Although the original plates were used and the stamps were printed in the same colours, these *reprints* can still be distinguished from the original old issues. The design is exactly the same, due to the fact that the old plates were used, but the paper is practically always different, the composition of the inks has changed and the gum too is no longer the same. Naturally, reprints could not be used for postage; they were destined only for stamp collectors. Some of these reprints are listed in catalogues and a fair price is quoted. Nevertheless, the price of reprints does not reach the value of the original mint stamps. Official reprints are listed in detail in specialized catalogues.

570 Black print of a Czechoslovak airmail stamp.

Reprints represent a great danger for inexperienced stamp collectors. They can easily be mistaken for the original rare stamps, and it is therefore best to consult an experienced philatelist or an expert before paying large sums for them. Reprints have been issued by Austria, British Guiana and other countries.

If such reprints have been issued by a postal administration they are called official reprints. They belong in a stamp collection. They can serve as temporary substitutes for expensive original stamps and they most certainly belong in specialized collections. In addition, they serve very well as basic material enabling experts to expose forgeries. Since reprints have been taken from the original printing plates, they have all the marks of the genuine stamps, and that enables the expert to detect forgeries by comparing them with the original, genuine stamps or reprints.

There are also private reprints. For example, the Berlin stamp dealer Goldner bought the original printing plates of the first stamps of Heligoland and had reprints made at three different printers.

Sometimes the postal administration no longer had the original printing plates or, in the case of multicoloured stamps, one plate had been lost or destroyed. Nevertheless, there were occasions when a postal administration decided to proceed with reprints. Such prints are called *official imitations*. An example is the British Penny Black, printed in 1864.

Printer's waste is also among the material which found its way from printers to philatelists. Printer's waste may consist of faulty sheets of paper (torn, folded etc.), sheets with faulty print, displaced second colour printing, displaced print, irregularly perforated sheets, incorrectly cut sheets, or imperfect gumming. When the printers are setting their machines and testing the depth of colours or the proper positioning of the plate in the printing press, they use auxiliary material. They take the next best available sheet of paper, frequently waste from the previous

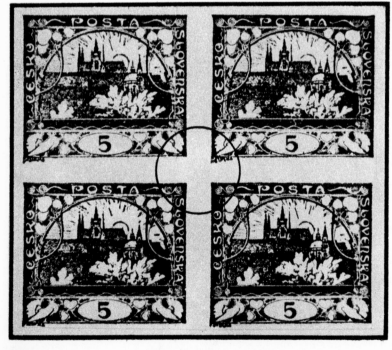

571 Official reprint.

printing of stamps, paper of different thickness and quality. On such waste all sorts of stamps are often printed in different colours, one across the other.

Some inexperienced stamp collectors think that this is valuable philatelic material. Printer's waste might be of interest to specialized collectors, but only as a freak of lesser importance, and not as study material. Printer's waste obviously has not the character of stamps; it has no franking value, and its use for study purposes is very limited. Nevertheless there are always customers for it. That

572 Printer's waste.

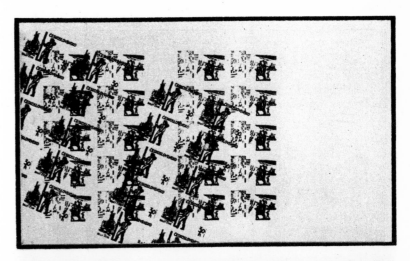

573 A normal printing sheet.

is the reason why printer's waste has been illegally smuggled out of printing shops and, in some cases, produced on purpose.

Very strict control is exercised in every stamp printing plant. All imperfect products discovered are eliminated and normally destroyed. Even so it happens that some imperfect stamp sheets are overlooked and reach post office counters and thus the stamp market. Such errors and misprints do have a philatelic value and are worth collecting, because they passed through the normal channels and frequently were genuinely used. These errors will be mentioned later in a special chapter.

There were, though, some attempts by postal administrations to make money out of printer's waste. The Bulgarian philatelic magazine, for instance, printed not so long ago advertisements of the State-owned stamp shop, offering for sale stamps of very recent issues in large blocks with displaced second colours, grossly displaced perforations, folds, etc. The provenance of this material was not disclosed.

PREPARED FOR USE BUT NOT ISSUED

Very often a postal administration had stamps printed which, for all sorts of reasons, were never issued. Sometimes the whole supply of these stamps was destroyed; in other cases the stamps were issued later, with an overprint of some sort. Almost in every case at least a part of the printed stamps reached the stamp market and the hands of philatelists.

The first stamp prepared for use but not issued was the British Penny Black of 1840, which looks exactly like the normal postage stamp but has in the upper corners, instead of the little stars, the letters 'V' and 'R', standing for Victoria Regina. This stamp was intended for use as an official stamp, but was not issued. A few obliterated copies of this stamp are known, but they come from experimental trials with obliterating inks, and a few copies slipped through the post by oversight.

Stamps prepared for use but not issued would not necessarily form part of a general stamp collection, but they most certainly belong in a specialized collection.

STAMP SHEETS AND THEIR ARRANGEMENT

The number of stamps in a sheet varies to a great extent. Sometimes there are 10 stamps in a sheet, or 25, 50, 60, 100, 240, and so on. The smallest sheets consist of four stamps. Such small sheets (of 4, 10, or 25 stamps) are usually printed on flat-bed presses. When using a rotary press it would be uneconomical to have just one sheet of, say, 100 stamps on a cylinder. This would mean that neither the surface of the cylinder, the capacity of the rotary press nor the surface of the paper roll would be used to the full extent. That is why larger units are usually printed, so-called *printer's sheets*.

A printer's sheet might be composed, for instance, of four *post office sheets* or *panes* of 100 stamps each, with the stamps arranged 10×10 in each pane. The printer's sheets are separated

574 Printing sheet composed of four stamps.

at the printer's and reach the post office counters as individual panes of 100 stamps each.

Sometimes unseparated printer's sheets reach the post offices. When marginal stamps of two adjacent panes are taken off the sheets together with the white space between them, we get so-called *gutter pairs*. During the period 1891—1927 post offices in France received stamp sheets consisting of two halves of 150 stamps each. Between the two halves of the sheet was a white gutter with the year of printing on it. French specialists call such gutter pairs with the date *millésime*.

Philatelists are always on the look-out for gutter pairs. In addition to gutter pairs which reached philatelists by way of post office counters there are quite a number which were removed from the printer's illegally.

In most cases the margins of stamp sheets are clean, without any printing. According to need, in some countries all sorts of information, instructions and figures were printed on sheet margins. The margins of the Penny Blacks bore instructions on how to use the stamps. Another example of what can be found on a sheet margin is a *plate number*. British stamps of 1880, for instance, always had a large letter denoting the plate under the last but one stamp in the bottom right-hand corner. Issues of 1911—13 had the plate number on the left-hand side. It consisted of a letter with a figure underneath. Czechoslovak stamps of the prewar period always had a plate number at the foot of the bottom left-hand corner stamp. On stamp sheets of other countries the plate number is in another place, or it is missing altogether.

Quite a number of countries followed the example of the first British stamps and put the sheet margins to good use. Not only

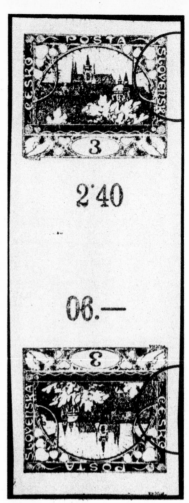

575 Gutter pair.

576 Gutter pair with printing on the gutter.

577 The plate number on these British stamps is denoted by a letter under the penultimate stamp.

578 British stamps of 1911-3:
the plate number is on the side of
the sheet.

579 In these Ghanaian stamps
the plate number is printed in
the three colours used.

580 Sheet number of
nineteenth-century Turkish
stamps.

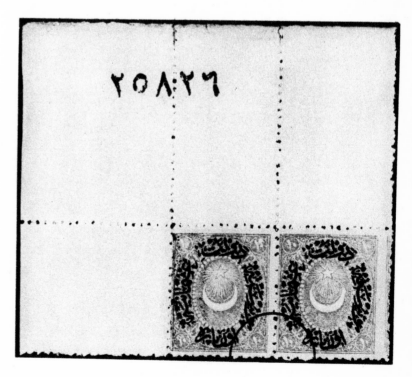

were instructions on how to affix the stamps printed on the margins. As far back as the classical period advertisements were in use; the stamp printers printed their name on the sheet margin. In many cases a decorative design was printed on it as well. To ease the work of post office clerks in Germany and other countries, numerators were printed on sheet margins. This made it easy for them to count the stamps left on a part sheet and to calculate their value. Above the top row of stamps there was always a number, giving the value of complete vertical rows of stamps. Suppose, for instance, that there are 100 stamps of one Deutschmark each on the sheet. Above the first stamp in the top row will be the figure 10 (Deutschmarks), above the second stamp 20, etc. In the left-hand margin, from bottom to top, are the values of individual stamps (not of whole rows): to the left of the bottom stamp will be the value 1 (Deutschmark), above left of the second stamp from the bottom 2, and so on. Beneath the bottom row of stamps are, from left to right, the serial numbers of the vertical stamp rows: 1, 2, 3 and so on.

A number of postal administrations sold the margin space for publicity purposes. There are sheet margins with publicity texts for a number of commercial firms. Stamps with such publicity text in the margin are a welcome addition to specialized collections.

The most common arrangement of stamp sheets in the United Kingdom and the Commonwealth is 240 stamps to a sheet, or

581 Sheet margin of Italian stamps with printing.

582 Text on the sheet margin of Turkish stamps.

583 Ruanda-Urundi stamp with printing on the sheet margin.

584 Sheets of recent US stamps incorporate a cartoon in the corners to promote the Zip Code.

585 Numerator on a German stamp sheet.

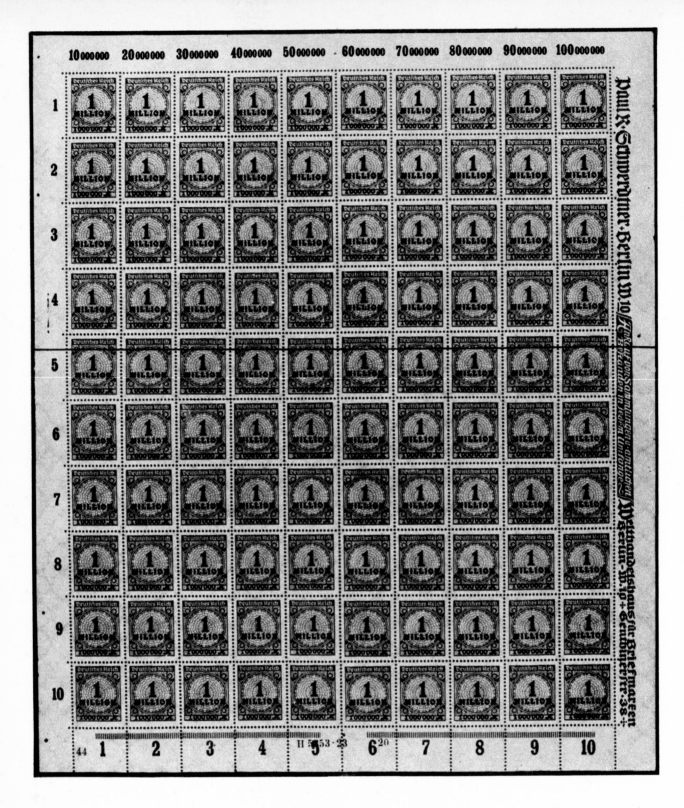

586 Sheet of German stamps with advertising matter on the right-hand side.

XIX Philatelists of every country begin by collecting their own native stamps. The postage stamps of the British Commonwealth are popular in all English-speaking countries, including the United States.

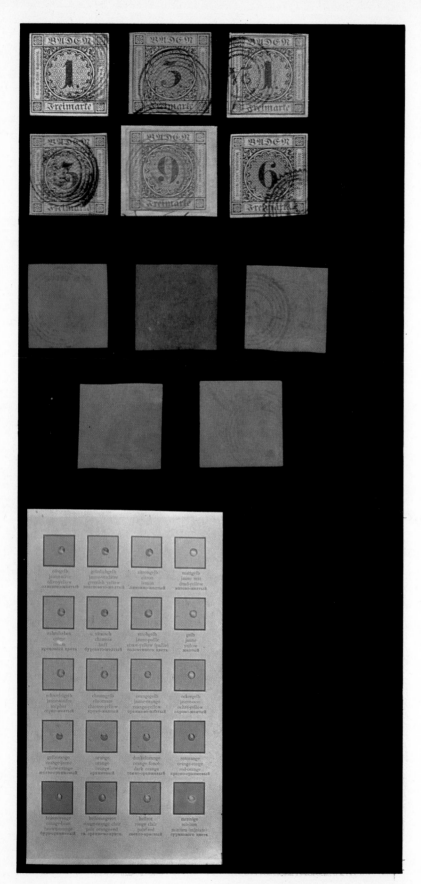

XX The quality and colour of the paper on which stamps are printed is frequently of great importance to the collector. Here are classical stamps of Baden printed black on coloured paper (1) and the backs of the various stamps (2). Philatelic colour guides are a great help in the determination of stamp colours (3): the exact shade can be matched up by placing the stamp under the round holes in the colour field.

1

2

3

120 or 60. But in the rest of the world where the decimal system is in use the most common sheet arrangement is 10×10, i.e. 100 stamps to a sheet. The reason for both these arrangements is obvious. The first stamps of 1840 were printed in sheets based on the British monetary system — twenty rows of twelve stamps each. A complete sheet of Penny Blacks consisted of 240 stamps and the face value was exactly one pound. It is a great pity our great-grandfathers did not put away a few of these sheets.

In the decimal system the currency unit has 100 smaller units, and so it is easy to count the face value of complete sheets.

When Austria issued its first stamps in 1850 there was a similar problem to be solved. The currency unit in 1850 was one gulden, which was equal to sixty kreuzers. The first Austrian stamp issues were printed in sheets of 8×8, which is sixty -four units. To make the counting of sheets and their face value easy, though, each sheet had to have only sixty stamps. This problem was solved in such a way that four stamp units of the last stamp row were left empty. Instead of a stamp there was a cross composed of two thick diagonal lines printed in the colour of the stamps. That was the case of the stamp issues of 1850—4. Later stamp issues had a white cross on a background in the colour of the stamps.

These are the so-called St Andrew's Crosses. As the stamp-sized units with the cross were not stamps, and had no franking value, people usually threw them away. But the St Andrew's Crosses were part of the sheet of stamps and were printed together with the

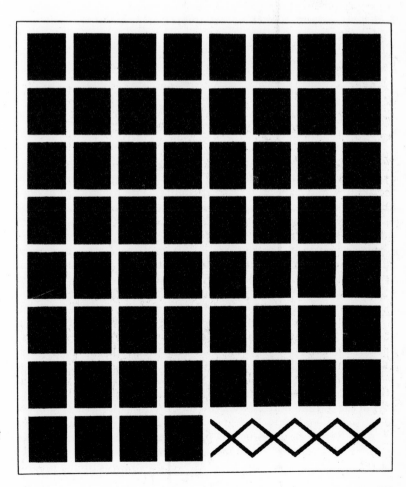

587 Schematic arrangement of a sheet of Austrian stamps showing the position of the St Andrew's Crosses.

589

590

stamps, and collectors of Austrian stamps are looking for them. They are rare and valued much more highly than the stamps themselves. Even a single St Andrew's Cross not adhering to a stamp is valued highly, which gives you an idea of how valuable a strip of all four St. Andrew's Crosses is. If somebody owns a stamp *se-tenant* (one that is joined to another stamp of a different colour or denomination) with a St. Andrew's Cross, he has a very rare item indeed. Sometimes an imperforate stamp was left with a wide margin, or a stamp of a later issue was so far off centre, that a fraction of the adjoining St Andrew's Cross can be seen. That, too, is a most attractive item.

TABS

From 1935 to 1949 Czechoslovak stamps of larger format were printed in panes of one hundred stamps, but the arrangement of the stamps in a pane was rather peculiar. The top row of stamps (in sheets of vertical stamps) has sixteen stamps followed from top to bottom by a further six rows of fourteen stamps each. On each side of the rows with fourteen stamps one stamp space remained empty, whereas in the top row of sixteen one stamp protruded on each side from the vertical rows. That means that on each side of the sheet one stamp jutted out at the top, leaving six empty spaces under it. At first these *tabs* were left as they were, without any printing. Later some texts and designs were printed on them, relating to the occasion for which the stamp was issued. Other countries issued stamps with tabs too, either perforated all round or with marginal tabs perforated on three sides. One of the popular 'tab countries' is Israel.

A specialized stamp collection should also include all variations of tabs (for instance a stamp with a tab on the left and right, with a tab at the top and bottom etc.), but tabs do not belong in a thematic collection unless there is a text or design printed on them and such a text or design bears some relation to the theme of the collection.

As time passed, more and more postal administrations started to use tabs. They had become a means of acquiring additional income

593 Belgian stamp
with label.

594 French stamp
with publicity label.

because of the collectors' interest in them. When tabs were introduced, specialized collectors could no longer be satisfied with just one, normal stamp. They had to buy two such stamps, or three or more in order to have all types of tabs and their variations. Soon tabs started to appear not only on sheet margins but right in the centre of post office sheets. Stamps and tabs in such a sheet are arranged (e.g. tessellated), so that it is possible to form all sorts of combinations of stamps and tabs. Such 'rarities' produced for philatelists are encountered even in recent stamp issues of some countries.

LABELS

In 1893 the Belgian post office introduced a novelty. Postage stamps were printed in such a way that underneath every stamp was a special label separated from the stamp by a perforation. A bilingual text was printed on the label in French and Flemish: 'Do not deliver on a Sunday.' The purpose of these labels, which were in use until October 1914, was to give the postmen a free Sunday, and stamps with these labels are called *Sunday stamps*. If someone insisted on the delivery of his mail on Sunday he tore off the label. Otherwise mail bearing stamps with the labels had to wait until Monday. The catalogue prices of these stamp issues include the label (unless both prices are listed); stamps without the label are cheaper.

Another speciality to be found in some countries is the *publicity label*. Publicity texts of business firms can be found not only on sheet margins, but also on special labels of stamp size se-tenant with stamps (Belgium, Britain, Italy, etc.). Italy issued in 1924—5 stamps with a publicity label of various firms. In this case the label was not separated from the stamp by a perforation, but was directly joined to the stamp.

TÊTE-BÊCHE

In classical stamp times, when the printing plates were grouped together from individual reproductions in metal (called *clichés*), it sometimes happened that one or more clichés were inverted. Such an inverted stamp, together with a stamp in the normal position on the left, right, on top or bottom, form a *tête-bêche*. The reason why a French expression is used for such a pair of stamps is that the first tête-bêche stamp pairs were found in France in sheets of the first stamps issued in 1849; they are very much in demand and highly priced. Especially high prices are paid for blocks of four, six or more with an inverted stamp.

Inverted stamps are seldom to be found in normal post-office sheets. They are much more frequent in overprints which often had to be produced at short notice. There was not always enough time to check the overprinting plate, and an inverted block could easily escape notice.

On the other hand, there are tête-bêche stamps which have not been caused by a printer's error but were produced on purpose. In 1863 Turkey issued its first stamps. The arrangement of the sheets was most peculiar. A pane of these stamps which were printed by lithography was formed of 144 stamps, twelve rows of twelve stamps each. The first row of stamps was in the normal position; the second row underneath was turned upside down; the third was again in the normal position, and so on right to the bottom of the sheet. At the bottom end the stamps had a much wider margin and so, where the bottom ends of the stamp rows met, a wide space appeared going across the width of the sheet. On this space a coloured control band was printed in red or blue with the Turkish text in Arabic script: 'Ministry of Finance of the Sublime Government.' A vertical pair or block of four of these stamps must be, therefore, in tête-bêche arrangement. There were altogether four postage stamps issued and four postage-due stamps,

595–596 Two Italian stamps with publicity labels not separated by perforation.

597 Block of six classical 20 centime French stamps with inverted stamp in top right corner.

598 *Tête-bêche* pair from a Czechoslovak stamp sheet printed for stamp booklets which were not issued.

each of the denominations being 20 paras, 1 piastre, 2 piastres and 5 piastres.

There was also, however, a normal arrangement of sheets of the 2 piastre and 5 piastre postage stamps. They were the first to be printed, but later the tête-bêche arrangement was adopted and these stamps issued. Only when the supply of stamps ran out was the first printing, the so-called Setting A, released for postal use. That means that vertical pairs and blocks of Setting A stamps are in the normal position. The space between rows is narrower and the coloured bands usually go into the stamp design. The number of Setting A stamps is much smaller and non-tête-bêche vertical pairs and blocks are especially rare.

Tête-bêche pairs of stamps are found in modern times as well, and have also been produced on purpose. When stamp booklets were introduced, stamp sheets had to be printed in a special arrangement to get the booklet panes in proper sequence. Some of these sheets were taken out of the printer's workshop legally or illegally before they were made up into booklet form. Such stamps are of interest to specialized collectors and can fetch high prices.

In addition, in recent years, other stamps not intended for booklets were issued in tête-bêche arrangement. Usually one stamp in the sheet is in the normal position, the other inverted, and the whole pane is in tessellated arrangement. There was no real necessity to print this way. It was done only to make such stamps 'more interesting' to philatelists and to make them buy more (for instance, part of the issue of a Turkish stamp against alcoholism of 1956).

599 Complete strips of Israeli stamps from sheets printed for stamp booklets. On the left are three stamps in normal position, next comes a gutter, then three inverted stamps and finally three stamps again in normal position.

600 Turkish stamps printed *tête-bêche*.

601 *Se-tenant* German stamps for South West Africa.

STAMP BOOKLETS AND SE-TENANT STAMPS

The introduction of *stamp booklets*, which are very popular in a number of countries, brought other peculiarities as well. It has already been mentioned that stamps imperforate on one or two sides and tête-bêche stamps come from stamp booklets.

If stamps for stamp booklets were printed on watermarked paper it frequently happened that, due to the special arrangement of stamps on a printer's sheet, they were found with the watermark in a different position. Take for instance British stamps since 1912. Stamps with inverted watermarks come from stamp booklets, whereas stamps with the watermark sideways (turned by ninety degrees) come from coil stamps for machines.

Stamp booklets always were and are on sale for a certain round figure (in the United Kingdom, for instance, for 1s, 2s, 2s 6d, 5s, 6s, 10s). Stamp booklets had to contain the stamps which were most needed, i.e. stamps for letters, postcards, registered letters, etc. The sum of the face value of stamp booklet panes sometimes did not produce the required round figure. This problem was solved in different ways. Either one or more stamp spaces in the booklet were left empty, or a stamp of different colour and denomination was printed among the rest of the stamps on the booklet pane. That is how most se-tenant pairs of different stamps came to be printed.

The postal administrations soon started to use the empty spaces on booklet panes as well as the covers of stamp booklets for all sorts of postal instructions, rates, etc. Soon publicity found its way into this field as well, and all sorts of advertising texts can be found on spaces se-tenant with stamps. This, too, is a very rewarding field for specialized stamp collectors.

Like other printing peculiarities which were either caused by an error or by some special need, the field of se-tenant stamps has during the last few years become a playground for unscrupulous stamp producers. The stamp market is being flooded by all sorts of se-tenant stamps produced for the 'benefit' of philatelists.

602 *Se-tenant* stamps from a British stamp booklet.

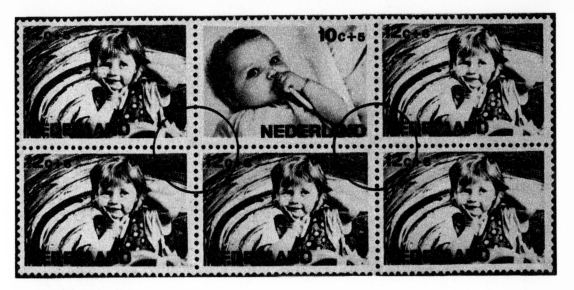

603 Dutch *se-tenant*
stamps, also from
a stamp booklet.

WHAT IS A TYPE?

Have a look at a catalogue. Even when going casually over the
lists you will soon come across the term *type*. The different types
of stamps are not only listed and priced but also detailed descriptions and sometimes drawings of how to distinguish different types
are included. Every specialized stamp collector will be pleased to
demonstrate different types of stamps and will describe their
characteristic marks and tell you what their origin was.

As soon as a certain permanent change occurs in a normal stamp

---

604 Empty fields of a British stamp booklet
used for postal rates.

605 Empty fields in a British stamp booklet
used for publicity.

606–609 A selection of *se-tenant* stamps.

607

a new type is born, most frequently in stamps which have been in use for a long time. A printing plate, even if it is made from the very best material, is bound after a time, to show signs of wear. In such a case there are two possibilities. Either the plate is repaired or it is replaced by a new plate. In both cases the stamps produced after the printing is resumed will practically always differ from the previously printed stamps. Thus a new type is created.

As far as the specialized stamp collector is concerned, this is a separate new stamp, although the postal administration or a thematic stamp collector will regard it as the same stamp since they do not take types into consideration. Incidentally, a thematic collector and the post office will always consider a stamp to be the same, even if it is issued with a different perforation, on another type of paper, or with a different watermark.

608

609

610 French stamps of 1876, first type. The letter 'N' of the abbreviation 'INV' is under the letter 'B' of '*République*'.

But let us return to types. Under this heading philatelists understand a divergency evident in the design of the stamp or in the overprint. This is the moment to point out the basic difference between a type and an error or printing fault. A type is a deviation from the normal or previous design of the stamp or overprint which is to be found in the whole sheet or a large part of it. It is, therefore, a constant, permanent change which has originated in the primary production of the printing plate.

It is best to explain the term 'type' with the help of an example. In 1876 France issued a set of definitives showing two allegorical figures, Peace on the left and Commerce on the right, holding

611 Second type. The letter 'N' of 'INV' is now under the letter 'U' of '*République*'.

their hands above a globe in front of which is the tablet with the denomination of the stamp. A new issue designed by J. A. Sage and engraved by E. Mouchon, appeared a year later and remained in use for many years. At first glance the stamps of both issues are identical, as, in most cases, is their colour. The catalogue, though, draws our attention to the striking marks of difference of the two types. The stamp designer's name is to be found on the bottom left underneath the word 'république'. After the name J. A. Sage there is an abbreviation, 'inv', meaning designed. The enlarged detail of the stamp in the catalogue shows that in stamps of the first type of 1876 the letter 'n' of the abbreviation 'inv.' is under the letter 'b' of the

612 Czechoslovak miniature sheet of 1963 of which there exist twelve types.

word 'république'. In the second type of 1877 the letters of the designer's name are closer together, so that the letter 'n' is to be found underneath the first 'u' of 'République'. There are other differences in the two types, but the placing of the letter 'n' is so clear that it is quite sufficient for the identification of the types. The catalogue will also show you why the correct identification of the two types is so important. The prices of stamps of type one are in most cases considerably higher than the prices of the other.

The above example deals with a case where the whole pane of stamps consists of the same type. This is not always so. Take, for instance, the three-mark stamp of Germany issued in 1899–1900. Here, too, two types are distinguished. In the first type the horseman in the forefront is leaning backwards; in the second type he sits upright. In this example both types are found on one sheet. The second and third horizontal rows of the sheet are always composed of stamps of type two, whereas all the remaining stamps in the sheet are of type one. That, of course, means that vertical pairs exist se-tenant with different types.

But types of stamps can have another origin, too, even in recent times. In 1963 there was an exhibition in Prague on 'Man and Space Flights'. For this occasion Czechoslovakia issued a miniature sheet with a face value of three crowns, showing the flight of a space station to Mars. The printing was done with two plates, each of which was composed of six miniature sheets. The stamp in the centre of the miniature sheet was taken from an original engraving and transferred to the printing plates with the help of a roller-die. All twelve stamps are identical. The decoration of the miniature sheet margin, though, which is composed of little stars, was engraved after the transfer of the stamp. Although the engraver was very careful there are a number of minute differences in the complicated drawing. And so specialized collectors list twelve different types of this miniature sheet.

There are quite a number of cases where the whole of a stamp issue had some grave mistake in the text. The mistake was quickly corrected and the stamp reissued. Again there are two different types.

All that has been said about types of stamps applies equally well to types of overprints.

PRINTING ERRORS AND FLAWS

Every philatelist, according to his line of interest, takes note of the different aspects of a stamp. Thematic collectors are not interested in types of stamps, errors or flaws. A philatelist forming a general collection will not be interested in errors, but he has to be on the look-out for types, as they might belong to his collection. On the other hand a specialized collector or a philatelist forming a study collection will be on the look-out, not only for types, but also for all sorts of printing errors and flaws.

Now that the meaning of a type has been explained, printing errors and flaws can be dicussed. There are two main groups of printing varieties: primary varieties and secondary varieties.

A *primary variety* or *error* has its origin as far back as the production of the printing plate or cylinder. It could have been caused by one cliché in the plate or one stamp on the cylinder being damaged. Such a fault will repeat itself for the full period of printing (as long as it is not corrected by an exchange of the cliché or a retouch of the cylinder) and is always found in the same position on the sheet or pane. If it was a fault in one of the original clichés and the printing plate had been grouped, say, from two clichés which are repeated on the plate, then such an error will occur more often in the sheet, but always in the same position. If these different faulty clichés form a larger part of the overall number of stamps in a sheet then this is usually called a *different type*.

The position on a sheet where an error is regularly found has been mentioned. The *position of an individual stamp* on a sheet is determined by a simple method, Stamps on a sheet are always counted from left to right, starting with the top row. If a sheet of 100 stamps is said to be arranged 10×10, then the first row consists of stamps numbered 1 to 10, the second 11 to 20, and so on. That means if you read somewhere that a certain error is to be found on stamp number 37, you will know that this is the seventh stamp from the left in the fourth row from the top.

A *secondary variety* or *error*, as different from a primary one, occurs during printing when the cylinder, printing plate or cliché is damaged. That is why a secondary error is always found only on one stamp. The same error cannot be repeated on several stamps on the sheet. A secondary variety will reappear in printing always in the same place and for as long as the damaged cliché is not replaced or the fault removed by a retouch.

Let us now have a look at the different errors occurring in the production of stamps in relation to their origin.

1	2	3	4	5	6	7	8	9	10
11	12	13	14	15	16	17	18	19	20
21	22	23	24	25	26	27	28	29	30
31	32	33	34	35	36	37	38	39	40
41	42	43	44	45	46	47	48	49	50

613 Scheme showing the position of a stamp in a sheet.

1. Errors caused in printing

a) **Plate error.** Printing plates, cylinders and clichés have to withstand high pressure and wear. Sometimes the material cannot stand the wear and after a while tears or bubbles appear, or a part breaks off. Every such change will be immediately reflected in one or more stamps. Much depends on how soon a fault is discovered in the printing shop, and what is done about it. Sometimes the fault is removed very soon and the error is found only in a small part of the whole printing of the stamp. In other cases it takes a long time, and then the number of stamp copies with the variety is much larger. Such errors are very frequent, especially in typography and sometimes every stamp in a pane has some *typical error*. That enables specialized collectors to reconstruct the original sheets of stamps, which means rebuilding like a jigsaw puzzle the original sheet from individual stamps, blocks and strips. This is a most praiseworthy task and also a very difficult one in cases when no complete sheet of a stamp has survived.

b) **Cliché.** In the past, when printing plates were grouped from individual clichés, and some major fault occurred in one of the clichés, it was sufficient to replace the damaged cliché with a good one. As long as it was a cliché produced from the original die everything was in order. Sometimes, though, a cliché was inserted upside down and the result was tête-bêche stamps. It was also possible, though, for no spare cliché to be available, and in that case a new one had to be produced. It could easily happen that the newly produced cliché was somewhat different and therefore printed a stamp of different appearance. There were also cases when a cliché had to be replaced but, by mistake, a cliché of another stamp of similar appearance or of another value was inserted, which resulted in most interesting errors of colour and *se-tenant* stamps of different value.

174

614 A 50 haliru stamp from Czechoslovakia, 1920, with typical plate error — the 'egg' over the figure's waist.

615 A stamp with retouched plate error on the left and a normal stamp on the right.

616 Russian stamp with double printing.

c) Retouching. In printing plates which are in one piece and in printing cylinders it is impossible to change damaged clichés. If a fault appears the printers try to correct it by retouching. With the help of a scorper they re-engrave the blocked spots, remove faults, etc. Even the smallest intervention of this type changes to some extent the design of that particular stamp and philatelists are bound to spot the change.

Here is an interesting example. In 1920 Czechoslovakia issued a set of definitives in two designs: the first was a dove carrying a letter in her beak and the second was an allegorical figure of a woman breaking her chains. The fifty heller stamp with the figure of the chainbreaker was printed up to January 1923 in red, but from January 1922 to the end of 1925 it was printed also in green and the same printing plates were used as for the red stamp. The thirty-ninth stamp in every sheet had a typical plate error — a white spot known among philatelists as 'The Egg in the Waist'. This error can be found on red as well as green stamps. In 1940, a full fifteen years after the printing of these stamps had ceased, Dr J. Munk discovered that probably in the first half of 1922 this error was retouched on the green stamps, and the 'Egg in the Waist' was removed by an additional intervention. (The red stamps were not retouched.) Although the printer doing the retouching job was very careful and tried to make it so that these stamps looked just like all the others, he did not succeed. An experienced specialist can distinguish the retouched stamp by some minute marks of distinction. The retouching was done on the finished printing plate. As there were more plates, the result of the retouching is different on each of the printing plates. So far four different types of retouching have been discovered and they are marked A, B, C and D.

d) Double impression. If the worker handling a printing press is not careful it can happen that a sheet is put through the press twice and each stamp distinctly shows two impressions. This is an error which does not occur very frequently, and if it does the faulty sheets are in most cases discovered by the checkers, eliminated and destroyed.

e) Inverted printing. When stamps are printed in two or more colours another printing error sometimes occurs; the worker, when putting a sheet of stamps into the press for a second time to print another colour, turns it round by 180°, and then the second colour will be inverted. Such an error is most striking in stamps where the frame is printed in one colour and the centre design in another. In 1918 the first airmail stamps of the United States were printed. The highest value of the set, twenty-four cents, has a deep carmine frame and a blue centre. One sheet of this stamp was printed with an *inverted centre* so that the aeroplane is flying upside down. Only one hundred copies of this error exist and they are most expensive. Such errors occur in modern times as well. In 1959 the United States and Canada issued commemoratives for the opening of the St Lawrence Seaway, featuring in linked ovals the Canadian Maple Leaf and the United States' Eagle. In Canada a limited number of sheets was printed with the centre inverted.

There was a great row in connection with such an error of printing a few years ago in the United States. In 1962 a stamp was issued to commemorate Dag Hammarskjöld, the Secretary General of the United Nations, who had died a year before in a plane crash not far from the frontiers of the Congo. L. Sherman of Irvington (New Jersey) bought a whole sheet of the four cent stamp, depicting on the right Dag Hammarskjöld, and on the left the building of the United Nations. At home he discovered that the yellow underprint under the brown print was inverted. He knew the history of inverted prints and was very happy. Together with Mrs Sherman they figured how much money they would get for this rarity and they kept their find a secret. One day, though, Mr Sherman read in a newspaper that some philatelist in Ohio had bought another sheet of fifty stamps with the yellow printing inverted. Before he realized that he had a sheet of errors he had already used most of his stamps on letters and was left with only nineteen copies. Sherman could no longer keep his secret. He boasted that he owned a complete sheet of fifty of this rarity and valued it at $400,000. As soon as the Postmaster General of the United States, J. Edward Day, learned of the existence of these errors he ordered some more Hammarskjöld stamps printed with the yellow printing inverted, so as not to have a rarity in the original copies. Sherman started a court action against the Post Office, stating that by the PMG's action he would be deprived of his treasure. He was successful, and the court ordered the printing to be stopped. But the court order came too late. In the meantime 320,000 copies of the faulty stamp had found their way to philatelists and stamp dealers, and today the price of the faulty stamp is just a little higher that the price of the normal stamp.

The United States Post Office learned their lesson from this case. The measures for inspection in the printing shop were tightened. When, in 1964, a stamp was printed showing an abstract painting by Stuart Davis, exceptional precautions were taken. An error could very easily occur in the printing of this multicoloured stamp with a design not readily recognizable at first glance. Before the printing started all sheets of paper were perforated on the left so as to make sure that no sheet would be put into the press in the wrong position. The printing was controlled by a photo-electric cell which immediately stopped the printing when a sheet was not in the right position. In addition a random visual inspection of the finished sheets was introduced. To give the inspectors an idea of what a sheet should *not* look like a few sheets of the stamp were printed on purpose with inverted colours for comparison. But these inverted printings will probably never reach the philatelic market.

f) Omitted colour. Just as it is possible, when printing stamps in several colours, for a sheet to be put into the press twice, it is also possible that one production process is left out. Two sheets might stick together and the worker puts them into the press both at once. Then this particular colour will be printed only on the top sheet, whereas it will be omitted from the bottom sheet. There are a great number of examples of this error, and the checker does not always find the faulty sheets. Such errors occur quite frequently on recent stamps printed on very up-to-date machines.

Here are some examples. In 1958-9 additional values for the set of airmail stamps were printed in the Soviet Union. Forty-kopek stamps were found with two colours omitted, black and red. These errors, which reached philatelists, show neither the value nor the name of the country.

In almost every new stamp issue of Great Britain printed in recent years sheets of stamps have been found with one or even two colours omitted. Such modern varieties fetch very high prices.

g) Printed on both sides. There have been cases when a sheet of stamps already printed was put into the press for a second time but with the reverse side on top. As a result stamps are produced on both sides with both printings normal. Such an error rarely

617 Rare error in the US 24 cent airmail stamp of 1918, see the inverted centre.

618 Canadian stamp of 1959 with inverted centre.

619 Extremely rare Indian error of 1854; the Queen's head is inverted.

620 Bolivian stamp with inverted centre.

XXI Some examples of points to watch out for: a Bolivian stamp with an inverted centre (1); an airmail stamp of the USSR with the overprint inverted, an extremely rare error, and a small 'f' in the word San Francisco (2); a stamp of the Federal Republic of Germany with a hand overprint 'Muster' which means 'specimen' (3); a bisected Turkish red 5 piastre stamp (4); stamps of unorthodox shape from Sierra Leone (5) and Burundi (6).

XXII An extremely rare Soviet miniature sheet of 1932 with stamps issued for the first All Union Stamp Exhibition in Moscow (1). Only 500 copies of this miniature sheet were issued. Courier cover from a stamp exhibition, Brno 1966 (2); Gibraltar cover for the inauguration of a cable-car service (3); Modern US private local issue (4).

1

2

3

4

621 Pair of US stamps dedicated to Dag Hammarskjöld. A printing error in this issue caused a great row.

happens in a modern printing shop as gummed paper is usually used for printing. This practically excludes the possibility of a sheet being put into the press with the gum on top. In the case of rotary presses it is not possible at all. Not many errors of this type exist and all of them were originated in the past. To this group also belong stamps with an underprint printed by mistake on the back, or on both the front and the back.

h) Set-off. You may quite frequently come across stamps printed on both sides but with a mirror print on the back. This error is known as a set-off. It can happen in two ways. The first possibility is that the press runs once without a stamp sheet having been inserted and the colour is printed on the overlay. When the next sheet of paper is entered into the machine and the print on the overlay is still wet the sheet will be printed on both sides. In this case both impressions on front and back will coincide exactly with each other. Another possibility is that a sheet is put on another sheet which is still wet. Again a set-off is produced but the two impressions need not coincide at all. The mirror impression on

622 Abstract painting by Stuart Davis on US stamp.

623 On the left of this card is a normal Soviet stamp and on the right a stamp in which the name of the country and the denomination are omitted.

624 US stamp with a colour omitted.

the back can be displaced or inverted. When stamps are being overprinted, or when they are printed on gummed paper, set-offs can be found on the gum as well. They are listed in some catalogues but in character they are not so very different from flaws.

i) Flaws. It happens quite frequently that extraneous material gets into the printing press. It might be a piece of paper, dust or something else. This causes *white spots*, sometimes quite large, to appear on the stamps. Dust may get mixed up with the ink and adhere unnoticed to the stamp. When the stamp is soaked, though, the dust dissolves and a white area appears on the stamp surface.

To the category of flaws belong also imprints of *leads* (printer's interlinear space, blanks) which are inserted between the clichés

625 Turkish stamps set off, sheet margin.

626 Back of a pair of Russian stamps from the sheet margin. On one the centre and the denomination are set off, whereas the other is without set-off.

627 Russian stamp with frame printed on the back; the centre is also printed on the back but inverted.

628 Pair of cheap Rumanian stamps. The right-hand stamp carries a white blot instead of the face.

of a plate. As soon as the printer notices this fault he pushes the leading down again and no more impressions are made. The same applies to the *nails* which are used to fix the plate to the press. The nails also tend to protrude and their marks can be found on or next to the stamps.

Sometimes the machine does not apply enough ink to parts of the plate or the pressure is insufficient here and there. As a result of this fault imperfect prints with the colour fading, or altogether missing in places, are produced. These are sometimes called 'dry prints'.

2. Overprint errors

When stamps are overprinted, practically all the errors and varieties possible in the printing of stamps can occur: there are plate errors of the overprint plates, inverted clichés (resulting in tête-bêche overprints), with retouching of the overprint, double overprints, inverted overprint, an overprint on the back and a set-off overprint. Flaws, too, are sometimes found in overprints.

Some catalogues list the position of overprints, and the most important overprint varieties, and show them with special marks:

↑ Normal overprint
↓ Overprint inverted
↘ Diagonal overprint from top left to bottom right-hand corner
↖ Diagonal overprint from bottom right to top left-hand corner
↗ Diagonal overprint from bottom left to top right-hand corner
↙ Diagonal overprint from top right to bottom left-hand corner
↑↑ Overprint double
↑↓ Overprint double, one inverted
↓↓ Overprint double and inverted

3. Errors of colour

Errors of colour must be clearly distinguished from colour shades which can cover quite a wide range, almost passing into other colours. Errors of colour occur mainly in two ways. Occasionally, when the printer had to replace a damaged cliché in a printing

629 Strip of three Soviet stamps with inverted and displaced overprint.

630 Block of four Soviet stamps, with an error in the top left stamp. Instead of the correct wording '100r.+100r.', the overprint reads '100r.+r.100'.

631 Rare overprinting error on a Danish stamp: in the centre row the left-hand stamp has an inverted overprint.

632 *Tête-bêche* overprint on Turkish stamps.

633 Turkey — inverted overprint.

634 Chile — double overprint, one inverted.

plate, he inserted by mistake a cliché of another value with the same design, which was normally printed in a different colour. Such a mistake produces an error of colour and interesting se-tenant pairs of different values. This happened, for instance, in 1861 with the local provisional Cape of Good Hope stamps, the so-called 'woodblocks'. Rare errors of colour exist — the 1d pale, milky blue or pale, bright blue, and the 4d vermilion or carmine. Wrong blocks of different value were inserted into plates of the other value and therefore copies of stamps exist in the colour intended for the other value. A similar thing happened in Roumania in 1893. Into a plate of 5 bani stamps printed in blue a cliché of the violet 25 bani stamp was inserted. Due to this error the 25 bani can be found in blue, and also in pairs with the normal blue 5 bani stamp.

It is much more common, though, that a printing plate or cylinder is mounted in a machine which had been previously printing stamps of a different colour, or that by mistake ink of a wrong colour is fed into a press. If such sheets of stamps printed in the wrong colour manage to pass the inspectors, philatelists get a most interesting variety. This happened, for instance, in 1935 with the top value of the GB Silver Jubilee stamps. Colour trials of the $2\frac{1}{2}$d in Prussian blue were sold at one post office.

Stamp collectors must pay great attention to the colours of stamps. Some colours are unstable and are apt to change under the influence of water, benzine, sunlight or chemicals. Such *colour changelings* are not considered rare. On the contrary, this change of colour represents damage of the stamp and diminishes its value. Stamp forgers have used all sorts of chemicals, to achieve changes of colour and to produce fantastic 'colour varieties'. Such stamps are naturally worthless. Therefore the best advice for a beginner is to consult an experienced philatelist.

4. Paper and watermark errors

Many varieties belong in this category, but they are not called printing errors. For instance, *laid paper* is used for the printing of a stamp. Suppose the lines in the paper should normally be vertical but a part of the stamps is printed with the lines horizontal. Very often different positions of the watermark are caused by the sheets of paper being inserted into the press incorrectly. Another cause is the change of paper during the process of printing.

Among the flaws caused by the paper must be included numerous *folds*. A corner of the sheet might be folded when it is put into the press or it may become crumpled in printing. The machine will print a normal stamp on the paper but if the fold is opened the design of the stamp splits into two parts. A large part of such folds in the possession of philatelists comes directly from the printers. There exist, nevertheless, stamps with small or larger folds which have been normally used on letters, that is, they have passed all controls and reached the post office counters.

Here is an example of a rare error produced by a mistake of the printers who used a different paper. The German definitives which had been previously printed on unwatermarked paper were reissued in 1905 on paper with a watermark of lozenges. These stamps were printed until 1921. In 1921 three sheets of the three mark value were found at two post offices, printed by mistake not on paper with the lozenge watermark, but on paper with a watermark formed of circles, which was used for the printing of insurance stamps.

5. Perforation errors

Varieties of perforation are not usually called errors, but the catalogues list them.

On the other hand, though, a great number of flaws are caused by perforating. If a perforation is displaced to such an extent that it goes deep into the stamp design then it is a very interesting variety for a specialized collector. In addition there exist on stamps of almost all countries *double perforations*, *omitted perforations*, *blind perforations* (when the pins are blunt and make only impressions without punching the paper) and other flaws.

6. Gum errors

Only very few errors in connection with the gum of stamps are known. In 1923 Czechoslovakia issued a series of stamps commemorating the fifth anniversary of the Republic. The yellowish gum is quadrillé, and has in the centre of each stamp a protective design formed by the letters 'CSP' — the abbreviation for Czechoslovak Post. Some copies of these stamps were found with this *gum watermark* displaced and even with the gum watermark inverted.

Stamps which have been gummed not only on the back but also on the front are also considered to be flaws. In some cases the gum on the backs of stamps has a vertical pattern. Stamps with a horizontal pattern are considered to be errors.

CANCELLATIONS

It has already been mentioned where handstamps come from and where they were first used. It is also known that handstamps are much older than postage stamps. Starting with the first simple handstamps, with just a few abbreviations, and later the name of the place, they subsequently changed their form and shape. According to the changes in their function the handstamps became more and more 'eloquent'. The name of the town was no longer sufficient; handstamps had to give details about the date of posting, the hour, etc. Whatever the post wanted to mark on an item of mail was at first written by hand. Later these functions were taken over

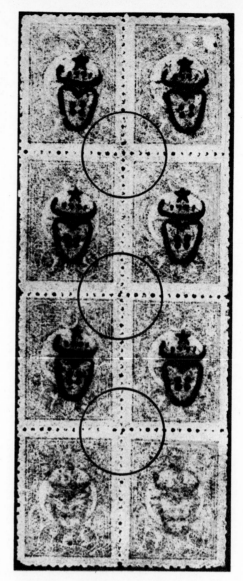

635 Block of eight Turkish stamps. Six of the stamps are overprinted on both sides.

636–637 Examples of abnormal paper folds.

638 Paper fold on Turkish stamps.

by handstamps. Frequently one handstamp was not sufficient, and several were used, each type of handstamp serving a special purpose.

Before postage stamps were invented handstamps often served a particular purpose. Take, for instance, the handstamp 'Franco'. Such a stamp on a letter indicated that the postage had already been paid and should not be collected from the addressee. Exactly the same was expressed by the handstamp 'PD', which is the abbreviation for Payé au Destinataire — paid up to addressee. In other words the handstamps 'Franco' and 'PD' are in some respects forerunners of the postage stamp. The same applies to figure

639 Strip of four Czechoslovak stamps with fold.

640 Large fold on a block of twelve.

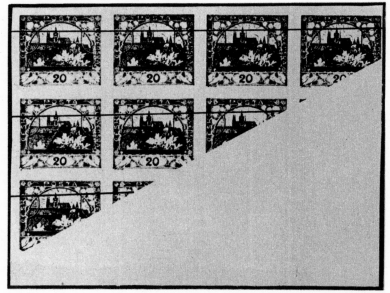

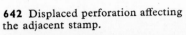

641 Unusual folding error.

642 Displaced perforation affecting the adjacent stamp.

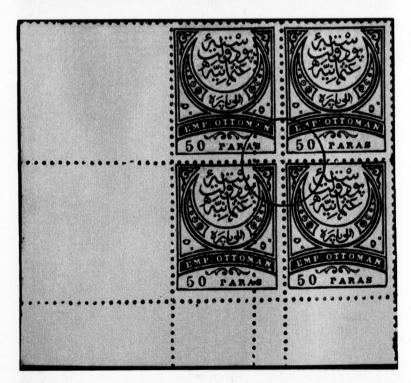

643 Block of four with double vertical perforation in the centre.

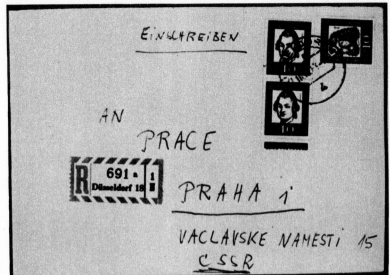

644 Double perforation on the bottom of a pair of German stamps.

645 Horizontal perforation omitted on stamps from Montenegro.

646 Imperforate margin.

647 Horizontal perforation omitted.

handstamps, which indicated not only the fact that the postage had been paid but also the amount paid.

The 'Franco' handstamp served the post not only in pre-philatelic times, but nowadays, too; for instance, when there were no postage stamps available or they could not be used for some reason. In 1953 there was a monetary reform in Czechoslovakia. Postage stamps could be used up to the time when new stamps were issued but in a ratio of one to ten. That meant that an inland letter which, up to the day of the monetary reform, had to be franked with a three-crown stamp now had to be franked with stamps of thirty

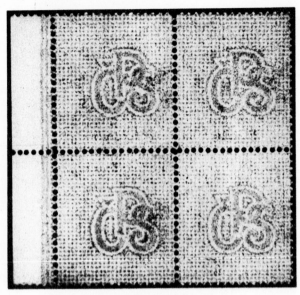

crowns. Since high-value postage stamps were in short supply many letters in the post were covered with stamps of lower values. Some post offices ran out of stamps long before the new stamps arrived. The problem was solved in such a way that, instead of stamps, the postage was paid at the post office counter in cash, the post office affixed the handstamp 'Franco' to the letter, and the postage paid was entered by hand in the new currency.

PRE-PHILATELIC HANDSTAMPS

A very satisfying field of collecting, although by no means easy or inexpensive, is a collection of pre-adhesive covers. Such a collection comprises old letters bearing handstamps dating back to the times before the first adhesive postage stamps were issued. Due to the fact that postage stamps were introduced at different times in different countries, in England the pre-adhesive period ended on 5 May 1840, but in Austria, where postage stamps were introduced on 1 June 1850, the pre-adhesive period ended on 31 May 1850. In some countries, for instance in Great Britain, it was possible to send letters to be paid by the addressee even after the introduction of stamps. Therefore stampless covers of later dates can be found.

Among the Austrian handstamps from the pre-adhesive period are some which are commonly called by philatelists on the Continent 'nobility handstamps'. This is because in front of the town's name they have the prefix 'von' or 'v'. This, of course, has nothing to do with nobility as it simply means 'from' in this case. On the

650 Letter from Brno sent before postage stamps were issued and bearing two different handstamps 'Franco'.

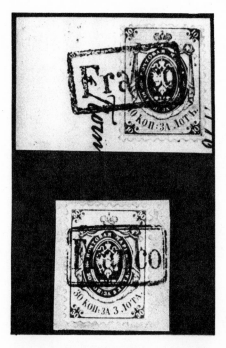

651 Russian stamps cancelled by the handstamp 'Franco'.

652 Cover from the period of the currency reform in Czechoslovakia, 1953. Stamps in the old currency were used but had only one tenth of their former franking value.

other hand, elsewhere in the world handstamps were used which stated the destination of the letter or which route it was going to take. Sometimes the route of a letter was given on a special label even after the introduction of stamps.

The introduction of postage stamps, though, did not necessarily mean the end of pre-adhesive handstamps. Usually they continued to serve their purpose until they were replaced by other, more modern handstamps.

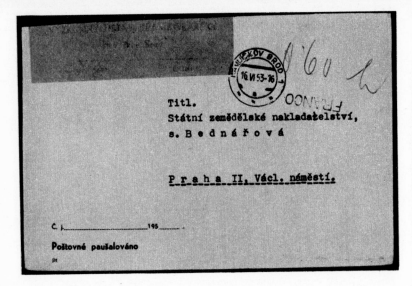

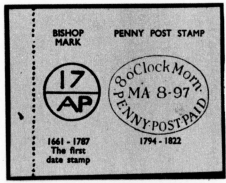

653 Another cover from the same period but instead of stamps a handstamp 'Franco' has been used and the postage amount written by hand.

654–655 British handstamps from the period before the introduction of postage stamps.

656 Attractive Italian registered cover.

THE FIRST CANCELLATIONS OF STAMPS

In England, and also in other countries, the existing handstamps at the time of the introduction of stamps were not intended for the cancelling of postage stamps. Simultaneous with the introduction of the first postage stamps England introduced special handstamps in the shape of a Maltese Cross, without a text. The Maltese Cross was used for the cancellation of postage stamps, and in addition the other handstamp which had been in use was used to mark the letter with all the necessary details. Some post offices in England were issued with Maltese Cross type handstamps of a different design, which enables specialists to identify the place where the stamp was cancelled even if the latter has been removed from the cover.

The British handstamps served as an example for other countries where special, 'mute' handstamps for the cancellation of stamps were introduced, i.e. handstamps without any text. These handstamps are of different geometric shapes, bars, concentric circles, etc. Sometimes they are found with a common text like 'Annulato' (cancelled) in Italy. When Sicily introduced stamps in 1859 a special, decorative frame handstamp was designed. Its purpose was to cancel the postage stamp but not to 'desecrate' by its impression the portrait of King Ferdinand II.

In other countries at first no special handstamps were introduced for the cancellation of stamps. According to postal instructions the stamps had to be cancelled by pen, by a signature of the postmaster. etc. *Pen cancellations* were sometimes obligatory for certain types of stamps. For instance the German ten groschen and thirty groschen stamps of 1872, and the two-mark stamp of 1875, originally had to be cancelled by writing across them the locality of posting and the date. Only after several years was it permitted to cancel them with a handstamp. Pen cancellations must be distinguished from other pen marks. An official postal cancellation by pen does not diminish the value of a stamp. On the contrary, sometimes such stamps are even more highly valued. On the other hand stamps marked with a pen in cases when this was not a rule are worthless,

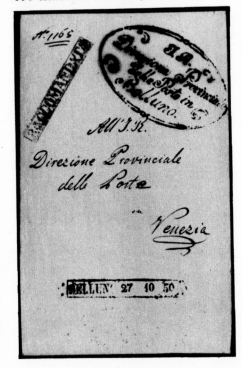

657 Austrian pre-stamp cover with handstamp 'Neutitschein'.

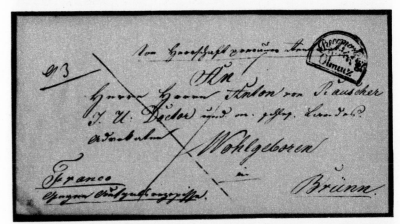

658 Registration handstamp from Olmütz.

659 Viennese handstamp.

or their value represents only a fraction of the value of a properly cancelled stamp.

In the same way as the British post started to distinguish different post offices by different shapes of the Maltese Cross, other countries also decided to cancel postage stamps with an obliterator

660 'Nobility' handstamp from Prague.

661 A Maltese Cross, the handstamp for the world's first stamps.

662 Another type of Maltese Cross.

which would show its place of use. That is how *number cancellations* were introduced. Every number denoted a post office. Such cancellers were used in England, France, Russia, Denmark, Bavaria, Baden and many other countries. With the help of the numbers in the cancellation it is therefore possible to state exactly where a letter had been posted. Obviously these numbers have tempted some specialized collectors to form collections of all number handstamps of a certain country.

As time passed and the number of mail items grew, postal administrations realized that the cancellation of mail with two or three handstamps (for instance a registered letter) was uneconomic and took too long. They therefore introduced one new handstamp which combined the functions of both previously employed main handstamps — it cancelled the postage stamp and at the same time stated where and when the letter had been posted.

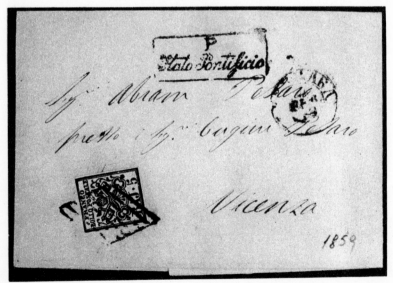

663 Danish mute handstamp.

664 Mute handstamp of the Roman States.

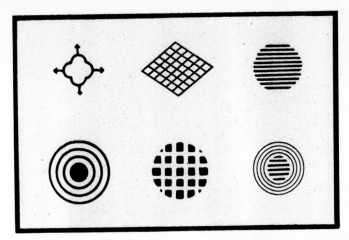

665–666 Different types of mute handstamps.

667 Stamp from Saxony cancelled with a mute handstamp and, next to it, a handstamp with text.

668 Stamp from Naples cancelled 'Annulato'.

669 Special cancellation handstamp for the first stamps of Sicily.

Originally only hand-operated cancellers were used, usually made of steel, but there were also handstamps in use made of wood or rubber. Modern techniques influenced the development of cancellers as well. The task of the hand-operated canceller is being increasingly taken over by roller and machine cancellers.

THE COLOUR OF CANCELLATIONS

The overwhelming majority of all cancellations is in black, but
even in pre-adhesive times other colours were used, such as, for
instance, red, green, blue. These other colours are not so common
and stamp collectors therefore value them more highly than black
cancellations. No doubt an additional reason is that a different-
coloured cancellation makes a collection more attractive and en-
hances the aesthetic effect.

The black cancellation, though, was not always the rule. When
England introduced the first stamps in 1840 post offices were instructed to cancel the Penny Blacks and Twopenny Blues with
a red Maltese Cross. Soon it was found that it was not very difficult

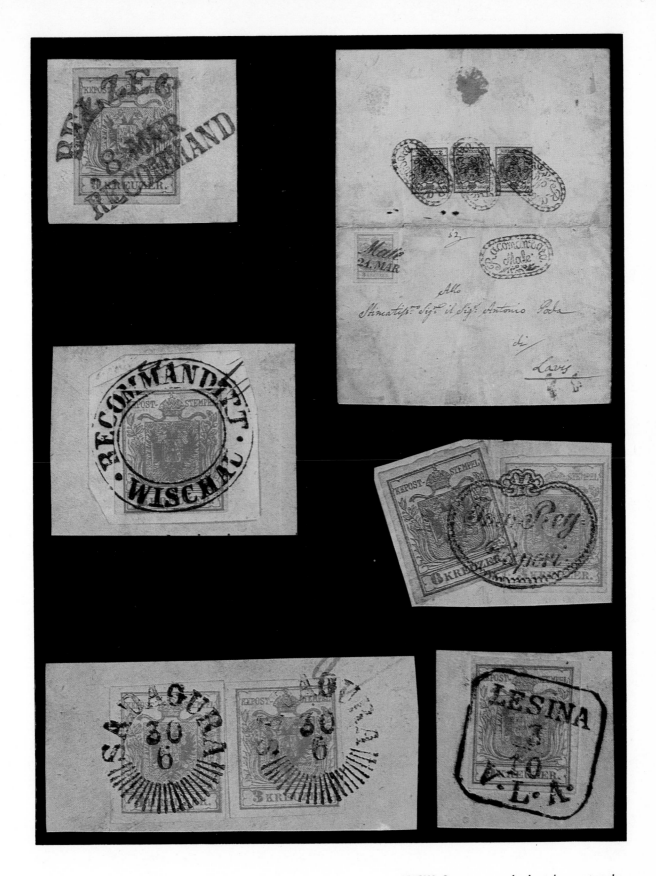

XXIII Some rare early Austrian postmarks.

XXIV Colourful Austrian covers. Below is an interesting mixed franking:
red three kreuzer and black two kreuzer stamps together with a yellow five
centesimi stamp of Austrian Italy.

to remove the red handstamp and some people re-used the postage stamps. Therefore the instructions were changed and all stamps had to be cancelled in black. As a black handstamp did not show very clearly on the Penny Blacks, the Penny stamps were reissued in February 1841, printed in red. Quite a number of postmasters did not strictly obey the rules of cancellation colours. When they ran out of normal ink they used whatever colour was available.

Different cancellation colours were also to be found later. They are still frequently used in many countries, especially for commemorative handstamps. All sorts of colours can be found, including gold and even multi-coloured handstamps.

TYPES OF CANCELLATIONS

With cancellations, just as with postage stamps, there are many different types. The most important ones can be listed in a similar order to stamps.

a) **Normal cancellation date stamps.** These are the most common cancellations and are used all over the world. They fulfil all the basic tasks which have been mentioned already. Cancellation date stamps are found in various shapes, but they are mostly circular.

b) **Airmail cancellations.** In the beginning, airmail letters, and other mail items transported by air, were marked with handwritten information. Later special handstamps were introduced with a text denoting that this was an airmail item, or with more detailed information about the type of flight, the date, etc. Some cancellations include a text like 'Posta aerea', the silhouette of a plane, or something similar. In addition special official, semi-official and private handstamps with details about the flight were used. Soon special airmail labels were printed for airmail items, but in some countries special cachets (usually of rectangular shape) with the French text 'Par avion', or a text in another language, were employed instead of the labels.

Aerophilately — the collecting of airmail items and stamps — is very popular all over the world. Postal administrations, airlines and other bodies dealing with special flights use special cachets on mail items carried on these flights, which are collected by aerophilatelists. (Aerophilatelists are internationally organized in the Fédération Internationale des Sociétés Aérophilatéliques — FISA.) There are cancellations for first flights on new routes or with new types of planes, cancellations for Zeppelin flights, balloon post, pigeon post, rocket mail, polar flights, etc.

c) **Newspaper cancellations.** Long before stamps were invented a newspaper tax was collected in some countries, and the payment of this tax was confirmed with the help of a special handstamp (in Austria this is called a *Signet*). These are not normal postal cancellations but predecessors of the newspaper tax stamps. There are, though, a few specialists who collect these handstamps.

d) **Official cancellations.** In a number of countries official mail is not franked with postage stamps and no official stamps have been issued. Therefore special, official handstamps are used on

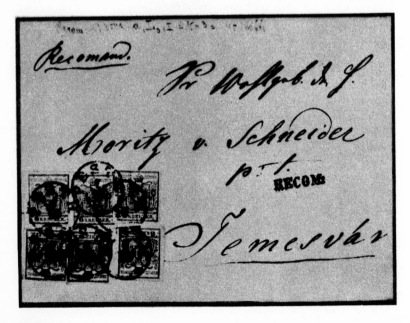

678 This cover meant a lot of work for the postal clerk. There are six handstamps on the six stamps and, in addition, a further handstamp 'Recom' for a registered letter.

679 Handstamps can have the most fantastic shapes: here a Turkish negative, so-called 'seal' handstamp from Bethlehem.

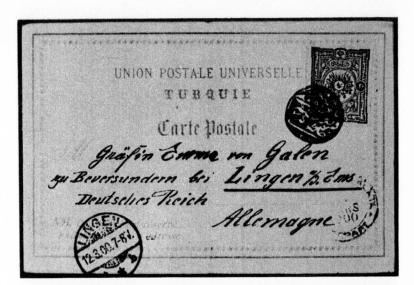

680 Hexagonal Turkish handstamp from Tekirdagh.

681 Ornate Mexican handstamp.

682 Handstamp from Travancore (India).

this type of mail. These handstamps denote that such a letter is official and free of postage.

e) Special cancellations. As far back as pre-adhesive times special handstamps were used to mark registered letters. They have texts such as 'Rekommandiert', for instance, and they were struck on letters in addition to the normal handstamp. The text 'Registered' or 'Rekommandiert' is sometimes included in cancellationdate stamps, which means that they have added a third function to their previous two. Furthermore, instead of labels for special delivery, cachets with the text 'Exprès' are used. The cachet 'A.R.' is used to confirm receipt; there are special telegraph cancellations, telephone cancellations, pneumatic mail cancellations, etc. When a letter was insufficiently franked and postage due was collected from the addressee, some post offices not only affixed the appropriate postage-due labels but also used a cachet stating that the letter was insufficiently franked. Furthermore, there exists quite a large number of special cachets used by post offices, as for instance 'Unknown', 'Return to sender', 'Zurück', etc. Nowadays specially printed labels are often used instead of these cachets, and in some places the post office cancels them with the normal CDS (cancellation date stamp).

683

684

685

684

683 Airport post handstamp, Zurich.

684 Airmail handstamp from Rome.

685 Airmail commemoratives on card. The stamps are cancelled with a handstamp commemorating the fortieth anniversary of the Czechoslovak Airlines; in the top left is a circular handstamp for the first Prague-Frankfurt flight and a rectangular cachet for the flight.

686 Newspaper of 1848 with an Austrian signet.

f) Travelling post office cancellations. The mail coaches travelling with trains on the main lines use their own cancellations. Such cancellations usually have a text telling the train's place of departure and arrival, or a number allocated to the TPO (travelling post office). Special cancellations are also used by the automobile post. The first TPO was used by Baden in 1848.

g) Maritime cancellations. These cancellations were introduced before postage stamps were invented. In some cases they just state that it is a maritime mail item; sometimes the name of the shipping company is added, the port of origin and destination and even the name of the ship. Cachets with the word 'Paquebot' are very common. Warships of many countries also had their own cancellations, either with a number or the name of the ship.

h) Fieldpost cancellations. These too date back to the period before the introduction of postage stamps. In later times military units not only had their own postal service but also their own cancellations. A most interesting and very large field for collectors is offered by the fieldpost during the First World War. At that time the military authorities were not so conscious of the need for

687 Official cover from Cyprus with the handstamp 'Service des Postes'.

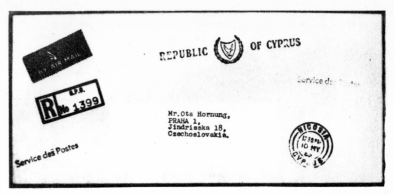

688 North Korean handstamp 'Taxe perçue'.

secrecy. Therefore there are not only cancellations giving the name and number of the unit in the cancellation date stamp, but also additional cachets with detailed information. During the Second World War the network of the fieldpost was even larger, but detailed information was no longer given and the names and numbers of units were not stated. Instead field post office numbers and abbreviations were used. For security reasons in some cases the fieldpost numbers were switched round and now it is very difficult, especially in the case of the German fieldpost, to tell from which unit a fieldpost item originated. It is up to specialized collectors to make their own studies and collect the necessary documentation. This is a most rewarding field of collecting which still has great possibilities.

i) Auxiliary cancellations. During wars and in postwar times, whenever there was a need, temporary and auxiliary cancellations

689 Brunswick stamp cancelled by mute handstamp; next to the stamp is a normal handstamp with text and also a registered letter handstamp.

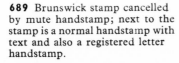

690 Viennese handstamp in red combining the CDS (cancellation date stamp) with the registration of the letter.

691 Letter from Haifa with registration handstamp. The letter was posted during the Second World War and was opened by the censor. There is also an arrival handstamp of the Czechoslovak fieldpost in England.

appeared. Either previously-used handstamps were adapted, or makeshift handstamps were produced. Due to the lack of time and shortage of means they were frequently produced not from steel but from rubber or even wood. In Denmark, for example, for a transitory period in the 1890s, newly established post offices used auxiliary handstamps which had to serve until the post offices were issued with proper metal handstamps. After Czechoslovakia was founded in 1918 the German and Hungarian texts were removed from the bilingual handstamps and only the Czech and Slovak texts left. This was repeated after the liberation of Czechoslovakia in 1945. In a similar way the post offices in Poland, Yugoslavia and other countries dealt with their handstamps.

j) Commemorative cancellations. This type of cancellation is very common nowadays. For important events and festivities special cancellations with an appropriate text and often with a draw-

692 'A.R.' handstamp with inscription on a Turkish stamp.

693 Cover from Russia to Sweden with cachets denoting insufficient franking: top left in German, bottom left in Russian.

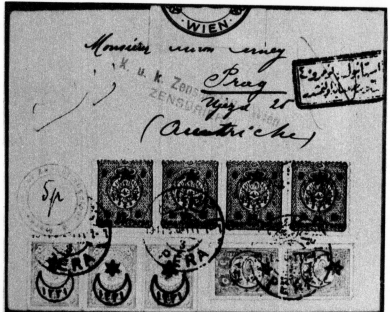

694 Censored cover from Turkey, First World War. The most interesting feature is the double circle handstamp in red on the left with the text 'Marke von der Zensur abgelöst' (stamp removed by censor) and the value '5p' (5 paras) added by hand.

695 This stamp was not cancelled at the post office of origin. It was cancelled later with a special handstamp for this purpose with text 'Nachträglich entwertet' (subsequently cancelled).

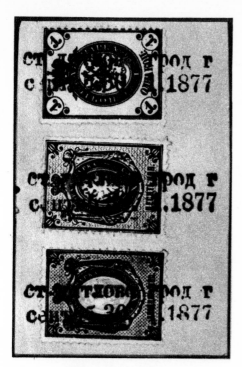

696 Russian railway station handstamp.

698 TPO handstamp from German South West Africa.

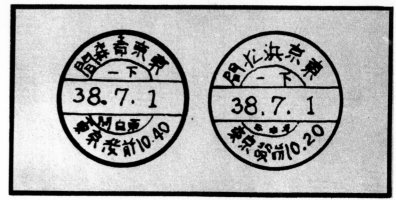

697 Two Japanese TPO (Travelling Post Office) handstamps.

ing are used. The shapes of these cancellations are varied. The first commemorative cancellation was in use from 26 July to 9 August 1863 in Leipzig for the German Gymnastic Festivities. The text on this cancellation read 'Thurn-Fest-Platz-Leipzig'. Since there was no date on this cancellation the normal CDS was used as well. There are also a number of publicity cancellations pointing out interesting sights of the places where they are in use or promoting products of the town, or drawing attention to local events (slogan cancellations). To this group of cancellations belong also the cancellations used on the first day of issue of new stamps.

k) Cancellations of special post offices. Sometimes post offices are established which use their own special handstamps. A good example is hotel posts. A special post office is open in summer on the highest mountain of Australia, Mount Kosciusko (7,328′). A post office also exists in the deepest Austrian mine, Wodzicky near Fohnsdorf in Styria, 3,721′ deep. It is very clear, of course, that these post offices do not serve any real need but have been established, together with the handstamps, for the sake of stamp collectors, and, perhaps, for souvenir hunters.

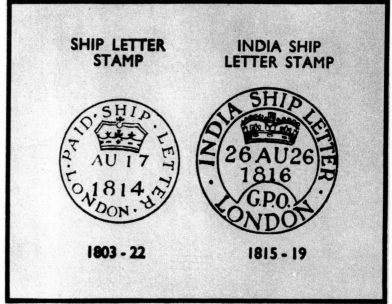

699 Old British ship-letter handstamps.

700 Classical cover from Greece with the rectangular cachet of the Austrian postal steamers.

701 Maritime handstamp 'Bremen — New York'.

702 Handstamp of the Israeli steamer *Moledet*.

l) Cancellations of local and private posts. Wherever a local or private post functioned with its own postal network and was not part of the State post, special cancellations were used; they were usually different in shape from the cancellations used by the State post.

ROLLER AND MACHINE CANCELLATIONS

Roller cancellations represent the first step towards the mechanization of the cancelling of mail. They are 'endless' cancellations. A normal cancellation date stamp followed by parallel or wavy lines or an instructive or publicity text appears on the roller. Nowadays post offices use machine cancellations to a great extent.

Machine cancellations belong to specialized collections and, whenever their text or design is related to a theme, also to thematic collections. From a purely philatelic point of view many stamp collectors prefer stamps cancelled by hand to stamps cancelled by roller or machine. Wavy lines and publicity texts very often spoil the stamp design, especially if they are smudged or too heavy.

The first cancellation machine was constructed by the armourer Salles in France in 1857. This machine had a remarkable performance for those days — up to 200 cancellations per minute. Salles'

703 Picture postcard sent by Austrian soldier in 1916 from Jerusalem to Prague. It has a circular handstamp of the German Military Mission in Turkey and in addition a three-line cachet 'Bevollmächtigter des I. Expeditionskorps für deutsche und österr.-ungar. Heeresangehörige' (Authority of the 1st Expedition Corps for German and Austro-Hungarian Army Personnel).

704 Handstamp of the Italian fieldpost in Istanbul.

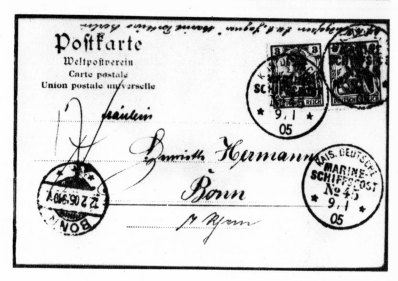

705 Postcard with cancellations 'Marine-Schiffspost'.

706 Back of a cover with handstamp commemorating the Conference of Algeciras, 1906.

707

machine was introduced in several places but after some time discarded and forgotten. In England a cancelling machine was introduced in the 1860s and the performance reached was 118 cancellations per minute. Modern machines have performances of 700 cancellations per minute, or more. To improve the automatic

707–708 Two German commemorative handstamps.

709 British commemorative handstamp.

710 Austrian commemorative handstamp.

sorting and cancelling of letters, Great Britain, West Germany and other countries have introduced stamps with phosphor lines or stamps printed on fluorescent paper. The machine 'finds' the stamps on the letter and cancels them.

BULK POSTAGE AND PRECANCELLED STAMPS

The great amount of mail dispatched by large firms represents a heavy burden for post offices. The same problem occurs with newspapers, magazines, etc. In some countries it is therefore possible to pay for the postage in bulk and this is noted by the firm on each mail item by a rubber handstamp or a printed text. Sometimes such mail receives an additional CDS.

711 Christmas handstamp from Austria.

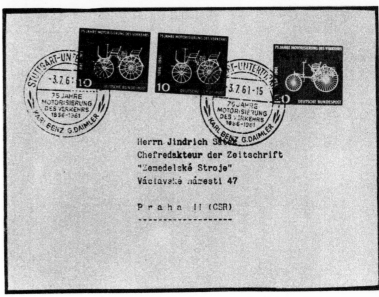

712 Cover with West German commemorative handstamps.

713 Argentine First Day Cancellation.

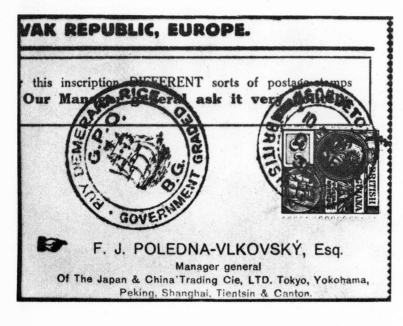

714 In addition to the normal CDS, a special handstamp promoting the export of rice was used by the post office of Georgetown (British Guiana).

715 Egyptian hotel handstamp.

The United States, France, Belgium and other countries introduced so-called *precancelled stamps*. These are normal postage stamps obliterated in advance with an overprint. Such precancelled stamps are supplied to large firms only — other people cannot use them. If a mail item with a precancelled stamp is returned to the sender it is usually cancelled by a handstamp 'Return to Sender' to make re-use impossible.

France ceased to overprint normal stamps for use as precancelled stamps, but issued special stamps for this purpose. A cancellation handstamp is included in its printed design.

METER MARKS

In postwar years meter machines have become very common all over the world. For large firms this is a useful way of franking

716 Handstamp of the Tin Can Mail of Tonga. Swimmers brought the mail in a large tin can to the waiting steamer.

717 Handstamp of the Libyan local post.

the mail. No postage stamps are needed, the postage is set on the meter and the mail is dealt with quickly. Furthermore, the employees of the firm cannot use the firm's stamps for their private mail.

According to a rule of the Universal Postal Union the colour of meter marks should be red. The mark is composed of a part usually similar to a common CDS with all the normal text; then there is a design (a circle, square or other shape) with the name of the country and the postage, and the rest of the space is filled with the name of the firm or with a publicity text. Meter marks from individual countries vary in shape and arrangement.

Philatelists are obviously not pleased with the introduction of meter marks, as they eliminate stamps and limit their use. On the other hand there are a number of specialized collectors who have chosen meter marks as their field of interest. This is a most complicated and difficult field. The number of meter marks in use is very large, no general list of users is available and nobody really knows how many such meter marks there are, who employs them

718 Machine handstamps from different countries: England.

719 France.

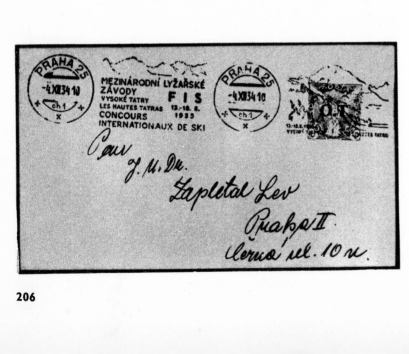

720 Czechoslovakia.

721–724 Pre-cancelled stamps from different countries.

725 French stamp with the pre-cancellation included in the design.

and what texts are being used. A firm can frequently change the advertisement text without telling anybody. Meter marks can be included in some specialized collections and some of them most certainly belong in thematic collections.

CANCELLED BY FAVOUR AND TO ORDER

Such cancellations deserve to be mentioned and explained. 'Cancelled by favour' is an expression used for stamps cancelled in a special manner, generally at the request of a philatelist. Such items did not usually go through the post. There were times when a great number of philatelists were convinced that only cancelled stamps were worth collecting and were of value. So they affixed newly issued stamps to postcards or pieces of paper and had them cancelled at a post office. Sometimes all sorts of 'rarities' were produced in this way. Until 1914, for instance, foreign post offices operated in Turkey. In Istanbul there were, in addition to Turkish post offices, also German, Austrian, British, French, Italian, Russian, Rumanian and Egyptian post offices. A visiting 'philatelist' would visit these post offices one after the other, buy a stamp, affix it to a postcard and have it cancelled. In the end he would post this 'collection' from one of the post offices. Such a 'combined franking' has hardly any philatelic value, but nevertheless, after more than half a century, it is a document of historic interest and reflects the situation existing at the time.

Some postal administrations (mostly of Eastern Europe) supply stamp wholesalers with large quantities of complete sheets of gummed stamps already cancelled. These stamps are cancelled to order and frequently sold at a fraction of their face value. The majority of stamps cancelled to order is used for stamp packets. It is obvious that the philatelic value of such stamps which have never seen a letter or gone through the post cannot be compared with the value of stamps normally used on mail. Stamp catalogues do not make any distinction between genuinely used stamps and stamps cancelled to order. Obviously, though, the fact that some stamps have been put on the market in great quantities CTO, results in a much lower catalogue price for used copies. Although CTO stamps are a source of income this policy has created a great deal of mistrust of the issuing countries and many collectors have given up their collections of such States or do not include stamps cancelled to order in their collections.

In some countries *first day covers* are sold to philatelists at the post office with stamps affixed and cancelled, and sometimes such covers are valid up to two weeks after the actual date of issue. Some postal administrations issue *first day sheets* specially printed for new issues which are affixed to them and cancelled with the *first day cancellation*. Both are issued for stamp collectors.

FORGERS AND FORGERIES

Forgeries of stamps have been mentioned in earlier chapters. They represent a problem of such importance, especially for beginner stamp collectors, that it is necessary to deal with them in detail.

726

727

728

729

The history of stamp forgeries is very old, almost as old as the history of stamp collecting itself. As soon as the circle of stamp lovers started to grow it became apparent that the quantity of stamps available could by no means meet the demand. Everybody knows that there are quite a few stamps which exist only in very limited numbers, perhaps a few dozen, or even less, of some issues. These stamps were rare and therefore already much in demand when philately was young. In those days there were neither philatelic literature nor experts. Our great-grandfathers did not greatly care about the origin of the stamps they put in their collection. They were not too particular about the quality of a stamp, so why should they go to any trouble to find out whether it was genuine?

A few enterprising individuals saw their great chance: There is a demand for Post Office Mauritius, it's in short supply; fair enough, let's print it. Very often they did not even pretend that they had the original of a stamp and they even advertised them as imitations. And our great-grandfathers bought them. A genuine stamp was not available and it was also more expensive, so they stuck an imitation into their stamp album. At least they could fill an annoying, empty space. And their grandson or great grandson is nowadays very surprised when he takes his forbears' collection to a stamp dealer and is told that the best stamps in the whole collection are forgeries.

FERRARI AND FOURNIER

The greatest stamp collector of the last century and the beginning of this century was without doubt the French nobleman Philippe Renotière de Ferrari. He was a millionaire and he spent many of those millions on stamps. He formed a gigantic collection of

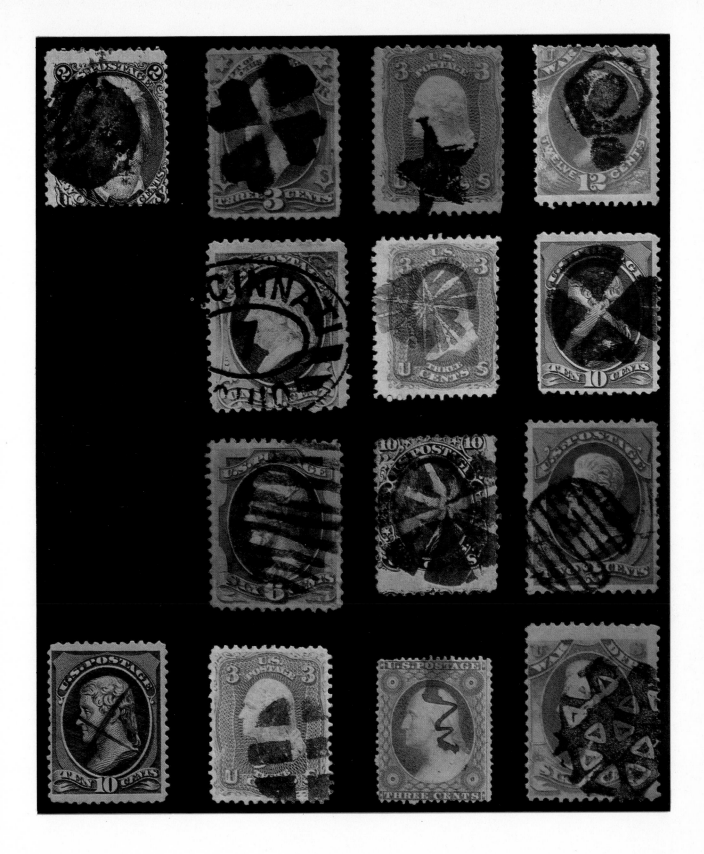

XXV Classical stamps of the United States with different types of cancellations and postmarks.

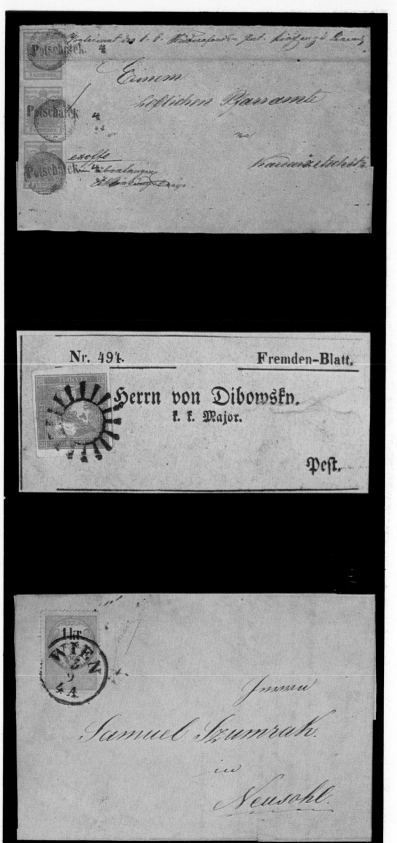

XXVI More early Austrian covers: a vertical strip of three yellow 1 kreuzer stamps and the rare postmark of Potschatek on cover (1); the Blue Mercury, the world's first newspaper stamp on piece with a clean strike of the rare mute cancellation of Budapest (2); and a rare cover bearing an Austrian fiscal stamp instead of a postage stamp (3).

1

2

3

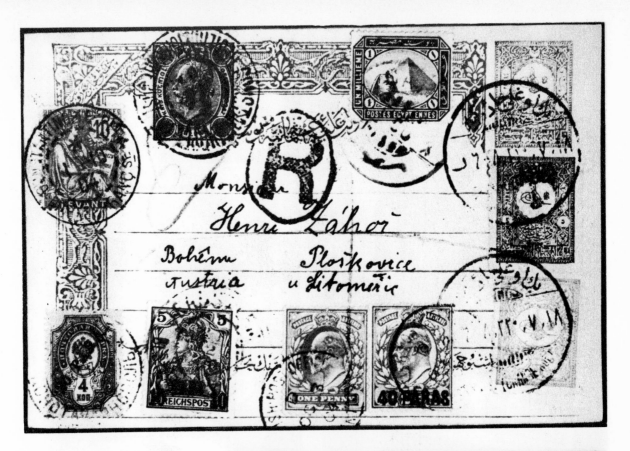

730 Postcard with stamps and handstamps of post offices of different nations existing in Constantinople before the First World War.

731 Hungarian First Day cover.

732 First Day cover from Cyprus which travelled through the post.

733 First Day covers of different countries: France.   **734—735** United Kingdom and USA.

735

736 Czechoslovakia.

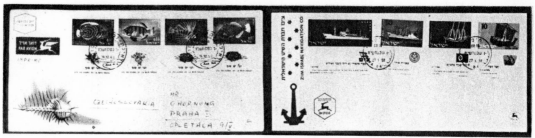

737 Israel.

738 First Day cancellation on British stamps.

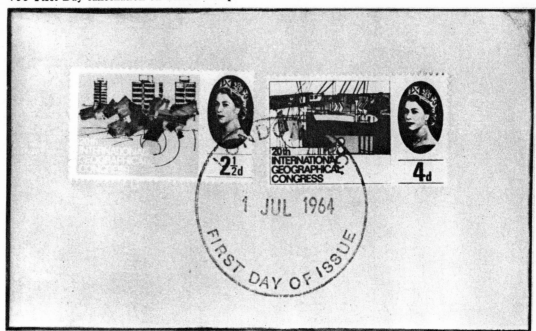

absolutely fantastic value which comprised the greatest stamp rarities of the world. When Ferrari died and his collection was put up for sale it was a world sensation. It was not just one sale — his collection was so huge that there were a number of special sales.

Ferrari had his agents all over the world. They were on the look-out for rare stamps. The stamp forgers were very much aware of it, and they produced some unique items for Count Ferrari and more then once he was duped: so often, in fact, that in those days good stamp forgeries were nicknamed in philatelic circles 'Ferrarity'.

To the 'assistance' of philatelists who were in vain looking for some of the rare stamps came François Fournier. As far back as 1892 a certain M. Mercier started to print imitations of stamps in Switzerland. But business was not very good. It was up to Fournier to bring new life into the enterprise. He decided not to produce individual copies of stamps, as the other stamp forgers were doing, but introduced mass production of his goods. If you were looking for rare Cape of Good Hope triangulars, or for old Saxony stamps, then the firm of Fournier was ready to supply them. The only good thing to be said about this mass forger is that he did not pretend that his products were genuine stamps and that he was selling them at a cheap price. He mass-produced more-or-less successful forgeries of all sorts of classical stamps, not only of expensive stamps but also of cheaper ones.

In 1910 Fournier published a catalogue of his products which comprised over 1,200 complete forgeries and 636 forged overprints. Fournier's products became so dangerous that philatelists decided to take action. Fournier died during the First World War and his successor, Christian Hirschburger, no longer successful in business, decided to sell his complete workshop with all the machinery, blocks and remainders to the Philatelic Society of Geneva. Out of the supplies of forgeries 480 sample albums were compiled as basic material for philatelic experts and the remaining stamp forgeries were burned under official supervision. The printing blocks and the rest of the equipment were destroyed. All this happened in 1928. Just as a point of interest, philatelic experts have calculated that the available supplies of forged stamps in the business represented, if valued as genuine stamps according to the French Yvert Tellier catalogue of 1928, an overall value of 2,846,500 francs!

Fournier's goods bear all the signs of cheap mass production. They can by no means be compared with the laborious, hand-made products of the master forgers. Very frequently they are just rough imitations. Neither their design, nor their paper, colour or cancellation correspond to genuine copies. Nevertheless they represent a great danger, even nowadays. There are probably a million copies or more in circulation all over the world. Present-day owners either genuinely believe that they possess the genuine stamp or knowingly take advantage of the insufficient knowledge and credulity of an exchange partner or customer. Their victims are in most cases young philatelists. The danger of Fournier's forgeries is that there are so many of them and that some of them are forgeries of cheaper stamps.

A MASTER OF HIS PROFESSION

739 Genuine Turkish 5 piastre stamp.

740 Fournier's forgery. (The cancellation is also forged.)

There was a most interesting incident in France during the Second World War. French customs officers intercepted a suspicious mail item sent to Portugal in 1942. The contents were declared to be art reproductions of stamps. When these stamps were handed to some philatelic experts they declared them to be genuine and the contents of the parcel to be of extremely high value. Therefore Jean de Sperati of Aix-les-Bains was put on trial for attempting to evade customs duties of 300,000 francs.

The trial became a sensation that nobody had expected. Sperati declared that the consignment did not contain genuine stamps but imitations produced by himself. He called them 'Philatélie d'Art'. When the court cited the expertise of well-known philatelists Sperati presented as evidence the material used for the production of his forgeries. He was a master indeed, and, in addition, he had given his work careful thought. He had managed to obtain remainders of the original paper on which the stamps had been printed long ago and he printed his forgeries on sheet margins and free spaces, or removed the original printing on the stamp and replaced it with his forgery. He thus overcame one of the great obstacles that usually defeats the common stamp forger — the original paper. He was also extremely careful in the production of his blocks, the selection of inks, colours etc.

How perfect de Sperati's products were can be seen from this episode which took place in the court room during his trial. By mistake some genuine stamps were mixed up with de Sperati's forgeries. Not even the greatest philatelic experts could distinguish them. The court had to ask de Sperati himself to show which stamps were genuine and which were his reproductions.

De Sperati was acquitted as far as the infringement of customs regulations was concerned, but he was put on trial as a forger. He managed, though, to extricate himself again by declaring that he had never said that his products were genuine stamps. He had always called them art reproductions!

De Sperati later wrote a book about his 'stamps' which became a philatelic best-seller and was soon out of print. The catalogue of his samples, which he had promised to publish, was never edited. The British Philatelic Association bought a part of his products for ten million francs in 1954 and de Sperati gave his word never to put his imitations into circulation. Three years later Jean de Sperati, master stamp forger, died at Aix-les-Bains at the age of seventy-three.

Most forgeries, and the most dangerous ones, are to be found in classical stamps. There are two reasons for this: first of all, it is with the rare and expensive stamps that the tedious and difficult work of the forger pays, and secondly they were printed by a more primitive technique, mostly by letterpress, and this makes them easier to imitate. Therefore it is a basic rule for all beginners, and even for more experienced philatelists, never to buy a pig in a poke, never to rely on one's own judgment. Show the stamp to an expert and get his advice!

KNOWN TYPES OF FORGERIES

The stamp forgers have never missed a chance to make money by forgery. Their activities are twofold, and therefore two major groups of forgeries are distinguished:
1. *forgeries to defraud the post;* 2. *forgeries to defraud stamp collectors.*

There have never been many forgeries of the first type. The forgers were usually soon discovered and severely punished. Every State protects its stamps in a similar way to banknotes, and the penalties are just as high. In spite of all precautions, however, a certain number of fraudulent stamps passed unnoticed, at least at first, and were not spotted by postal employees. They are normally found used and cancelled on covers. Such a forgery is of great interest to specialized collectors. It is a fraudulent imitation of a stamp, but it has served a postal purpose.

Stamp forgeries used on genuine letters or in another way are very rare and fetch high prices. Most interesting is the case of the famous GB 'Stock Exchange' forgeries. In 1898 supplies of forged copies of the 1867 green one-shilling stamps from old telegraph forms used at the London Stock Exchange Post Office came on the market. Although the forger was never identified it is assumed that one of the counter clerks used these skilful forgeries. He accepted cash from the sender and, instead of genuine shilling stamps, used his forgeries and kept the money.

Very similar is the history of forgeries of the first Czechoslovak stamps. In fact so similar that it is possible the forger in Czechoslovakia knew of the success of his London predecessor. The stamps forged were the 1919 brown 100 heller stamp, the ultramarine 200 heller and the olive-green 300 heller stamps, showing Hradčany Castle in Prague. These forgeries were discovered in 1934 in postal kiloware and all of them had been cancelled at Vejprty. Only the 300 heller fake was known as far back as 1920 in mint condition. Practically only cancelled copies got into the hands of philatelists; they were produced solely to cheat the post office. The *Vejprty Forgeries* are very rare. Since it took fifteen years for them to be identified the forger was never found. It is presumed that he was a post office clerk who did not sell these stamps for normal letters but used them on parcel cards. When a customer paid for these, the forger affixed them himself, knowing that parcel cards were not handed to the addressee but kept at the post office for a number of years.

Forgeries to defraud stamp collectors, on the other hand, are much more common. Since they were never intended to serve any postal purpose they have no philatelic value. There are some collectors, specialists and experts who are interested in forgeries. They serve as documentary material, their details and peculiarities are noted so that genuine stamps may be distinguished from them. They are described in a number of books on philately and specialized subjects.

a) Complete forgeries. These are imitations of stamps in which there is nothing genuine, neither the printing, nor the paper, cancellation, gum, perforation nor overprint. Such forgeries were, for instance, produced by Fournier. These forgeries are the least dangerous, as the forger never manages to copy all the detailed characteristics of the genuine stamps. Therefore even a beginner should be able to recognize such forgeries after a relatively short time. It is quite sufficient if he feels that something in the stamp

741 Genuine Czechoslovak stamp.

742 A forgery produced to cheat the post.

is suspicious, for instance the colour or the paper. He will scrutinize such a copy more carefully, compare it with a genuine stamp (a damaged copy will do) and discover the fraud.

The Stock Exchange or Vejprty forgeries could never have remained undiscovered for such a long time if they had not come into the hands of philatelists so late. After all, who otherwise would have suspected them when they all had genuine cancellations? Some copies of the Stock Exchange forgeries, for instance, have a combination of check letters in the corners which does not and cannot exist on genuine stamps. The Vejprty forgeries are complete forgeries; their design differs from the genuine stamp in many details, their colour is dull and their design is a millimetre narrower and almost a millimetre shorter than the genuine copy.

b) Forged imperforates. It has already been mentioned that, generally speaking, imperforate stamps are rare, whereas the same stamps issued at a later date and perforated are common. The stamp forgers simply got hold of a pair of scissors and cut the perforations off a cheap stamp. A philatelist must therefore know how wide a space was left in printing between stamps in a sheet. That will tell him how wide a margin must be so as to exclude the possibility of cut-off perforations. When you scrutinize such a stamp with cut-off perforations under a powerful magnifying glass, you will in many cases find traces of the perforation holes. The stamp forger had to cut off as little as he could to leave the widest possible margins. You have to be careful, though, especially with single-line perforations. A sheet of stamps was sometimes moved a little more than necessary during perforation and the result was a stamp with wider margins horizontally, vertically or all round. Such copies are a welcome find for stamp forgers. If you want to be on the safe side it is best to obtain copies of imperforate stamps with sheet margin or corner copies or pairs or larger blocks.

c) Forged perforations. In some cases perforated stamps are more expensive than imperforate copies. This led the forgers to the production of faked perforations. But they never succeeded in copying exactly the diameter and spacing of the genuine perforation needles. Forged perforations usually have an irregular spacing of the holes, they are not in a straight line and so on. It is rather difficult for an inexperienced stamp collector to identify these forgeries.

Even stamp forgers are human and make mistakes. They have managed to perforate stamps which were never perforated. Even a stamp on a cover with a genuine cancellation is no guarantee that the perforation is really genuine.

d) Forged overprints. Such forgeries are extremely dangerous, mainly because the stamp itself is genuine. If the overprints concerned are of a simple nature, produced by letterpress and composed of normal letter type, their exposure is difficult unless it is a very poor imitation. Therefore you can be sure only if you have long years of experience and good material for comparison. Otherwise it is best to consult an expert. There are a number of cases when stamps have been forged by removing an overprint. Quite a number of interesting varieties have been found in recent years on modern British stamps, for instance copies with the Queen's head missing when printed in gold. Stamp forgers have found a way to remove the Queen's head by chemical means and produce a 'rare variety'. The greatest care is advisable.

e) Forged colour. It has been mentioned that the colour of many stamps can be changed by chemicals to achieve a rare shade. The

743 Forgery of the 1850 3 pfennig stamp of Saxony.

744 Primitive forgery of a Sicilian stamp.

745 Forged Tuscan stamp.

colours listed in catalogues cannot be complete or accurate enough and are not very reliable. If in doubt consult an expert, unless it is an evident forgery.

f) Forged paper. Very few cases are known. The wrong type of paper is, of course, used in complete forgeries. Sometimes the colour of the paper is changed artificially. From 1901 to 1913 Turkish postage-due stamps were printed on red paper. Their design was the same as the design of the postage stamps. In 1909 a two piastre stamp was printed in greenish-black on white paper. Stamp forgers dipped such stamps into red ink to produce the much more expensive postage-due stamp. This forgery can be detected easily if compared with a genuine postage-due stamp printed on red paper.

g) Forged watermark. There have been attempts to produce forged watermarks, mostly on genuine stamps printed on paper without watermark, but with little success. The rare 1919-20 Malta ten shillings (SG 9b) is sometimes rebacked with watermarked paper.

h) Forged gum. This is very common and dangerous. Many old stamps are found only with partial gum or without gum and it is quite easy to replace it with gum of the proper texture and colour. The wholesale regumming of stamps has been caused by some collectors who insist on perfect mint copies only and refuse the most attractive copies of stamps if they have traces of a hinge. But there is a higher justice: the buyers of 'mint, no hinge' stamps, in many cases acquire regummed stamps. Stamp forgers have also forged the gum watermark of Czechoslovak stamps of 1923.

i) Repaired stamps. Quite a number of people make a living out of stamp repairs, and indeed some of them are past masters. They

746 Forged perforation of a French stamp.

747 This Austrian stamp was removed from the cover, the perforation forged and the stamp re-affixed.

216

748 Forgery of the Baghdad provisional overprint on a bisected Turkish stamp. The forger made a bad mistake: the date on the handstamp reads 14 December 1887 but the provisional overprint was issued in 1889!

749 The forger here tried to remove the overprint '25 and text' from the stamp. Careful inspection shows traces of the original overprint.

can cover a tear, cut or thinning so perfectly that you would hardly discover it. Sometimes you can spot a repair when treating a stamp with benzine. Stamp repairers add missing perforations, join torn stamps and produce attractive copies from several pieces. Stamps which had large patches of thinning before the repair job started are very dangerous. The repairer scrapes off the superfluous paper all over the back of the stamp and glues on a new layer.

It would not be right, though, to condemn all stamp repairers. They have frequently saved stamps which would otherwise have been lost to philately. A good repair job can improve the aesthetic appearance of a stamp. Repairs cannot be simply called forgeries. Philatelic experts authenticate repaired stamps but when applying their handstamp or giving a certificate they mark them as damaged copies. After all, even a damaged stamp is genuine, although it is not as valuable as a perfect copy. If such a copy is marked as repaired it can be safely entered in your collection. The fraud starts when a repaired copy is described as perfect and sold for an exaggerated price. But that need not be the fault of the man who has repaired the stamp.

j) Forged cancellations. These are found in abundance. Take, for instance, the German inflation stamps of the period after the First World War. Cancelled, preferably on a cover, they are much more expensive than mint. Forgers frequently had these stamps cancelled by some willing postal clerk with a genuine handstamp. Here it is imperative to know exactly the period when and where these stamps were in use. It is difficult to expose this type of forgery because of the use of genuine, postdated handstamps.

Forged cancellations were also produced, for example, by

Fournier. He employed them mostly for his own stamp forgeries or on genuine stamps with forged overprints. It normally requires great experience and knowledge to prove that a cancellation has been forged.

k) Forged entires. Another difficult field. Sometimes artificial 'rarities' were produced in the following manner: two stamps with properly placed, genuine cancellations were selected. Both stamps, or one of them, were bisected so that the remaining parts of the handstamps fitted into each other. Next they were affixed to a piece of old envelope and the 'piece with rare bisect' was ready for sale. Another method used was to affix a stamp (for instance a damaged copy with a thinning) to a piece of a cover and to complete the missing part of the cancellation on the paper. Sometimes a forged handstamp was used.

Here is an example from Rumania. Some time ago one of the well-known philatelic experts in that country was Baron Wertheimer-Ghica. He published several studies on Moldavia 'Bulls' and other classical stamps of Rumania, and thus established his good reputation. One day he sold some 'unique' items from his collection. At first the forgeries (mostly forged cancellations but also some stamp forgeries) passed undiscovered, as they bore the signature of the well-known expert. After some time the scandal became public and a warrant of arrest was issued. The Baron was warned in time and escaped to Latin America.

BOGUS LABELS

Do you remember the Paris affair with the 'stamps' of the non-existent State of Sedang? It was not the last swindle of its type. From time to time all sorts of so-called stamps from invented countries, or stamps of distant States which were never issued by the national authorities, appeared on the stamp market. For a short time the swindlers had some success, but sooner or later the trick was discovered.

Nowadays, with many philatelic magazines printed in tens of thousands, with detailed information from the issuing countries and the ability to check, it is a difficult task for swindlers. Nevertheless it has been done. In 1960 a set of Cuban Olympic stamps was offered for sale. The authorities of Havana declared them as fakes to the Universal Postal Union. It was discovered that the 'stamps' had been printed in Milan. Although the philatelic public was warned in time through societies and the press some eager collectors who did not want to miss the novelty had to pay. If they had read the philatelic press they would have saved their money.

750 Attempt to 'produce' bisects on a piece. Although the forger took great pains to find proper copies his product is far from perfect. A close look will show that the bottom of the triangular cancellation is broken where the two stamps meet.

WHO ARE THE STAMP EXPERTS?

Every large organization of philatelists has its *expert committee* whose members are amateur or professional philatelists with great knowledge who systematically study the stamps and philatelic material of their sphere of interest and speciality. If someone aspires to become a philatelic expert he has first to prove his

751 Bogus stamp from a non-existent country.

abilities and qualifications. This is usually done by publishing specialized studies dealing with certain stamp issues, lectures and practical work. Even so, a future expert is at first usually accepted only as a candidate; and only after a certain time, during which he has to prove his qualification, is he accorded the title of an expert.

The field of philately has become so wide that it is impossible for anyone to be a specialist and expert in everything, and so each expert has his own special, and sometimes very limited, field. There are experts for the whole field of classical philately, experts for British stamps, for German or Italian States, experts in aerophilately, etc. The best experts and specialists of a certain country are usually to be found in that particular country. They mainly collect their own country's stamps; these are available in sufficient numbers and most is known about their background, production, printing and use.

Expert committees need not be large bodies, and not all fields of philately are represented on them. That is why a close co-operation has been established between the expert committees of the individual national philatelic societies. The international contacts and the activities of national expert committees are organized by the Association Internationale des Experts Philatéliques (AIEP), affiliated to FIP. Out of the lists of experts registered with AIEP, the judges for large, international stamp exhibitions are usually chosen. If at home no expert specialized in a certain field of philately and stamps can be found, such stamps can be sent by the expert committee to a country where one is to be found.

Members of the expert committee have the right and obligation to examine stamps. When an expert finds that the stamp he is scrutinizing is genuine he may apply his signature (handstamp) to the back of the stamp. This is the practice on the Continent. In England the examination is made by expert committees of the Royal Philatelic Society of London or the British Philatelic Association. If a stamp is genuine a photograph is taken and a certificate issued with photograph and number. Another photograph is kept in the records of the committee for further reference.

When expert signatures are printed on the back of a stamp, their position, according to international rules, is of great significance. The attached illustrations explain the meaning of the position. If an expert finds that a stamp is a forgery it is his duty to mark it as such. Everybody handing in his stamps for scrutiny must expect that, if they are forgeries, they will be marked to make it impossible to sell them as genuine.

Sometimes other handstamps are found on the backs of stamps, which have nothing to do with the experts' decision. Some of these are *property stamps*. Some large stamp-dealing firms, for instance Senf in Germany, applied a small firm's stamp on the back. If someone bought stamps from them and later had a claim they could always tell if the stamps in dispute really had been bought from them. In the case of reputable firms such a property stamp is to a certain extent also a guarantee of genuineness, but it is not completely reliable. In addition, some stamp collectors also used to mark their stamps with a tiny handstamp on the back so as to be able to recover them in case of theft. This is a nuisance as it spoils the stamp unnecessarily.

The signatures of internationally recognized experts in certain fields of philately are well known among specialists. If you come

752 Another stamp from a fictitious source.

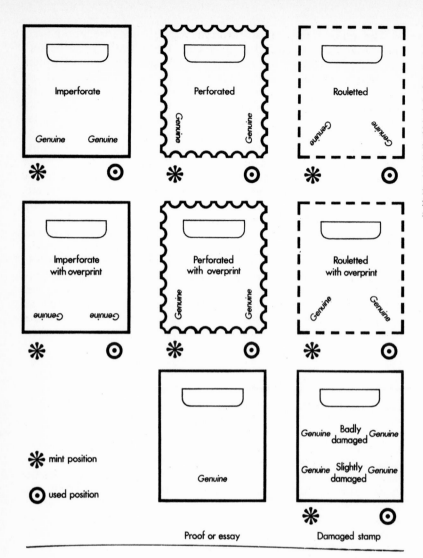

across a stamp with a signature on the back, ask a specialist. He will be able to tell you if this is an expert's signature which thereby proves that the stamp is genuine. Do not underestimate this and do not accept any signature on the back as a proof of genuineness. It has been found that stamp forgers not only forged stamps and overprints but experts' signatures as well.

HOW TO BECOME AN EXPERT

There are millions of philatelists all over the world, in fact according to the latest estimates of UNESCO some one hundred million, but there are only a few hundred philatelic experts. Not every stamp collector can become one of the few, but every philatelist has the ability to acquire a deep, specialized knowledge in his field of collecting which will bring him near the level of philatelic experts. There is only one way to achieve this — devoted study of specialized literature, following up everything published in that particular field, study of historical sources and, most important of all, a serious study of the stamps in question.

The more stamps pass through your hands the better your knowledge will become: that is the basis of success. Only a perfect knowledge of the genuine stamp, of all its typical characteristics and marks, enables you to discover forgeries. This is within the reach of every philatelist. Who knows, perhaps today's young beginner who has to pay a high price to stamp forgers will one day be a well-known philatelic expert, an authority whose word carries international weight?

Let me suggest something which will be very useful and enable even beginners to discover forgeries. A piece of strong, white cardboard with two black threads tied to it will do. Put under one of the threads a genuine stamp (see illustration 754 overleaf) and check thoroughly where the thread passes over the stamp design. Next, take the stamp you want to scrutinize and put it under the second thread in exactly the same position. With the help of a magnifying glass compare how the thread passes over the design and which details it touches. You can change the position of both the stamps several times but always make sure they are in identical positions under their respective threads. Since the design of a fake stamp is hardly ever absolutely identical to that of a genuime stamp, you should be able to discover forgeries with this method.

BEFORE YOU PUT THE FIRST STAMP INTO YOUR COLLECTION

If you go fishing with just a length of string and a bent pin you cannot expect to catch much. Every profession and every hobby has its utensils. Philately is no exception. Fortunately the accessories a normal stamp collector needs are not expensive, and even the pocket money of a schoolboy is sufficient.

a) Tweezers. All sorts and shapes of philatelic tweezers are on sale; you can even get gilt ones. There is no need to buy expensive tweezers; simple, cheap ones will do. Just check the pair you are buying to see that the ends meet properly and that the edges are not too dull or too sharp. Do not use cosmetic or surgical tweezers: they have grooves and could damage a stamp. Good philatelic tweezers must be absolutely even. It does not make any difference if they have a pointed or flat end, or if they are straight or bent. After all, every stamp collector has to get used to working with tweezers. As soon as he gets used to his pair he will never part with them and they will serve him for years.

b) Magnifying glass. The choice of magnifying glasses offered is very wide. There was a period when glass cubes were in demand; later magnifying glasses came with holders, on stands, etc. All types can be used. Normally a glass which magnifies between three and five times will be quite sufficient. Specialized collectors and philatelic experts, of course, need much stronger magnifying glasses, and frequently have to use philatelic microscopes. Quite useful are magnifying glasses with a built-in light. They are bulkier, though, and more expensive.

c) Perforation gauge. It does not make much difference whether a perforation gauge is made of paper, metal or plastic, so long as it is accurate. You can best check it by placing it on an accurate ruler and seeing whether the number of perforations on a length of two centimetres is exactly the same as is written on the perfora-

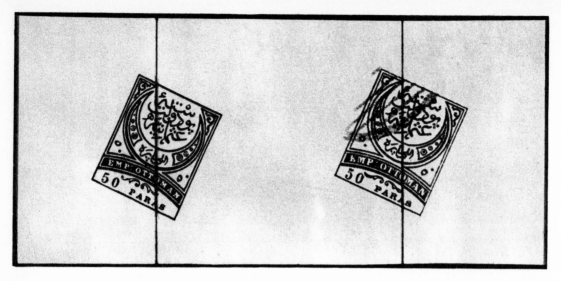

754 Comparing a genuine
and a forged stamp with
the help of two threads.

tion gauge. Perforations can be measured in two ways. Either place
the stamp perforations against the black dots of the perforation
gauge or on top of the lines. Move the stamp from one size to the
other until the one exactly fitting the stamp perforation is found.
If the perforation of a stamp is indistinct it is recommended to
check it under a magnifying glass.

d) Stamp hinges. Many types of stamp hinge are on sale. After
the sad experience with 'patent hinges', which left obstinate, greasy
stains on stamps, the quality of stamp hinges has greatly improved.
Therefore you are quite safe if you buy proper hinges from a stamp
dealer. Never use hinges of adhesive tape, stamp sheet margins or
scotch tape. They will be very difficult to remove and the glue of
adhesive tape might contain chemicals damaging to the stamp.
Some stamp collectors cut larger hinges in half to save money.
Such hinges are sometimes found in *approval booklets*. This cannot
be recommended. The stamps are not properly fixed; they tend
to move and can be bent.

e) Watermark detectors. Two basic types are used. The first
consists of trays made of glass, pottery or plastic for use with
benzine. They are cheap and good enough for most stamps. For
your benzine get a 'dropper' type bottle. The other type of
electrical watermark detector is much more expensive.

f) Brush or sweat box. For the removal of old hinges a soft, thin
brush can be used. Wet the hinge remainders on the back of the
stamp carefully and after a while pull them off with tweezers so
as not to disturb the gum. If you can spare a few shillings it is
best to buy a sweat box. It contains an asbestos or similar pad
which has to be saturated with water. Next, the stamps with the
remains of paper or old hinges are put on the pad face-downwards
and the box is closed. After about ten or fifteen minutes the hinges
peel off. When drying, the stamps tend to curl up. You have to
weigh them down in some way, bearing in mind that the backs
are sticky.

g) Writing utensils. If your handwriting is good it is as well
to write the descriptions on the album sheets by hand. You will
need a pen for indian ink (quite a number of useful new writing
utensils are on sale), a ruler, a stencil for letters, etc.

h) Ultra-violet lamps. These are not part of the equipment of

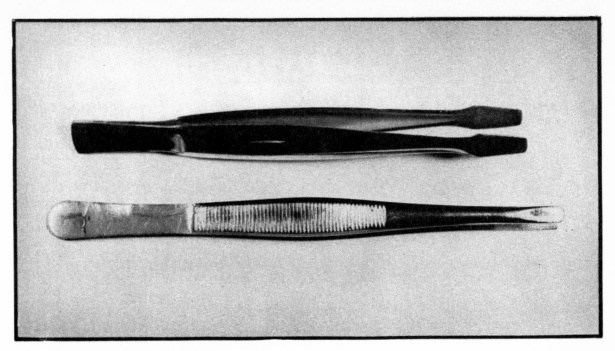

755 Different types of tweezers.

756 Different types of magnifying glass.

a normal stamp collector and you will find them only in the equipment of specialized collectors and experts. With the help of such a lamp it is possible to detect forgeries, different types of stamps, etc. If a stamp is put under such a lamp its colour will appear in a different way. Take, for instance, two identical stamps of the same colour. If put under the lamp they might show distinct differences of colour; one might be red, the other dark red. Such stamps must be compared with a genuine copy (it can be damaged) or with the description of the colours shown under a lamp in a specialized philatelic handbook. Thus it is possible to identify a genuine stamp and discover forgeries.

THE ALBUM

The history of *stamp albums* is very old, and dates back almost to the time when stamps were first introduced. The first album was printed in 1852 by A. Oppems in England. These old albums, however, can in no way be compared with modern albums. They were just simple booklets with normal covers. On each page were rows of 'fields' for the stamps, with no space between them. Our great-grandfathers did not know about stamp hinges. The stamps were simply stuck into the album, either with their own gum or with glue, and unfortunately many rare stamps have been ruined in this way.

Each stamp-issuing country was listed with the most important data — population, territory, ruler, etc. Sometimes short lists of stamps issued to date were also included, together with their prices. The first reproductions of stamps in the printed fields appeared later. More and more details were added, albums were printed in colour and some in several languages. The flag of the country was shown, together with the coat of arms and the portrait of the ruler.

As time passed albums improved. Soon it became evident that it would not do simply to leave a few empty pages in bound albums for future stamp issues. Album publishers decided to use loose leaves. All sorts of systems were tried, albums with screws, and so on. In the end album covers with spring-back binders proved to be best and were generally adopted.

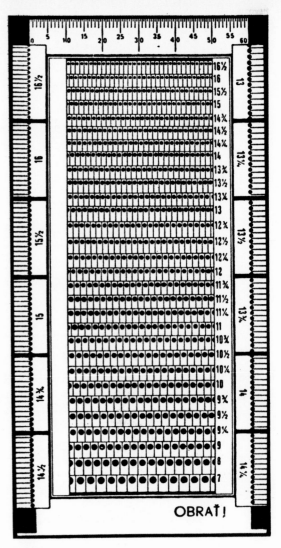

757 A perforation gauge.

758 Stamp hinges.

ALBUM LEAVES

The arrangement of *album leaves* changed, too. The stamp area was arranged with better taste; the useless reproductions of stamps were left out when it was found that catalogue numbers were quite sufficient. The printing became simpler, without unnecessary flourishes and decorations. The latest development is hingeless albums, with each printed field for a stamp covered by transparent foil. There is no need to affix the stamps with the help of a hinge; they just slide behind the foil and their gum remains perfect.

Printed albums can be used only by collectors forming general collections, or by thematic collectors forming a common thematic collection, as for instance a collection of flowers, animals, sports, airmail stamps, etc. For slightly specialized collections, albums

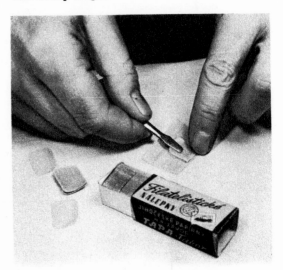

224

XXVII A newspaper of 1854 with copies of Austrian newspaper stamps. The strip on the left consists of five copies of the dull purple newspaper stamps, while those on the right are, on top, five copies of the Blue Mercury of 1851 and, below, a strip of four blue newspaper stamps of 1858.

XXVIII Old entires: a postal stationery cover issued for the local post of St Petersburg but sent to Moscow, as can be seen from the arrival postmark on the right (1); a commemorative postcard and three stamps of the jubilee series issued in Russia in 1913 for the threehundredth anniversary of the rule of the House of Romanov (2); and one of the first Turkish postal stationery covers of 1869, which were printed with the stamp on the flap at the back of the cover, bearing a colourful additional franking (3).

1

2

3

759 Schematic drawing showing the proper way to use stamp hinges. The top quarter is folded back, slightly wetted and affixed to the top of the stamp. Next the bottom of the longer part of the hinge is wetted and the stamp placed in position.

760 French album of 1864.

761 Inside sample of a hundred-year-old stamp album.

are printed with sheets including the main types of perforations, watermarks, and so on. For a specialized collector, or a philatelist forming a thematic collection, albums with printed fields for stamps are of no use. They mount their collection on blank leaves, either without any print at all or with a light grid making the arrangement of the stamps easier. Some philatelists have the name of the country they collect printed as a heading on the leaves. It looks neat but is not necessary. In fact, a number of judges in international exhibitions are definitely against it. Printed headings only detract; one does not have to be told where the stamps come from, nor does the judge.

In some countries album sheets are printed in various sizes.

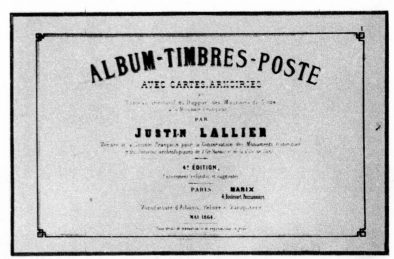

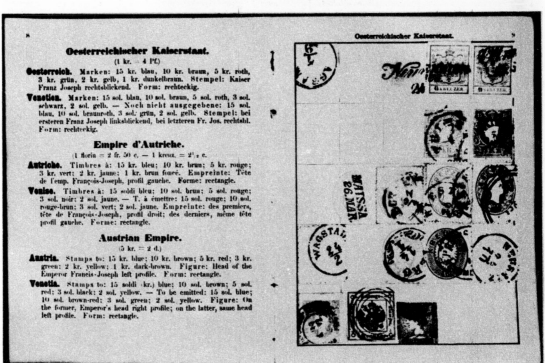

762   763

762–763 Album covers from the
end of the nineteenth century.

With some exceptions their sizes are more or less constant. Stamp
collectors will do best if they buy album sheets produced in their
own country by a reputable firm. Thus they will always be able to
get the same type of sheets of the same colour shade.

764–765 Two sheets of Olympic
stamps from a modern album.

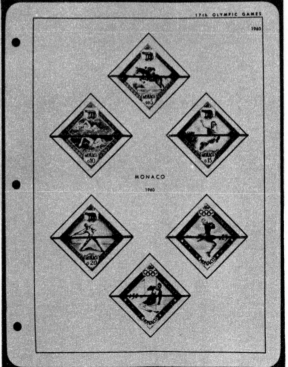

FRAMES AND BLACK PAPER

It adds to the appearance of a stamp if it is surrounded on the sheet by a black frame. If a philatelist arranges his collection on sheets without printed frames it means a lot of work drawing in all the necessary frames. He will, though, achieve exactly the same effect if he places under each stamp a piece of black paper slightly larger than the stamp itself. This method is even more practical, for it also enables him to change the arrangement of stamps on a sheet whenever he acquires new material.

The black paper should extend beyond the width of a stamp by about half a millimetre on each side. Most countries have adopted a certain, limited number of stamp sizes, which means the collector can cut long strips of black paper in the correct width or prepare rectangles or squares of the right size.

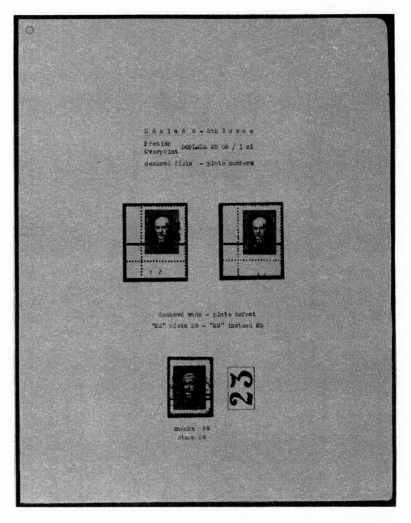

766 Neatly arranged leaf from a specialized collection of Polish stamps.

THE PROTECTION OF STAMPS

Many stamp collectors worry about their stamps, especially the rare and expensive copies. It therefore became common practice to place such stamps in transparent covers. In some places it is possible to buy these or you can make them yourself. It is not advisable to use cellophane, as it tends to absorb moisture. The best material is diophane. Place the stamp on a black paper rectangle of the same size as that used for mounting on a sheet. The diophane is cut to size (about $\frac{1}{4}$" wider on each side), bent to shape and glued to the black paper (it must not be too thin) with film glue, formic acid or acetic acid. Great care must be taken that the acid does not touch the stamp! It is best to leave one side (the top side) open to let the stamp be taken out of its cover.

You can also produce 'hingeless' fields for your stamp collection on sheets without printed fields. The diophane foil must be about $\frac{1}{8}$" wider than the stamp field on the top and on one side. Glue it to the sheet on the left and bottom only. Then insert the stamp from the top right-hand corner. Wait till the glue is dry, or you could damage the stamp.

In very wide use nowadays are the so-called 'Hawid' strips. These are produced from two layers of plastic foil. The top foil is transparent, the bottom layer usually dark and with gum on the back. Both foils are joined at the bottom. The strips come in a range of widths. First you must find the proper width for your stamp: the foil should protrude above the stamp by $\frac{1}{16}$" to $\frac{1}{8}$". Next, cut the right piece off, leaving again the same margin on both sides of the stamp. The joined foils, with the stamp, can be glued to the sheet.

The best way to protect your stamps is with the help of protective covers. These are a sort of transparent envelope for whole sheets. The first types produced were rather heavy and thick. Some protective covers are open at the sides and therefore the sheet can slide out. The latest types of protective cover are thinner and lighter and are open only on one side. These give your stamps the best protection. Make sure you get the right size of protective covers. They should be just large enough to let your sheet slide easily in and out.

STOCK-BOOKS

Some stamp collectors do not like album sheets or any type of album. They prefer stock-books. Stock-books are books of different sizes composed of cardboard leaves with transparent diophane strips in rows above each other on every page. The stamps are slid in behind the strips. Stamps are very well protected in a stock-book, and there is no need for stamp hinges. The appearance, though, of such a collection in a stock-book cannot be compared with a collection on sheets. Stock-books are altogether inadmissible for exhibition.

Nevertheless stock-books are a very useful accessory for philatelists. They come in very handy for accumulated material, and are useful for the preparation of your collection. Arrange the stamps you want to put on one page before you start with the mounting. If you visit a philatelist for an exchange you will find a stock-book

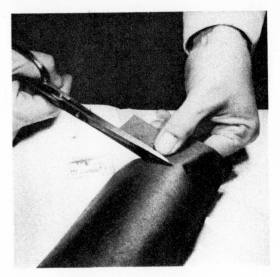

767 Cutting the black paper to put under a stamp.

768 Closing a transparent cover for a stamp.

769 Stamp in transparent cover.

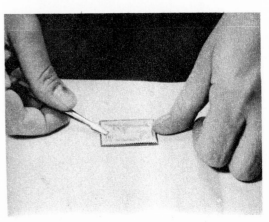

is most useful for the material you want to take along. You can buy stock-books from pocket-size up to the largest sizes. Special stock-book albums are produced for entires and postal stationery.

Some philatelists also use a filing system with filing cards fitted with transparent strips for their spare stamps and for the preparatory work before mounting.

WHAT TO DO WITH DUPLICATES

Stamps of which you possess two or more copies and which do not belong in your collection proper are called *duplicates*. Every stamp collector goes carefully through the material he owns and selects the best copies for his collection. The damaged and worthless copies are eliminated and the rest of the duplicates are put aside for sale or exchange.

The longer you collect stamps the larger will be the number accumulating in your desk or cabinet. The first principle of philately is good order and arrangement. This applies not only to the collection proper but to your duplicates as well. A good philatelist does not underestimate any stamp, even the cheapest one.

Who knows, maybe some day he will find among the forgotten, cheap material a rare variety. Therefore treat every stamp properly, no matter whether it is a copy for your collection or a spare stamp. The duplicates should also be properly soaked, pressed and stored.

At first this will be an easy task. Get a few envelopes, write the names of the countries on each of them, or the name or the theme, and put the stamps in them. After some time the envelopes will start to become bulky. There will be more and more stamps in each envelope, and to find a certain stamp will take a long time. Therefore it becomes necessary to sort the stamps in each envelope into issues or periods and to find a small, transparent envelope for each of them. There will be some countries where the number of duplicates will be smaller, and those can be left in their envelopes. In other cases the stamps will overflow and you will need a large envelope or a box. It is up to each stamp collector to find his own way of sorting. There are many different methods, and all of them are useful. The main thing is for your duplicates to be sorted out so that you can always find what you are looking for. If you have accumulated a larger number of covers it is best to put them into larger boxes.

Better stamps should not be left in the envelopes but put into stock-books. In this way they will always be handy and you will not have to look for them. Stamps for exchange or sale should also be kept in stock-books.

If you want to send stamps to someone for exchange, or if you have joined a stamp club and are participating in their exchange or sale service, another system is used. The duplicates will go into approval booklets. These too are an old invention, dating back to the end of the nineteenth century. Children sometimes use old exercise books, but this must be avoided, as the stamps might get damaged by ink.

The only effective way is to buy approval booklets, which are available in different sizes. Affix your stamps firmly with hinges. Above the stamp you can write the catalogue number, and below the price. If you wish you can write 'used' or 'mint' or write other

770 Stock books.

remarks as, for instance, 'pair', 'block of four' or draw the appropriate signs.

Some philatelists put 'secret' signs against their stamps. For instance, they draw little lines where the postmark comes to the margin of the stamp to prevent anyone exchanging them for other copies. This is quite unnecessary. True, there are some dishonest collectors, but only very few. If someone has cheated you or if you do not trust him, don't send him your stamps.

A number of collectors insist on unhinged mint stamps. If you want to include such stamps in your approval book, put them into a little transparent envelope and affix the envelope to a booklet page.

HOW TO DEAL WITH LARGER UNITS

When entering miniature sheets, blocks, entires or postal stationery in your collection, you can also use diophane covers for their protection; but most practical of all are protective covers for the whole album sheet. Larger units of philatelic material can be affixed to album pages with hinges, but they do not hold them very well. When the leaves are turned over the hinges easily come off

771 Colourful title pages of old approval booklets.

and the cover or miniature sheet can be damaged. The best way is to affix them in the same way as with photographs — using transparent corners.

It it not a good idea to keep entires or postal stationery in a stock-book, they take up too much space. Furthermore they are often thicker and could damage the transparent strips. Special stock-books for entires are produced with double, transparent folders where you can keep the entires in two layers; you can see one set from the top and the other from the bottom when you turn the leaf. If it is an interesting cover with important details on both sides, then it is kept in a separate pocket of the stock-book. If you want to mount such an important cover on a sheet the best way is to take a photograph of the back and to affix it underneath the cover with the front side showing. Another possibility is to cut both sides of the cover and to open it up. This, of course, damages the cover to a certain extent.

Stamp booklets should never be exhibited or entered in a collection as they are. The proper way is to remove carefully the threads or staples and to arrange them in proper order on a sheet, including covers and all instructions inside. Spare stamp booklets should be left as they are.

Interesting entires and postal stationery destined for sale or exchange can be kept in a stock-book or in envelopes.

Duplicates of entires and stationery should also be kept in envelopes. It is best to put greater quantities into a box or keep them as a file.

772 Page from a modern approval booklet, with prices marked below the stamps.

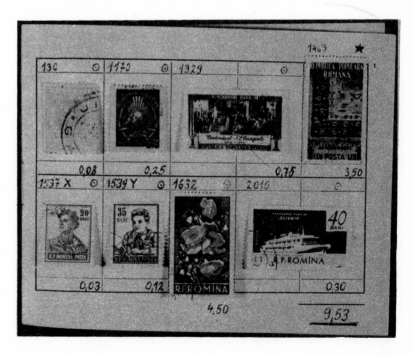

Whenever you are sorting out your duplicates and selecting copies for your collection always bear the future in mind. Perhaps some day you will decide to widen your scope of collecting and to specialize, and invariably you will need more material. Perhaps the very stamp which you have put among your duplicates and sold or exchanged will be needed, and you will have the greatest difficulty in finding another copy.

Whilst sorting out your duplicates have a look at your catalogue, even if you are dealing only with cheap and common stamps. There might exist some variety of a common stamp that makes it a rare find. And even if you should not find anything of interest, the constant use of a catalogue will widen your knowledge considerably.

It is advisable to have two stock-books for exchange purposes — one for mint stamps, the other for used copies. Before putting mint stamps (especially larger blocks or sheets) away it is useful to powder the gum side a little to prevent their sticking together. If this should happen try at first to pry them gently apart. Do not use force. If they don't come apart try to cover them with a sheet of paper and slide a warm iron across them. The stamps dry rapidly and separate. If even this method is unsuccessful you will have to put the stamps over steam. This, of course, will

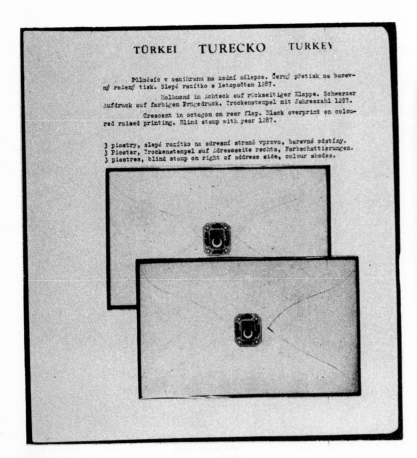

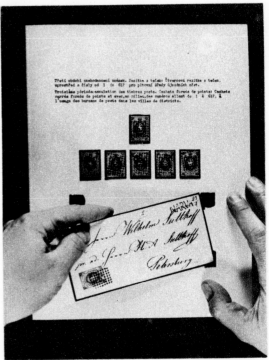

773 Affixing entires and stationery onto an album leaf.

774 Cover being put into place.

775 British stamp booklet.

776 The back of the same booklet. The cover of a booklet is as much part of a collection as the stamps it contains.

damage the gum. Should there be no other way of separating them you will have to soak them off. The gum will be lost but at least the stamps can be saved.

Stamps, especially mint stamps, are very sensitive to atmospheric conditions. Their worst enemy is dampness. They stick together and are attacked by mould. If the atmosphere is too dry they curl up and can be damaged. Stamps need air. Therefore do not stack heavy albums on top of each other. Make room in your cabinet and put them in upright next to each other, but do not press them together.

Stamps in an album have to be aired from time to time. It is quite sufficient to turn the leaves. This, of course, is a good opportunity to have a look at the collection and to check if the stamps are in good order. Some stamp collectors who keep their stamp albums stored for a long time without checking them discover that they are full of mites. The mites destroy the gum of all the mint stamps, which means a considerable loss in value.

Never forget that stamps are made of paper, of a most sensitive, delicate material threatened by many elements. And sometimes this paper is over a hundred years old!

A FEW WORDS ABOUT COLLECTIONS

We already know what types of stamps exist, how they should be handled and what types of collections can be formed. It is now entirely up to the reader to decide what to collect. In philately there are no limits to fantasy. There are only certain rules forged by generations of philatelists and by their experience. These rules must be kept, and therefore let us discuss the individual fields of collecting in greater detail.

THEMATIC COLLECTIONS

Thematic stamp collections have become tremendously popular. Young people, and not only young collectors, are naturally attracted by colourful, modern stamps and their designs. If they start a stamp collection, three out of four will form a collection of a thematic type. This is the youngest field of philately and many of the problems of thematic collecting have not yet been solved.

The well-known Luxembourg philatelist Bernard Fetter was the first stamp collector in Europe to exhibit a thematic collection. He caused a small sensation in 1928, and the judges were at a loss. If it had not been M. Fetter, a collector known not only in his country but also abroad as an outstanding philatelist and expert, the exhibit would perhaps not have been accepted at all.

Over forty years have passed since. The novelty of 1928 has not only become commonplace but nowadays it is hard to imagine any large stamp exhibition without thematic collections. Everybody wanting to follow Fetter's example would be very wise to take the first opportunity to visit a stamp exhibition. Such a display is interesting for non-collectors, let alone for beginners. There you will see the very best in stamps, and you will also see how experienced collectors build their collection. You will be able to acquire a lot of knowledge and get some ideas which will prove most useful when you start forming your own collection.

One thing should be clear right from the beginning. Even if a future philatelist has accumulated hundreds of attractive stamp sets, even if he has filled dozens of stock-books, he still has no collection. All this wealth lacks one important thing — thoughtful, creative work which transforms quantity into quality, which makes a stamp collection out of an accumulation. There are other, most important requirements, too — patience, persistence and knowledge.

Take for instance the theme 'The History of Medicine'. Merely to collect all the stamps showing portraits of doctors requires a great deal of diligence, the study of thick catalogues, and so on. The best effort, though, is not enough; an indispensable factor is wide knowledge. The catalogues listing the stamps and showing their designs do not always state that the man on the stamp was a doctor. You find many stamps with portraits of men celebrated as great statesmen of whom some were originally doctors. If there are weaknesses in the collector's knowledge, if he does not know a certain fact, then these gaps will necessarily show in his collection.

A thematic collector cannot expect great help from albums or catalogues. Only those who form the commonest subject collection, as, for instance, collections of animals, flowers, sports, etc., will find printed albums and specialized catalogues. All the remaining thematic collectors are entirely on their own. That is the nicest thing about thematic collecting. You are never just a 'stamp licker', handcuffed by the limited number of fields in your album, but a creator of your own work.

A TITLE

A child must have a name. In the case of a thematic collection this is certainly no secondary matter. I once knew a journalist who used to spend half an hour or more thinking about the title of his article and then write the whole story in fifteen minutes. It is even more important to spend some time choosing the title of a *thematic collection*. After all, you will struggle with your collection for years. Therefore don't hurry, but concentrate.

Let us suppose you have decided to collect ships on stamps. For home consumption it is good enough to call the collection 'Ships' or 'Boats'. This, of course, is a term so wide and comprises so many stamps that it is not very practical. A much better title would be 'On Rivers and Oceans' or 'Vessels of all Times'. These two are perfect titles for subject collections.

This means that all stamps showing vessels must necessarily belong to such a collection. It you are aiming at a higher target, if you want to show in your collection the development of navigation, all the discoveries and the technical developments, such a title will not be sufficient. How do you feel about a title like 'From Boat to Atomic Icebreaker'? Doesn't this sound better? The words already express an idea; the aim of the collection in this case is the development of vessels. This title, of course, is also rather wide. A staggering number of stamps come under it and still you do not cross the threshold of the higher stage of thematic collecting. If, equally, you call your collection 'Discoveries of the Navigators' it could already be a thematic collection. Such a collection could include not only stamps showing boats, but also stamps with portraits of famous navigators, stamps with maps or landscapes of

777 Leaf from an attractive thematic collection, 'The History of Medicine'.

778–780 These three stamps belong to a thematic collection dealing with medicine.

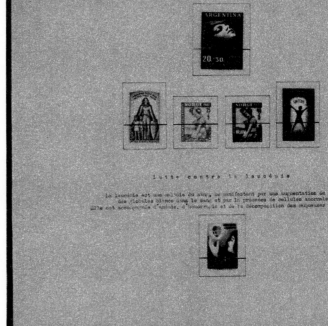

779

780

the discovered countries, their inhabitants, fauna and flora, etc. Much more rewarding, on the other hand, would be, for instance, the theme 'Following in the Tracks of Columbus'. It is narrower and can be better handled.

Let us, though, return to the collection called 'On Rivers and Oceans'. If you form it as a subject collection you can organize it in alphabetical order, both according to the countries issuing the stamps and chronologically. More adventurous would be a collection divided into individual sections: boats, sailing boats, steamers, men-of-war, shipwrecks, harbours, navigators, and so on. Even such a collection would still be a subject collection. If you should decide that you want to go further and build a proper thematic collection, you will have to deal with another important task.

LIBRETTO AND SCENARIO

The first step in the forming of a thematic collection is to work out a *libretto*. If you have reached this stage you must know by now what you are aiming at in your collection and you will also have chosen a title that clearly defines its limits. Now it is necessary to write it down, as shortly and exactly as possible. This description is your libretto and it will be the first sheet of your collection. It will express the idea and pattern of what follows.

With the libretto in front of you, you can start to classify your basic stock, but do not start to mount the material on sheets yet.

235

There is no hurry. The better you prepare for this last task the easier it will be and you will enjoy it much more. The results will be much better and not only your friends will appreciate it but perhaps even the judges in a stamp exhibition.

Next you will have to prepare your *scenario*. Take your libretto and go over it, paragraph by paragraph. Give every section careful thought and work it out in detail. You have to decide how many album sheets you want to allot to every part, how many stamps and of which sort you want to have on a sheet. The best way is to produce a dummy for every single sheet. Spread out in front of you the stamps which you intend to put on the sheet and try the best arrangement. It is even better to take an album sheet and try out actual positions, how many stamps to use, and so on. The best arrangement should be drawn on a sheet of paper, which need not be as large as an album sheet. There is no need for an artistic drawing; a few pencil lines serve the purpose just as well.

TEXT AND STAMPS

When doing this work you will come accross the first big question-marks. What text should you write, and how much? The descriptions must be as accurate and as short as possible. There must be only a minimum of text, and it should not cover a larger area than the stamps themselves. How much text is admissible can be tried out on a dummy sheet before spoiling an album sheet. The area of the text can be entered on the rough drawing of the

781–789 Samples of stamps showing ships and boats.

782

783

784

786

785

236

787

788

789

790–791 Stamps and covers from a thematic collection about the sea.

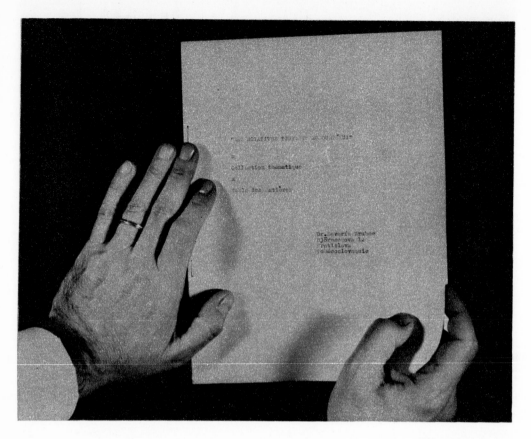

792 Title page of
a libretto for a thematic
collection.

793 A fully detailed
libretto for a thematic
collection.

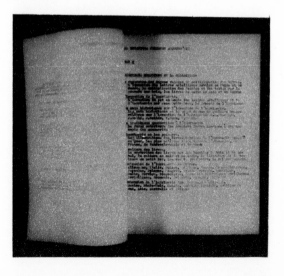

sheet with the stamps marked, in outline only, in the form of heavy lines. Your own good taste will tell you where you are right and where wrong.

Texts should be written in one colour only, and the best is indian ink. Main titles of chapters can be given emphasis, perhaps by writing them in red. It is better, though, to keep them in black, too, and use larger letters. The script used for your texts is another matter of importance. It must have a good appearance and if possible its character should fall in with the theme of your collection. If your handwriting is not good enough use a stencil. In thematic collections where there is a great amount of text this will be a herculean task. Therefore it will be necessary to use a typewriter. If so, choose a typeface that is both clear and not too small. You can write directly on the sheet, but if you make a mistake and correct it the appearance will be slightly spoiled. It is therefore better to write on paper of the same shade and colour as the album sheet and to affix the bits of text to the sheet. Try to ensure that all your pieces of text are aligned. Do not place the texts on black paper before affixing them to the sheet, and do not draw frames around them.

If you should decide to send your collection to a stamp exhibition abroad it might be useful to write the text in another language. In a thematic collection the text is of vital importance and must be understandable. Spelling errors must be avoided; they do not show the collector in a good light.

The best results, of course, are achieved by handwriting. Therefore, if your writing is not good and you can afford it, have someone else write your texts for you.

238

There must not be too much text on a sheet, but there must not be too many stamps either. In subject collections where there is just one title on top of the sheet, between twelve or eighteen stamps should be mounted on one sheet. The best arrangement is symmetrical in *shield form*. That means that the width of consecutive rows of stamps becomes wider from top to bottom; the shield can also be turned upside down. Entires (for instance, first day covers) mounted on a sheet together with stamps should preferably be placed on the lower half of the sheet.

When mounting a thematic collection it is sometimes impossible to avoid longer texts. The additional text naturally diminishes the space available for stamps. In thematic collections, therefore, the number of stamps on a sheet will be between six and twelve.

The writing-up of a thematic collection is obviously highly important. It is therefore advisable to choose an asymetrical arrangement. Even if every single sheet of the collection has a different appearance (variety frequently adds to the impact of a collection), the general arrangement should have a common character. It might be quite a good idea to ask an artist for his advice. He should suggest a sober and tasteful layout. And here you can win quite a number of points in exhibitions.

Of great importance also is the choice of colour of your sheets. Most attractive is white or cream paper. Some stamp collectors prefer black, grey or other colours for their sheets. Such a choice is not advisable. White or slightly toned paper is the best choice. Flashy colours are quite unsuitable.

WHAT BELONGS IN A THEMATIC COLLECTION?

The great discussion among thematic stamp collectors about what should and should not be included in a thematic collection still continues. If you are forming a subject collection, for instance a collection called 'From Log to Ocean Liner', and if you include stamps issued by different countries as long as they feature a vessel, then it is possible to put into your collection complete sets of stamps showing the same design of a ship in different colours. Not even a set of ship stamps with an overprint can categorically be refused.

If, on the other hand, you have decided to form a proper thematic collection the situation is quite different. The repetition of a design adds nothing to the theme and the collection becomes trite and boring. Therefore it is best to include only one stamp of a repeated design, the one with the most impressive appearance and colour. Stamps with an overprint must not be included at all, unless the overprint is somehow related to the theme of the collection.

Another unsolved problem is that of errors, varieties, colour shades, different perforations, and so on. In my opinion they do not belong in a thematic collection. The only exceptions are those varieties which are in some way related to the theme.

On the other hand a thematic collection should include first day covers, entires and postal stationery. But again there must be a reason for their inclusion; they must introduce a new element into the collection. A first day cover with a whole set of stamps, or such a set on several covers if there are too many stamps for one, can be entered in a subject collection. If you are forming a thematic collection, though, a first day cover should be included only if there is some design printed on the cover or a handstamp directly

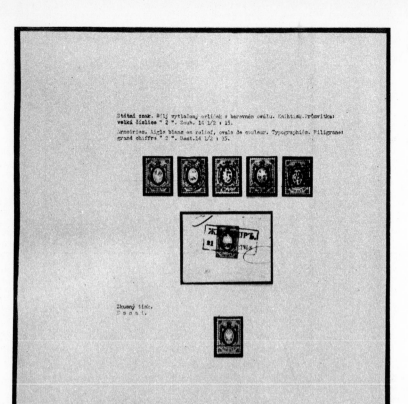

794 Shield arrangement of a leaf in a specialized collection.

795 Album leaf from a thematic collection, with shield arrangement of stamps and pieces.

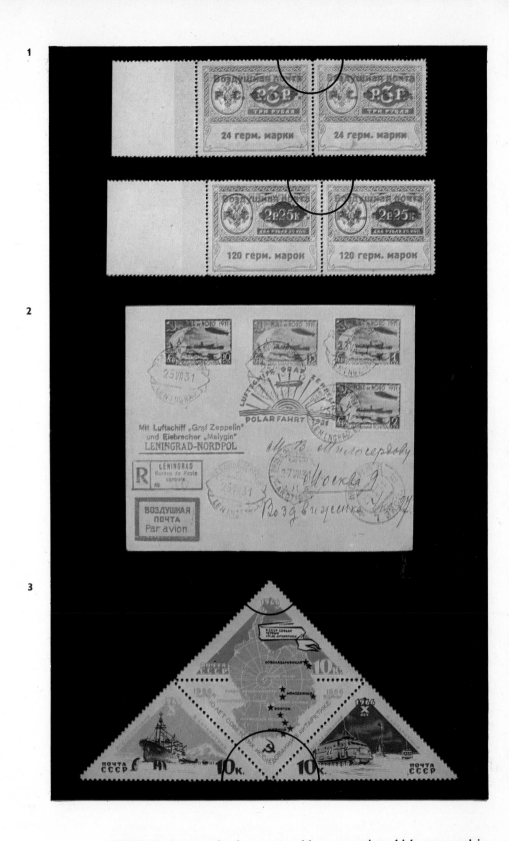

XXIX Soviet consular fee stamps with an overprint which were used in 1922 as airmail stamps for the Berlin—Moscow airline (1); An airmail cover carried over the North Pole, by the dirigible *Graf Zeppelin* and later transported by the icebréaker *Malygin* (2); Triangular Soviet stamps showing scenes and Soviet outposts in the Antarctic (3).

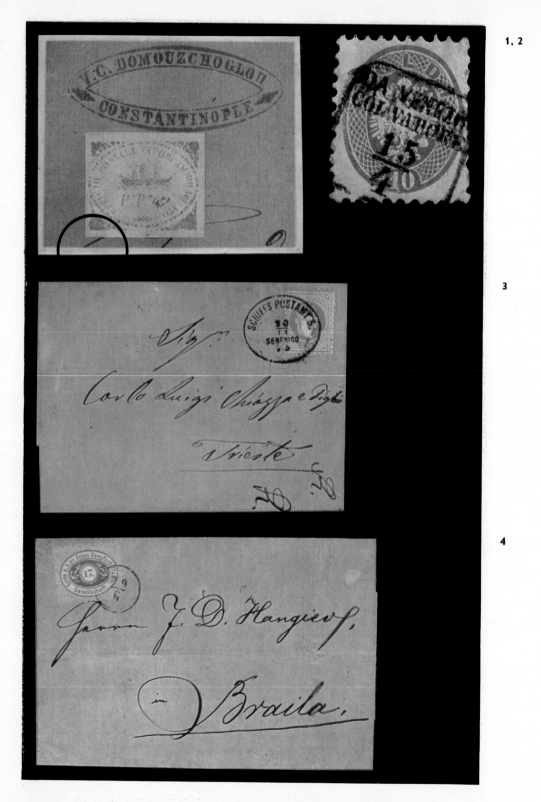

✗✗✗ Examples of maritime mail: a Turkish Admiralty stamp of 1859 on piece (1); a stamp of Austrian Italy with the handstamp 'Da Venezia col vapore' (from Venice by steamer) which indicates that this item of mail was carried to Trieste by boat from Venice (2); an envelope bearing a handstamp of the Austrian maritime mail in the Adriatic (3); and one with a Danube Steam Navigation Company stamp (4).

related to the theme. If it is just a cancellation stating 'First Day of Issue' there is no sense in including such a cover as it is just a repetition of the mint stamps.

Thematic collectors do not by any means share the same point of view in these matters. Some experienced philatelists who have formed outstanding thematic collections are of the opinion that sets of stamps showing the same design can be included in a thematic collection as long as there are not too many (sometimes the figures of two to five stamps are given). They are also in favour of the inclusion of stamps with an overprint and even of varieties of perforation and paper, of errors, and so on. Their argument is that collectors forming a thematic collection are philatelists and must take an interest in everything connected with their stamps. Very much will depend, of course, on the composition of the collection and on the writing-up. As yet there has been no definite decision on these points. Thematic collecting, after all, is a relatively young field of philately and is still developing.

There is one important warning which has to be given to all thematic collectors. Do not include in your collection non-philatelic material — pressed flowers and photographs, for instance. You must never forget you are a philatelist and are forming a stamp collection. Whatever you wish to express you have to do so with the help of stamps and philatelic material.

This is also the reason why you should not try to decorate the sheets of your collection with drawings. Bear in mind that stamps are in actual fact small graphic sheets produced with the greatest of care. The demands of stamps are very high and therefore outstanding artists are entrusted with their design. Your drawings can never reach the artistic level of the stamps and will therefore always give an inartistic, poor impression. It is much better to give the stamps a little more 'air'.

Only in exceptional cases should you mount on your sheets cuttings from newspapers, reproductions or photographs, but it is admissible to use maps whenever they are needed. They are much more instructive than a text. If it is a thematic collection for teaching purposes then you may include non-philatelic material to a greater extent.

A further important question is whether to form a thematic collection from mint or used stamps, or whether to include both. First of all you have to decide which you prefer, mint or used, but don't mix them. From an aesthetic point of view mint stamps are preferable. If you should decide to collect used stamps (it is cheaper), then see to it that the cancellation is clean, light and does not touch the design proper on the stamp.

Sometimes it will be very difficult or impossible to find a certain stamp in mint or used condition. In that case use whichever stamp you can get. Exchange it as soon as possible. Even a collection of mint stamps has to include handstamps related to the theme, mostly commemorative and propaganda handstamps. The same applies to miniature sheets, maximum cards and other philatelic material, if they are connected with the theme and add to its presentation.

If, in addition to perforated stamps, imperforate ones have also been issued you should usually include the perforated stamps (unless the imperforate are cheaper), and not repeat them. If stamps have been issued with tabs there is no need to include them in the collection with the tabs unless their text or design is of importance.

How large should a thematic collection be? That depends on the chosen theme and on the amount of philatelic material available. Normally the minimum of a good thematic collection would be

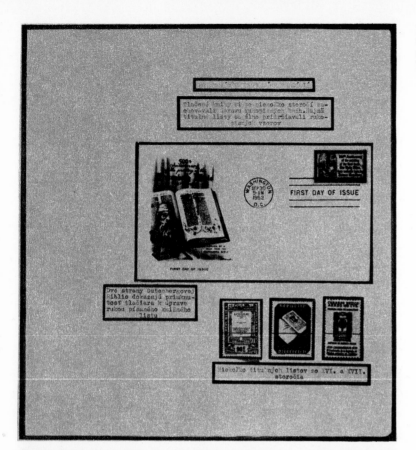

796 Asymmetric arrangement in a thematic collection. The philatelic material as well as the texts are placed on black paper.

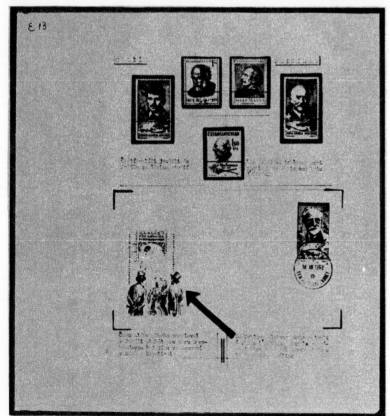

797 Leaf from another thematic collection. The arrangement is good but the decorative lines are unnecessary.

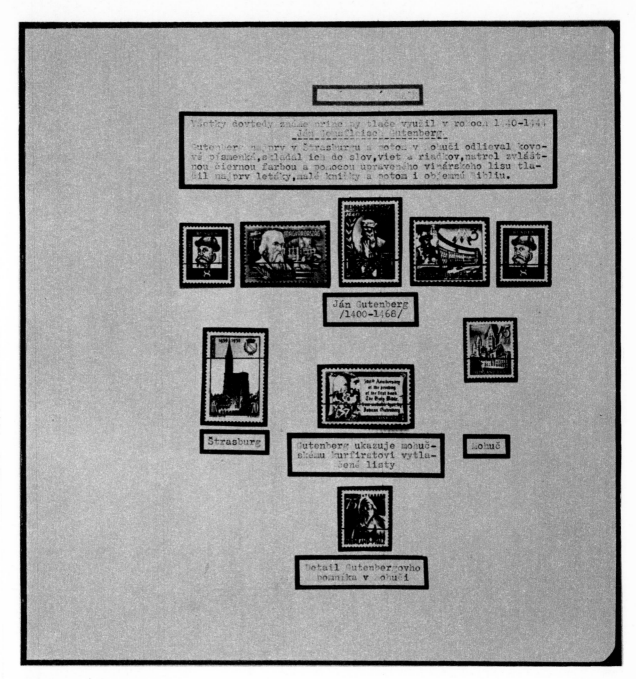

798 Perfectly arranged leaf from a thematic collection. The number of stamps is admissible, and the texts are not too long. Each item is mounted on black paper.

about forty sheets, the average being between eighty and a hundred sheets, but it can be much more. It would be very wrong to underestimate thematic collections and think you can get away with something like nine to twelve sheets, just enough for one exhibition frame. That will never win you a high award.

TEN REQUIREMENTS FOR A THEMATIC COLLECTOR

For the formation of a thematic collection, especially for a collection on the highest level, the following ten requirements based on the

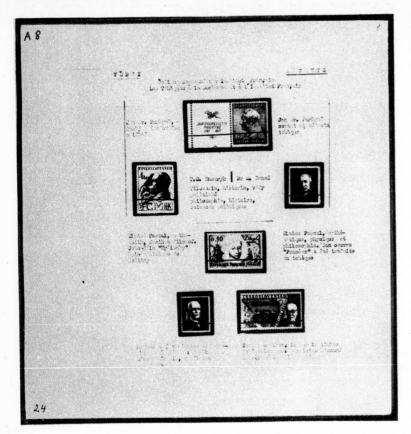

advice of Professor E. Olivier, the President of the French Society of Thematic Collectors will be useful:

1. Use a good and new idea which has to be worked out to the last detail.

2. Use an outstanding and attractive arrangement and also an attractive title.

3. Do not forget to include classical stamps; they add to the value of a thematic collection.

4. Use a clear introductory sheet with a short libretto.

5. The number of sheets in a collection is not limited, but in the case of a thematic collection it should be around thirty sheets. The number of sheets depends, naturally, on the size of the theme.

6. Work with simplicity, use sheets of light colour, and, if possible, put coloured paper under the stamps.

7. Use only perfect, well-centred stamps. If possible do not mix mint and used stamps on one sheet. If cancelled, use only those with light cancellations that do not impair the design of the stamp.

8. Use as little text as you can, written by hand.

9. Do not overcrowd the sheets and beware of 'daring' arrangements.

10. Write your collection up in such a way that a text in a foreign language or further stamps can be included.

CATALOGUES FOR THEMATIC COLLECTORS

A number of specialized catalogues have already been published for thematic collectors, naturally only for basic themes, such as Fauna and Flora, History of Medicine, etc. The possible number of themes is so large that catalogues cannot be expected to be issued for all of them. Therefore the thematic collector has to work with the normal world catalogues. He must scan them thoroughly and mark all stamps which come under consideration for the chosen theme of his collection. The best advice for a thematic collector is to compile a list or file for all the stamps he is looking for.

Any of the large world catalogues can be used for listing stamps for your thematic collection. The American *Minkus New Worldwide Stamp Catalogue* is perhaps the most suitable. The catalogue shows the stamps of the whole world in two volumes of over 1,400 pages. The advantage of this catalogue is that every stamp illustrated is accompanied not only by a description of the design but also by an explanatory text with many details about the stamp and about the meaning and contents of the design. When a stamp shows an important personality the catalogue lists the dates of birth and death and also gives a short biography. In the case of buildings the year of construction is given, mythological themes are explained, and so on. The heading of every country is accompanied by a short text about its history, and there are also details about its territory, population, currency, and language.

A FEW WORDS ABOUT CATALOGUE COLLECTIONS

The philatelist forming a catalogue collection is not limited in his choice. It is up to him which country or group of countries he decides upon. He can decide that he will collect only the classical stamps of Europe or America, or of the whole world. He can take as the final date for the stamps collected, for instance, England up to 1900; he can collect Germany from 1945 or the Soviet Union from 1917 onwards, or just Russia until 1917.

For the forming of a general collection a printed album will be quite suitable. It saves a great amount of work in the layout of pages, and the drawing of fields for stamps. The stamps are easily found in the catalogue as every field of the album is numbered according to the most popular catalogue of that country. Even a certain degree of specialization with perforations and watermarks does not constitute a problem, as the album publishers bear this in mind, too.

However, just as a thematic collector has to give his collection careful thought, so a general collector has to do likewise. It is quite impossible to collect stamps of the whole world. The beginner will have enough difficulties with the rare stamps of just the one country of his choice. It will be a good idea for him to concentrate on a country or a period on which he already possesses a fair quantity of material. In most cases this will be his native country. At home he can also obtain the best catalogues and the most detailed information. Later, when he has reached a certain level of completeness which can be surpassed only with great difficulty, he can think of adding a further country to his collection or can consider specialization.

Every experienced philatelist will advise you to specialize. The reason is that if you start a new country you become a beginner again to a certain extent. You have to get to know the stamps slowly, their peculiarities and characteristics. If, on the other hand, you decide to specialize you are building on experience already acquired; you step from the level reached to a higher level. Furthermore, your own general collection is an invaluable treasure for forming an interesting, specialized collection. After all, even the differentiation of watermarks and perforations becomes a specialization.

You have to realize, of course, that as soon as you join the ranks of specialized collectors you have to leave the narrow limits of your printed album and change over to blank sheets. Like a thematic collector, you have to reconsider the whole build-up of your collection. With a specialized catalogue on your desk you have to go over all your material and deliberate upon your intentions: that is how your libretto comes to life. There is no need to write it down; it is quite sufficient if it is clear in your head. On the other hand, as soon as you start to arrange your sheets, expecially for an exhibition, you will have to use a system similar to that of a thematic collector. The best thing to do is to draw dummies of your sheets, to evaluate the amount and placing of texts; to write them out you will need a stencil or typewriter or, if your handwriting is good, pen and Indian ink.

THE HIGHEST GOAL

One day you will find that your specialized collection has reached a very high level and that, by further enlargement, it slowly becomes a *study collection*.

There is no need, naturally, to form a study collection of an entire country. It is quite all right if you select just a short period of time or even just one stamp issue.

There is no rule stating that an advanced specialized or study collection can be formed only of classical stamps. This would be a task beyond the capabilities of a young collector. Classical stamps are usually expensive and hard to come by and it would be very difficult to accumulate the basic fund of material necessary for such a collection. Therefore have a look around for some later stamps, especially of the period after the First World War. You will find great possibilities for the building of a pioneering study collection. After all, time passes quickly and stamps considered modern a few years ago have now aged considerably.

I once knew a philatelist who chose for his study collection two very cheap Polish stamps of the period between the two wars. Without great expense he formed a quite outstanding study collection which won prizes in exhibitions and the felicitations of the jury. Not only does his collection include a wealth of beautiful material, but he has also discovered many unknown facts about these stamps. This is a road open to all.

INTERESTING FIELDS OF COLLECTING

Great, and often unexploited, opportunities exist in special fields of collecting. How about, say, a collection of cancellations? Have you ever considered a specialized aerophilatelic collection? Here are some examples and, perhaps, one of these fields may appeal to you.

800 Leaf from a specialized collection. Here there are too many stamps on the sheet and the text in three languages takes up too much space.

TÜRKEI   **TURECKO**   TURKEY

Hvězda a půlměsíc v ovále. Černý přetisk na hnědém podtisku. Knihtisk. Zoubkování 12½.

Stern und Halbmond in Eirund. Schwarzer Überdruck auf braunem Unterdruck. Buchdruck. Gezähnt 12½.

Star and crescent in oval. Black overprint on brown print. Typography. Perforation 12½.

20 para, barevné odstíny.
20 Para, Farbschattierungen.
20 paras, colour shades.

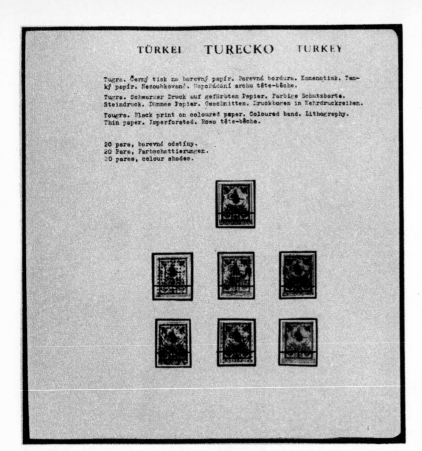

TÜRKEI　TURECKO　TURKEY

Tugra. Černý tisk na barevný papír. Barevná bordura. Kamenotisk. Tenký papír. Nezoubkované. Uspořádání archu tête-bêche.

Tugra. Schwarzer Druck auf gefärbtem Papier. Farbige Schutzborte. Steindruck. Dünnes Papier. Geschnitten. Druckbogen in Kehrdruckreihen.

Tugra. Black print on coloured paper. Coloured band. Lithography. Thin paper. Imperforated. Rows tête-bêche.

20 para, barevné odstíny.
20 Para, Farbschattierungen.
20 paras, colour shades.

801 This leaf in a shield arrangement from the same collection is much better and has a balanced appearance.

802 Attractive leaf from a collection of Canadian postal stationery. On the top are cut-outs, with complete items beneath.

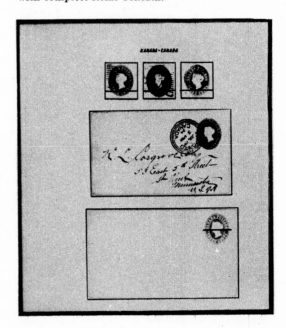

COLLECTION OF POSTMARKS

We know a lot about postmarks, but that is not enough for the creation of a specialized collection. Nevertheless, just as it is not possible to collect the stamps of the whole world it is also not possible to collect all postmarks. In fact, there exist many more postmarks than stamps. It is, though, quite possible to collect the postmarks of a certain country or, even better, postmarks used during a certain period, in a city or region. It is easiest, of course, to collect local postmarks. For a young philatelist a collection of classical postmarks will pose great problems. These are the most interesting of all but the stamps themselves are usually quite expensive and the number of complete covers or pieces with handstamps is very limited. Therefore it will be best to choose a more modern sector.

It must be said from the start that postmarks and collections of postmarks represent in themselves a documentary work of Postal History and the development of a given sector of the chosen country. That is why you must always try to obtain postmarks on entire covers or postal stationery. This is the ideal solution, but it is hardly ever possible to achieve it. Therefore the collector has to be satisfied in many cases with *pieces* comprising a stamp and complete handstamp. Very often he will be quite happy to find just a stamp with a fairly large, legible fragment of a postmark. Such a piece, or a stamp, never represents the same value as an

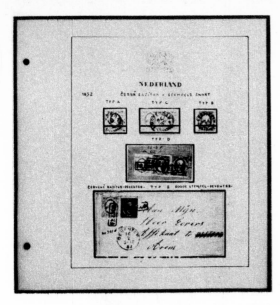

803 A pleasing arrangement from a study collection of the early Netherlands.

entire, but if almost the whole postmark is on a loose stamp it is certainly not without value. If the worst comes to the worst he will have to accept even a *fragment of a postmark* on a stamp. It has, of course, to be a fragment large enough to show clearly what sort of a postmark it is. As soon as the collector finds a piece with the required handstamp or even a complete cover he will replace the unsatisfactory fragment.

Collectors of postmarks are at a great disadvantage. The number of philatelic works dealing with postmarks is much smaller than of those dealing with stamps. There are quite a number of classical stamp-issuing countries where the field of postmarks is still an unexplored jungle on which no work of importance has been written. One of the most outstanding works on postmarks is the book by Edwin Müller, *Das große Handbuch der Abstempelungen von Altösterreich and Lombardei-Venetien (The Large Handbook of Cancellations of Early Austria and Austrian Italy)*. This book was first published in 1925 and has been revised a number of times since then. Nevertheless it is still not complete. Even nowadays specialized postmark collectors discover previously unknown postmarks or types of postmarks.

If no complete handbook with reproductions of all handstamps is available, there are still plenty of opportunities for making

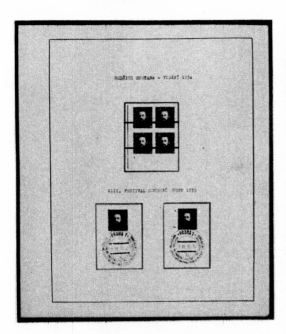

804 Leaf from a collection of modern stamps.

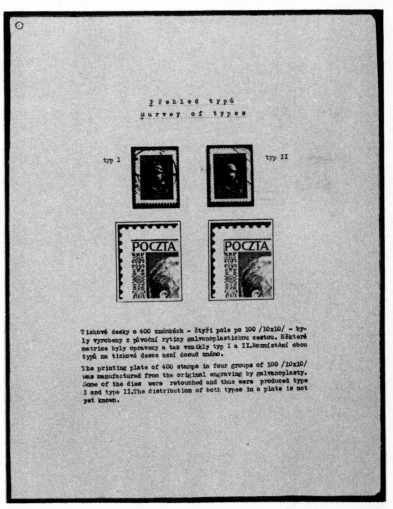

805 Example of a neatly made-up leaf of two modern Polish stamps from a specialized collection.

new discoveries. And that is the most exciting thing about a collection of postmarks.

If you should decide to collect the postmarks of a country on which no work of reference has yet been written, you are starting a completely new venture. You are forming something entirely new and original, something unknown and undiscovered.

Let us mention here a few basic principles for forming a collection of cancellations. The collector is interested in the postmark, and therefore it is not absolutely necessary to have it on a stamp. It can be on postal stationery, on a label or money order or even on a certificate of posting of a registered mail item. These are postal documents and as such perfectly acceptable in a collection of postmarks. If you can find a cover with a clear handstamp you can ignore the fact that the stamp on the entire is a little damaged. The philatelic value of such an item will be much smaller, but it is admissible for a collection of postmarks.

The arrangement of the sheets will be different from the arrangement for stamps. Sheets have to be used without printing. To improve the aesthetic appearance of the sheets, try to have pieces of approximately the same size. This applies to modern stamps only. In the case of old pieces use your scissors with the utmost caution. It will be best to leave an old cover as it is, even if it is a little tatty. Only if it really is a wreck should you try to produce something better. Never try to copy the shape of the postmark when cutting out your piece. Stick to a rectangular shape, and, if possible, a vertical rectangle.

It is a good idea to produce samples of postmarks. This can be done by taking a photograph or photostat of the handstamp from a publication, by redrawing it with the help of tracing-paper, or by photographing the piece with the stamp and postmark. In that case it will be necessary to concentrate solely on the postmark. Reproductions of individual postmarks are needed if they are different or if there is a change of some sort. If it is the same type of postmark with just a difference in the name of the post office, then it is sufficient to show a reproduction at the beginning of that particular sector of the collection.

The main facts about the handstamp will be in the heading of the sheet or, if there are more postmarks on one sheet, above or underneath the postmark in question. The reproduction of the postmark will be mounted either on top of the page, if the whole page deals with that particular postmark, or against the row containing that postmark; and next to it in line there should be samples. Try to place a postmark in its proper position. In other words, if necessary you can mount a stamp upside-down or sideways. But do not overdo it; diagonal positions should be avoided where it is possible to use a vertical or horizontal position, even if the postmark is a little lopsided. Next to the reproduction of the handstamp place the best copies of the actual handstamp. The postmark should be legible and not smudged. The text must be as short and as accurate as possible. In the case of mute postmarks it is important to state where they were used.

In the case of classical postmarks it is of importance to try and present them on different stamps of different issues. Try also to present the earliest possible date of use of a particular postmark and also the latest date. Don't be satisfied with just one strike of a handstamp, even if it is absolutely perfect. Try to find more copies to make the collection more attractive. There is no reason why you should not mount next to the reproduction of a postmark a perfect strike, and then slightly poorer strikes on other stamps

806 A perfect piece with stamp and cancellation.

807 Pieces should never be cut out like this.

and even fragments. Very much will depend on the philatelic material which you have succeeded in acquiring.

Postmarks also come in different colours. They are much more attractive and more legible on stamps of light colours than on dark stamps, though sometimes, of course, there will be no choice.

Closely related to collections of postmarks are Postal History collections. They represent a further step. The idea is to show the postal development in a certain area or city, or the development of a Travelling Post Office, and so on. Their basic material will be

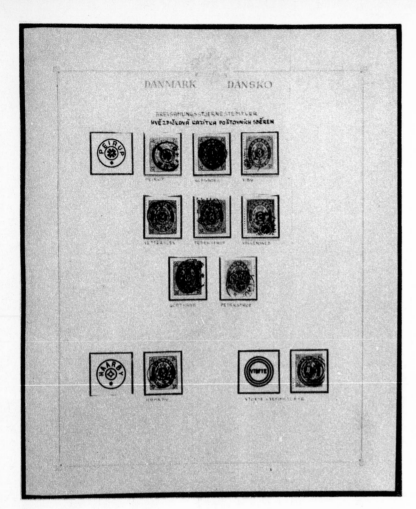

808–809 Two exemplary album
leaves from a collection of early
Danish handstamps.

809

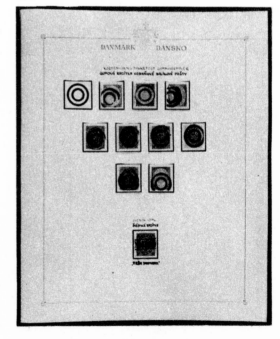

handstamps, if possible on covers. A limited amount of non-philatelic material can be added, maps, contemporary newspaper cuttings, old prints, and cards, for instance. Such a collection requires a high degree of knowledge and study. Every Postal History collection is in fact a very advanced historical paper presented, not by a written or spoken text, but by factual and frequently unique philatelic material.

AEROPHILATELIC COLLECTIONS

Normal collections of airmail stamps or stamps with aeroplanes need not be discussed in detail. The principles mentioned in connection with catalogue collections or thematic collections apply here too, depending on the way such a collection is planned and written up. A philatelist, though, who has ventured into the field of aerophilately, is practically never satisfied with stamps alone. He will obviously add to his collection such airmail documents as *First Flight Covers* and postcards and other interesting entires and postal stationery. It is these specialized collections that deserve more detail.

a) Pigeon post. The number of stamps showing a pigeon is very large. This is not surprising, for pigeons have been used for the speedy delivery of news since human history began, especially in China. When the crusaders besieged Jerusalem a pigeon wounded by a bird of prey fell into their lines. Under its wings they found a piece of paper giving a detailed account of the enemy's plans. The defenders of besieged Acre also used a pigeon post. The crusaders brought their acquired knowledge back from the Holy Land to Europe.

In Europe, though, pigeons were used only occasionally. On the other hand Nurreddin, caliph of Baghdad, introduced, as far back as the twelfth century, a regular *pigeon post* from Cairo to the Euphrates river. In Europe the banker Nathan Rothschild made clever use of pigeons. He included with the armies fighting against Napoleon reliable men who sent pigeons to London with news of all battles and of important developments. This enabled him to do very profitable financial transactions.

The greatest attention was given to the pigeon post during the siege of Paris of 1870—1. News from the besieged city was carried to the outside world very effectively by balloon. But some way had to be found of getting news into Paris. The only way was by pigeon. The balloons leaving Paris carried pigeons with them and the birds later returned, carrying news. Out of an overall number of 363 pigeons used for this service only 57 survived the war.

The pigeons carried mainly military and official news, but some private letters were brought into the city too. Although such letters were written on the thinnest paper and were very short, the pigeons could take only very few. Here modern technique stepped in. All letters destined for Paris were concentrated at Tours. There they were *microphotographed* on thin membranes. There was room for a great number of messages on one membrane, and each pigeon could carry eighteen membranes weighing altogether half a gramme. In Paris each membrane was projected on to a white wall. A number of copyists reproduced each message and it was delivered to the addressee. In actual fact this was a predecessor of

810 Attractive airmail cover from Russia, 1931.

811 Airmail cover of 1927 carried by a postal plane accompanying one of Lindbergh's flights.

the airgraph used by the British during the Second World War.

Another attempt to introduce a pigeon post was made in New Zealand. In 1896 a regular pigeon post service was established between the Great Barrier Island in the Hauraki Gulf, where ships were sometimes wrecked, and Auckland. The letters were written on tissue paper and tied to the pigeons' legs. In 1898 Henry Bolitho had the idea of franking these letters with stamps. A one-shilling stamp was indeed printed and used for this pigeon post service until 1908, when the island was linked to Auckland by a telegraph line.

On the opening day of the First World Postage Stamp Exhibition in Prague, PRAGA 1962, 5,000 pigeons were released carrying a special Pigeon-gram with a peace message. Similar pigeon posts were used later in Czechoslovakia and other countries on special occasions.

b) Balloon post. It has already been mentioned that besieged Paris had a regular balloon link with unoccupied France. The first flight was undertaken on 30 September 1870, eight days after the Prussian siege started, by the airman Tissandier flying the balloon *Le Neptune*. He carried out of Paris 30,000 letters and landed safely at Dreux where he handed them to the post for further carriage. To make the most of the restricted capacity of the balloons the weight of the letters was limited to a minimum and the Paris post issued special balloon cards and covers. The postage for a letter measuring 43×28 centimetres (about $17'' \times 11''$) was twenty cents.

Altogether sixty-five balloons flew from Paris up to 22 January 1871. They carried across enemy lines some two and a half million letters and postcards (of an overall weight of approximately ten tons), 91 passengers and 363 pigeons. The Germans captured only five balloons. Out of the remaining sixty ballons four landed in Belgium, three in the Netherlands, two in Germany and one in Norway. Only two balloons were lost. Later the wreck of one of them was found as far away as Port Natal on the south-eastern coast of Africa!

The lines of flight of each balloon are known. Every postal item bears the datestamp, so that it can be ascertained which balloon carried a particular letter. In addition there is also the datestamp of the post office which accepted the mail for further delivery. Very

812 Airmail cover from the Aeronautical Salon in Paris, 1936.

813 Interesting airmail cover with mixed franking.

814 Soviet stamp with carrier pigeon.

815 Pigeon post cover from the Siege of Paris.

816 Membrane from the pigeon post showing sixteen letters reduced in size.

815   816

817 Projection of the membrane with letters brought into Paris by pigeon.

soon philatelists discovered this highly interesting field of collecting. Several large collections exist comprising philatelic documents of each flight. They are always a centre of interest when they are shown in a stamp exhibition. Although the number of mail items carried by the balloons is fairly high these letters are seldom available, and philatelists value them highly. Some balloons carried larger numbers of mail items, other balloons less. This naturally influences the valuation. Of importance, too, is the state of preservation, the general appearance and other factors; for instance, the address on the letter.

Nowadays a philatelist will find it practically impossible to form a collection of the Paris balloon post. Every aerophilatelist would be very happy if he could boast of at least one such cover. Balloon posts, though, are found in modern times, too. For special occasions, stamp exhibitions and fairs, for example, balloon flights are staged. The balloons usually carry mail with commemorative handstamps and labels. Although such flights are not necessary to the postal system, there are many aerophilatelists who concentrate on such

818 Stamp of the New Zealand pigeon post, 1898.

819 Commemorative cover issued for the fiftieth anniversary of the New Zealand pigeon post.

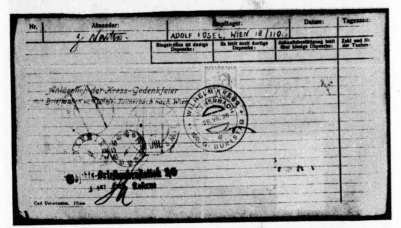

820 Austrian cover carried by pigeon in 1936.

821 Airletter of the Praga 1962 Stamp Exhibition pigeon post.

XXXI Fieldpost covers: one from the German fieldpost in Turkey during the First World War (1); another from the British fieldpost in Palestine, 1918 (2); and lastly one from the Czechoslovak fieldpost in France, 1940 (3).

1

2

3

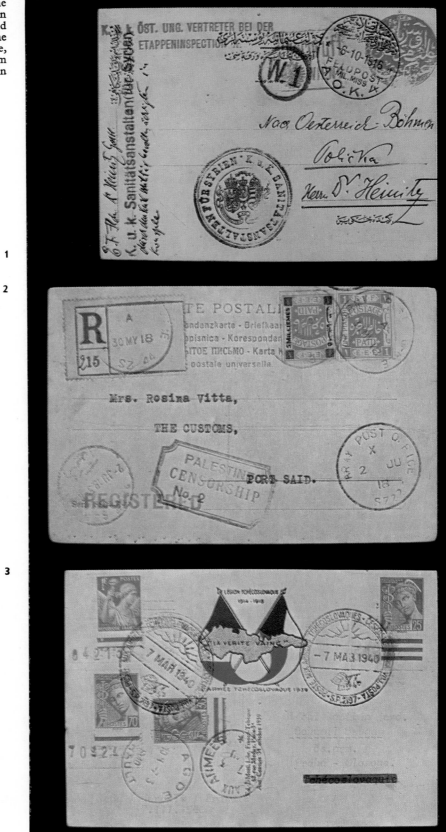

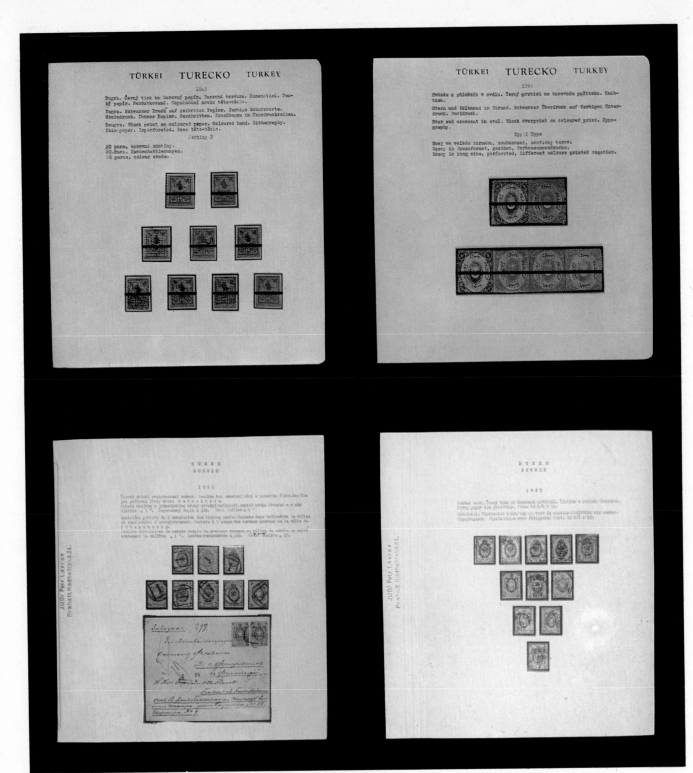

XXXII Some of the ways in which a collector might set out the stamps and other philatelic items in his album.

822 The launching of a balloon always caused a sensation. This old drawing shows Blanchard taking off at Nuremberg on 12 November 1787.

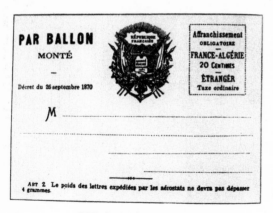

823 Special card issued in Paris in 1870 for the balloon post.

824 Balloon cover which travelled from besieged Paris to Vienna.

items and collect them. In any case it is advisable to be very cautious. Only by regularly reading the philatelic press can a collector make sure that such a flight really has taken place. A collection of balloon posts should not contain letters with a wealth of postmarks and cachets, be they ever so attractive, if they have not really been carried by a balloon. Also watch out for the exorbitant prices sometimes asked for these modern balloon flight items.

c) The origins of aerial posts. The pigeon post, and especially the balloon post, represent the oldest methods of mail transport by air. These methods of transportation, however, did not last

825 Postcard carried by balloon from Przemysl, besieged in 1915.

long, as they were unsuitable as a reliable means of mass transportation. *Airmail* started to develop only after the introduction of efficient flying machines, of aeroplanes and airships.

The origins of airmail services date back to the year 1911. In those days there were no regular airlines, only the first trial flights. Mail carried on such flights was either franked with normal stamps or special private labels. The letters and postcards were stamped with commemorative postmarks and cachets, and frequently signed by the pilot. For some flights special postcards were printed, for instance for the flights from London to Windsor in 1911, or for the flights of the aeroplane *Gelber Hund (Yellow Dog)* in 1912 in Germany. The aeroplanes of those days were very fragile and could carry only a small load. Original airmail items from those days are therefore in great demand and frequently fairly expensive.

Regular airlines were opened after the First World War. On 20 March 1918, even before the war was over, the first regular airmail service was started on the Austrian line Vienna-Cracow-Lemberg-Proskurow-Kiev. As far as *airmail stamps* are concerned Italy was first in the world to produce them. On 20 May 1917 an express delivery stamp was issued with an overprint for the trial airline Torino-Rome. In June another express stamp was overprinted for the trial airmail service Naples-Palermo, served by seaplanes.

More and more special flights were undertaken and regular airlines opened. The custom of issuing special stamps, very often overprints, commemorative cancellations and special airmail covers and cards for first flights of new lines and for some special flights, was kept as a tradition dating back to the times of pioneer flights. First flight postmarks and covers are still being issued, and now there are so many that aerophilatelists have the greatest difficulty in coping with them. Naturally these modern *first flight covers* cannot be compared to genuine material from early times as far as philatelic interest and value of the material goes. First flight covers are issued nowadays in tens of thousands and no pilot can be expected to sign them. This sector of philately has been commercialized, too, and collectors have to specialize in order to deal with the great flood.

In a special section of their own are the *catapult flights* of the

827 Postcard carried by the first British postal flight on the occasion of the coronation of King George V, 9 September 1911.

828 British cover commemorating the fiftieth anniversary of the historic flight.

829 Postcard carried in 1912 by the German plane *Gelber Hund* (Yellow Dog).

830 Postcard with the world's first airmail stamp.

twenties. Large transatlantic boats carried an aeroplane which took off when the boat reached a safe distance from land. The planes carried airmail which thus arrived much sooner than if it had travelled the whole way by boat. Airmail carried on catapult flights was marked by special postmarks and cachets. Not many catapult flights were undertaken as it was not long before planes could fly across the Atlantic unaided, and the number of catapult mail items is therefore rather small.

d) Zeppelin post. Zeppelin posts are practically a closed sector. The slow and not too safe Zeppelins — remember the disastrous fire and wreckage of the *Hindenburg* before the Second World War in Lakehurst, USA — were soon superseded by aeroplanes. Zeppelins, though, played a big role in the development of airmail services between the two wars. Many countries issued special *zeppelin stamps*. In addition, documentary postmarks and cachets were used for the individual flights. All these items are in great demand. From some flights, mainly in the later prewar years, there exist quite a number of items; but from other flights, especially from pioneering days before the First World War, the number of covers and cards is very limited, and as the number of collectors is much greater, the prices fetched by such flight documents are very high.

This type of collection is therefore rather difficult and expensive for a beginner unless, of course, he inherits an existing one which can be continued.

e) Rocket mail. The first steps in conquering space fascinated the whole world, and philatelists were no exception. At the time of writing mail has yet to be carried by spaceship. There are though, quite a number of items carried by *rocket mail*. The origins of rocket mail experiments date back to the twenties. Like the beginnings of airmail, the first rocket mail experiments had a private, or at best semi-official, character.

831 Airmail item from the first Moscow — Teheran flight.

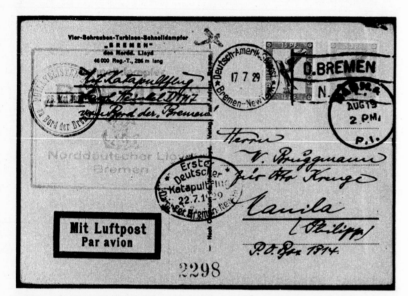

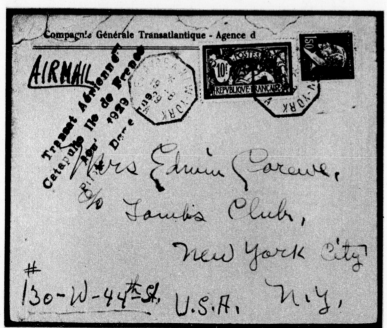

832 Postcard carried on the first German catapult flight from the deck of the *Bremen* on 22 July 1929.

833 Cover from a catapult flight off the deck of the *Ile de France*, August 1929.

834 Count Zeppelin — the constructor of modern airships.

835 The top value of the set of three stamps issued for the flight of a German zeppelin to the World Exhibition in Chicago, 1933.

836 Zeppelin stamp from Iceland.

837 Zeppelin stamp from Paraguay.

838 Soviet zeppelin stamps.

839 Zeppelin cover from the United States carried by the *Graf Zeppelin* on its flight round the world in 1929.

There is a great future in rocket mail service. It is, therefore, a philatelic sector of great promise, even for a beginner. You must be very careful, though. In many cases 'rocket mail experiments' have been staged by enterprising individuals who sometimes produced great numbers of rocket mail items which had never seen a rocket. Obviously such 'documents' are of no philatelic value. Rocket mail collectors must therefore closely follow all news and information in the philatelic press in order to keep abreast of developments and not to pay good money for fakes.

f) Helicopter mail. This aerophilatelic sector is not very wide. Helicopter mail services were originally established for special occasions as, for instance, stamp exhibitions, and were more or less an attraction for visitors, acting as a source of additional income. Such occasional flights are documented by handstamps or cachets. A few regular helicopter lines are in service, but mail carried on these flights is not marked in any way and cannot be distinguished from ordinary airmail.

In 1950 Belgium issued a charity stamp for the inauguration of the Helicopter Airmail Service and the National Aeronautical Committee's Fund. In 1962 Czechoslovakia issued a helicopter label, on which there was no value printed; nevertheless it was a postal adhesive sold at post office counters at the World Stamp Exhibition PRAGA 1962 for fifty hellers. It paid the additional postage for the transportation of mail by helicopter.

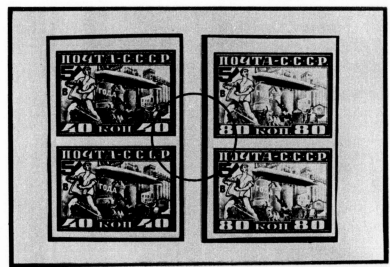

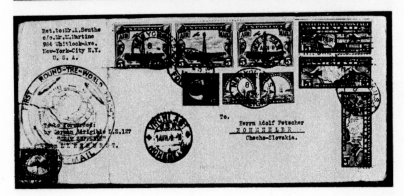

Aerophilatelists have a great advantage over all other specialized collectors. Specialized catalogues exist listing not only the prices of airmail stamps but also of airmail entires and of special and first flights.

Albums have also been printed for aerophilatelic collections. These albums, though, satisfy only the requirements of a limited number of collectors. Most aerophilatelists have to use sheets without print or just a grid when forming their collections. The same rules apply for the arrangement and write-up of aerophilatelic collections as for collections of entires and stationery. The sheets must not be overcrowded. Not more than two covers or postcards should be put on a sheet. The text must be short but comprehensive.

POLAR MAIL

The great scientific explorations and discoveries of the last decades were naturally reflected in philately, especially as far as the exploration of the polar regions and space is concerned. A great number of thematic collections were formed dealing with these two subject areas. Their level, though, is very varied. In neither case will a simple accumulation of material produce a good collection, no matter how interesting it is.

Those who want to take up a collection of polar mail will have to study the history of Arctic and Antarctic exploration and to follow all new items in the daily and scientific press. They must know which countries send expeditions, which ships sail and when, what stations are being established, what flights undertaken. The philatelic press will be useful; some magazines carry regular columns on polar mail items. The deeper the collector's knowledge the better his collection.

The number of stamps showing polar themes issued in recent years is large enough, but stamps alone cannot satisfy an intelligent philatelist. Naturally he will include in his collection polar postmarks and will be looking for mail items — covers and cards. There

840 Paraguayan zeppelin cover.

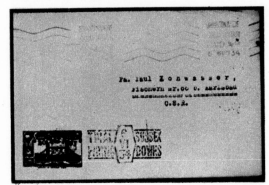

841 Russian zeppelin cover.

842 Item from a trial rocket flight in England, 1934.

843 Rocket flight cover, Italy, 1934.

262

844 Swiss rocket flight cover of 5 November 1961 with special handstamp.

845 Polish rocket flight, 1962.

is enough modern material available, but important items can be missed. It will therefore be useful to establish contacts with reliable exchange partners abroad, preferably in countries which send expeditions to the polar regions. There the necessary material can best be found. It will be much more difficult to acquire mail documents and philatelic material from pioneer times. For instance, how many postcards carried in 1914 by *Fram*, the boat used for Amundsen's expedition, are offered for sale? Try to obtain a cover from Byrd's Antarctic expedition of 1929. It is very difficult and expensive.

No specialized catalogue dealing with polar mail exists. This makes things difficult for the collector but, on the other hand, he has more chance of discovering something unknown or forgotten.

THE EXPLORATION OF SPACE

This sector of philately has become very popular in the past few years. After the first space flights a flood of stamps featuring space themes was printed all over the world and also many first day covers and postmarks were used.

Mankind is on the threshold of space exploration and it is relatively easy to obtain the philatelic material. A collector starting now has a great future, but it is also absolutely necessary that he follows all news items. There have been some cases already when clever organizers abused the interest of philatelists and produced all sorts of 'space mail items' with private postmarks which, obviously, have no philatelic value. In this connection it has to be pointed out that in the Soviet Union a great number of covers have been issued and cachets used to commemorate space flights. A large percentage of these covers and cachets are of a private or maybe semi-official character and often do not merit the high prices asked for them.

846 Soviet stamp dedicated to the memory of the polar explorer F. Nansen.

847 Norwegian stamp showing a map of the Antarctic.

848 Stamp showing the claims of Chile to Antarctic territory.

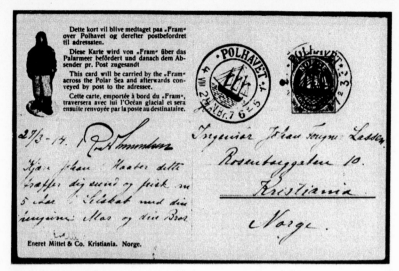

849 Card carried by
Amundsen's ship *Fram* in 1914.

851 Cover from the Soviet polar
station on the ice floe 'North Pole 4'.

851 Cover from the Soviet polar
station on the ice floe 'North Pole 4'.

852 Attractive cover with
handstamp 'North Pole 9'.

850 Letter from Byrd's
Antarctic expedition in 1929

853 Cover from a Japanese polar expedition.

MAIL ITEMS FROM WRECKS AND CRASHES

Mail items can endure much more than a human being. It happened more than once that in a shipwreck practically everybody aboard was drowned, but a great part of the mail was saved. Whenever a plane crashes the chances of human survival are often slim but mailbags are frequently saved. Such mail items are collected by a number of specialists.

The state of preservation of the salvaged covers and postcards is often very poor. In water the stamps come unstuck and the addresses are partially illegible. Covers from crashed aeroplanes are often singed. Even so the post office is usually able to decipher the address and to deliver the mail. Every cover bears a handstamp

854 Mail item from Australian Antarctic Territory.

855 Document showing the participation of Czechoslovak scientists in a Soviet Antarctic expedition: photograph with Czechoslovak stamp cancelled by handstamps of the Antarctic expedition and the station, Mirny.

856 Antarctic expedition from Chile.

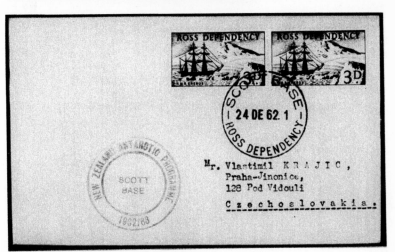

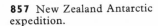

857 New Zealand Antarctic expedition.

858 French Antarctic expedition on board the Danish ship *Thala Dan*.

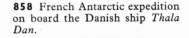

or a special label explaining that the mail was damaged in a disaster.

Wreck and crash mail items must be handled carefully. These covers are very fragile and disintegrate easily. Frequently such covers are sent to the addressee in an official GPO cover, as they probably could not stand normal handling.

It is not easy to form such a specialized collection as the number of available items is very limited and they are difficult to come by. The text in such a collection is of pre-eminent importance and must give all the basic information as, for instance, the name of the boat or the number of the plane and its type, the starting point and destination, the cause and date of the disaster and any other relevant facts. The write-up must be short and concise. It is a good plan to have a separate sheet for every disaster.

DISINFECTED MAIL

In the eighteenth and nineteenth centuries, at a time when widespread epidemics such as cholera ravaged large areas of Europe, mail from the stricken countries was officially disinfected. The letters were either opened, cut or pierced with special tweezers and exposed to sulphur fumes or disinfected with vinegar or simi-

859

859–865 Samples of philatelic material suitable for a thematic collection covering the exploration of space.

860

lar substances. Such mail items were marked with special cachets stating, for instance, that a letter was disinfected only from the outside or on the outside and inside as well.

It is practically impossible for a young philatelist to form a specialized collection of disinfected mail. It is scarce and expensive. Sometimes, though, he might be lucky, and such a cover is certainly a welcome addition to his collection.

861

862

863

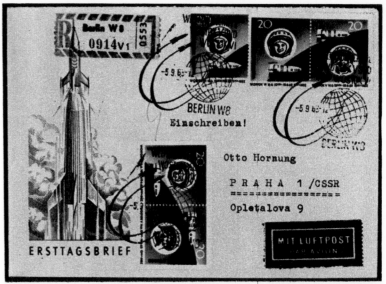

865

866 This cover survived a plane crash in 1939.

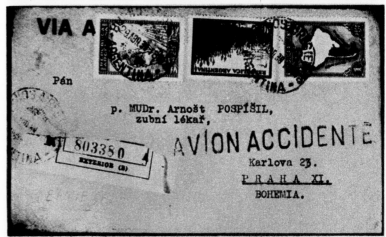

867 On 22 March 1946 the ship carrying this cover hit a wartime mine and sank, and the stamps came off the cover. The letter was delivered with postage-due stamps and the post office affixed to it a label explaining that it was found near the island of Lolland.

868 Cover from a plane disaster in Singapore, 13 March 1954. It was partly burned and was therefore forwarded to the addressee in a British official cover with an explanatory handstamp.

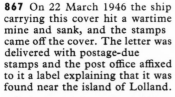

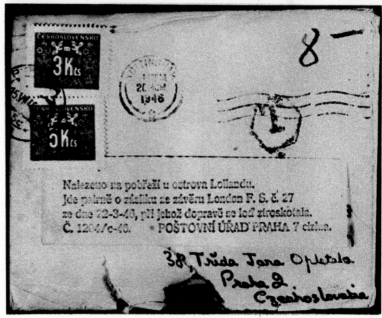

FIELDPOST AND PRISONER OF WAR POST

A most interesting field of philately is that of fieldpost items. Although the number of philatelists specializing in such collections is fairly large this is still virgin territory. Wartime events and the obvious need to keep facts relating to military matters a secret caused confusion over the use of certain postmarks in various periods of the Second World War. It is easier to collect fieldpost items from preceding wars as the facts are better known but, on the other hand, the items tend to be more expensive and harder to find. This makes things attractive for advanced collectors.

Fieldpost postmarks were used as far back as the eighteenth century. During the war of the Austrian succession, 1741—8, the Austrian army, together with allied British and Dutch armies, fought the French in the Netherlands. Three postmarks are known from the year 1744: a circular handstamp with the letters 'AA' — 'Armée Autrichienne' (Austrian Army); a circular handstamp with the letters 'AB' — 'Armée Britannique' (British Army); and a rectangular handstamp with the text 'A HOL' — 'Armée Hollandaise' (Dutch Army). These postmarks are naturally very rare and a normal collector will usually see them only in stamp exhibitions.

In the same way, to form a collection dealing with the fieldpost of the Crimean War or the 1870—1 Franco-Prussian war is very difficult. Nevertheless, collectors will find a most promising field in the period covering the First and Second World Wars. Here, of course, it will be best to specialize, to limit the collection to a certain country or group of countries or to a limited sector. I have seen, for instance, a most interesting collection dealing with the fieldpost of the Austrian Navy before and during the First World War. Some of the postmarks or cachets give the names of the individual warships. Frequently picture postcards with photographs of the ships are found.

A closely related field of collecting is Prisoner of War mail. This mail was sent through the International Red Cross. Special Red Cross postcards and envelopes were printed for this purpose.

Fieldpost items and other wartime mail was usually censored when it was going abroad. On such covers censor handstamps,

869 Prussian fieldpost in the war against France 1870—1.

870 Fieldpost handstamps of 1744.

871 Cover from the Boxer Uprising in China, 1898.

872 French fieldpost card of the First World War.

873 Czechoslovak fieldpost in France, 1940.

874 Cover showing the handstamp of the Czechoslovak fieldpost in England, 1945, and the censor's handstamp with his signature.

875 Triangular folded letter (a so-called 'scarf letter') of the Russian fieldpost of the Second World War with censor's handstamp.

876 Red Cross card sent by a prisoner of war in Russia in 1916.

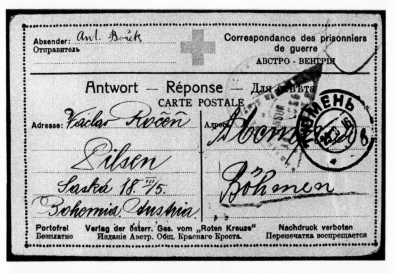

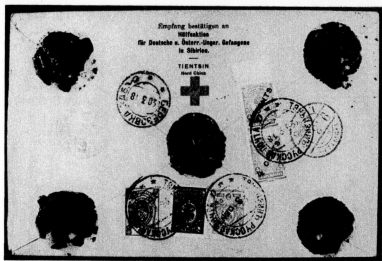

877 Cover sent via China by an Austrian POW from a camp in Siberia.

878 The first message sent home during the Second World War by a German POW captured by the British.

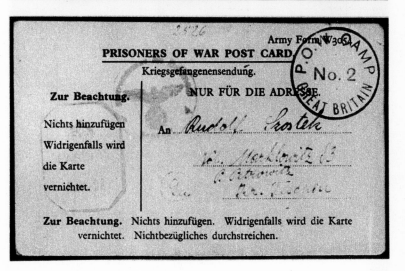

censor labels and sometimes the censor's written remarks and his signature can be found. They are all important requisites of this type of mail, confirming its authenticity and frequently disclosing many interesting facts about the fate of such items.

CONCENTRATION CAMP MAIL

The Second World War is slipping further and further back into history. In 1945, when all the gruesome facts about Nazi concentration camps became known, the world was shocked. Hardly anybody realized at the time that this dark chapter of human history would be a most interesting field of philately. A few collectors have taken it up since, but, unfortunately, not many. The mail items from concentration camps and Nazi prisons are scarce and become more valuable as time passes. There is still time to start a collection now, whilst items are available and survivors are alive. It is almost a closed philatelic chapter and in the future it is bound to become just as exclusive, and the documents as elusive, as for instance, balloon post items of the siege of Paris.

Special covers and postcards were printed by the German authorities for the larger concentration camps. Only a limited number of prisoners had a chance to send letters, but some of these can still be found. The relatives of victims, perhaps, treasure such letters, but as time passes they might become available.

In such a collection there might well be included letters sent from different prisons where resistance fighters were held, and also kites smuggled from concentration camps, prisons and in transit.

Again, when writing up such a collection, unless it is evident from the item itself, a detailed text is important; where possible it should include a summary of the prisoner's story.

879 Turkish censor's label from the First World War.

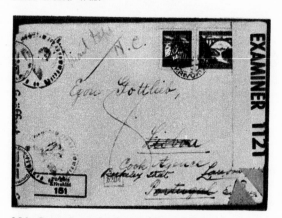

880 Cover from the Second World War opened first by the German censor and later by the British.

881 Airletter censored by the Anglo-Russian-Iranian censor in Teheran.

882 Second World War cover opened by censor.

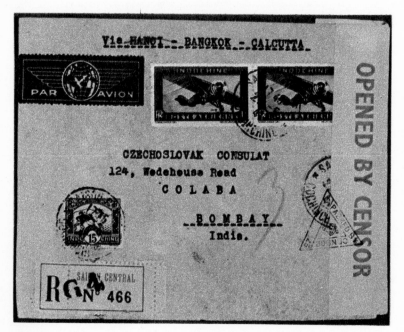

883 Postcard from the Sachsenhausen concentration camp.

884 Cover from the concentration camp at Dachau.

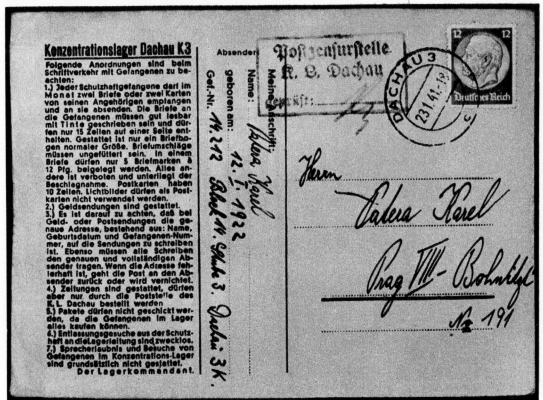

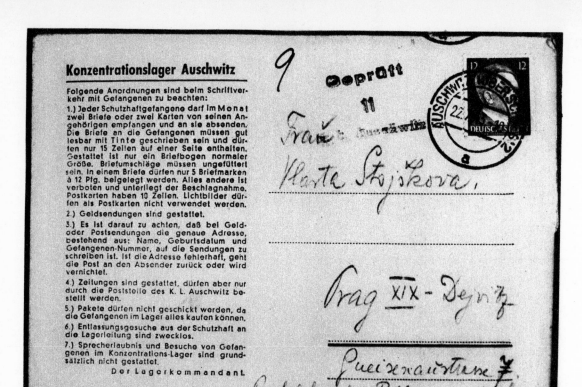

Konzentrationslager Auschwitz

Folgende Anordnungen sind beim Schriftverkehr mit Gefangenen zu beachten:

1.) Jeder Schutzhaftgefangene darf im Monat zwei Briefe oder zwei Karten von seinen Angehörigen empfangen und an sie absenden. Die Briefe an die Gefangenen müssen gut lesbar mit Tinte geschrieben sein und dürfen nur 15 Zeilen auf einer Seite enthalten. Gestattet ist nur ein Briefbogen normaler Größe. Briefumschläge müssen ungefüttert sein. In einem Briefe dürfen nur 5 Briefmarken à 12 Pfg. beigelegt werden. Alles andere ist verboten und unterliegt der Beschlagnahme. Postkarten haben 10 Zeilen. Lichtbilder dürfen als Postkarten nicht verwendet werden.

2.) Geldsendungen sind gestattet.

3.) Es ist darauf zu achten, daß bei Geld- oder Postsendungen die genaue Adresse, bestehend aus: Name, Geburtsdatum und Gefangenen-Nummer, auf die Sendungen zu schreiben ist. Ist die Adresse fehlerhaft, geht die Post an den Absender zurück oder wird vernichtet.

4.) Zeitungen sind gestattet, dürfen aber nur durch die Poststelle des K. L. Auschwitz bestellt werden.

5.) Pakete dürfen nicht geschickt werden, da die Gefangenen im Lager alles kaufen können.

6.) Entlassungsgesuche aus der Schutzhaft an die Lagerleitung sind zwecklos.

7.) Sprecherlaubnis und Besuche von Gefangenen im Konzentrations-Lager sind grundsätzlich nicht gestattet.

Der Lagerkommandant.

885 Cover from Auschwitz.

886 Postcard from the Jewish Ghetto in Lodz with sender's address, 'Der Älteste der Juden in Litzmannstadt' (The Senior of the Jews in Litzmannstadt).

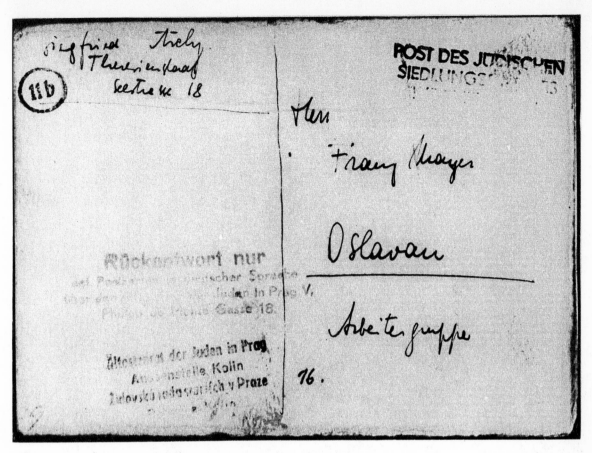

887 Postcard from Theresienstadt concentration camp.

888 Letter to a Czechoslovak prisoner in Breslau prison.

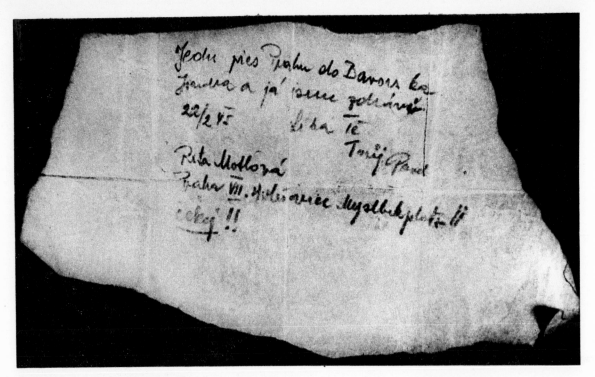

FIGHT FOR FREEDOM

This theme is closely related to the previous type of collection. It is possible to build it up into a very interesting thematic collection. Every country features on its stamps the most important freedom fighters. There exists further interesting philatelic material; the Second World War especially offers a wide choice of material. This period has still not been exhausted and there are great possibilities for research and discoveries. It is a field of collecting which can be recommended to any thematic collector who has not yet made up his mind about his speciality.

889 Paul Motl, a concentration camp prisoner, managed to throw this message out of the railway wagon in which he was being transported with other prisoners to Bavaria towards the end of February 1945 . . .

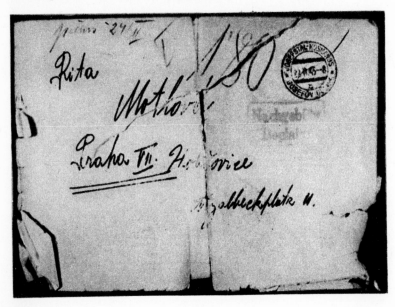

890 . . . a railwayman found the letter and sent it in this cover to Paul Motl's wife.

891-892 A collection of
concentration camp items may
be extended to include other
appropriate themes, such as
these two stamps issued in
memory of Lidice, the village
whose male population was
murdered on 10 June 1942.

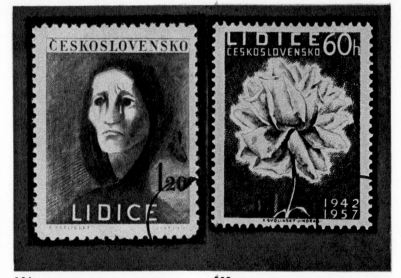

891   892

893 Fifteenth-century leader
of the Hussites, Jan Zizka, on
a Czechoslovak stamp.

894 US stamp with a
portrait of La Fayette, hero of
the American War of
Independence.

895 Marshal Suvorov, a
great military leader from the
Napoleonic period, portrayed
on a Soviet stamp.

894   895

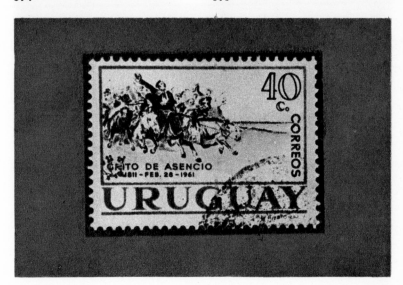

896 Uruguayan stamp
commemorating the fight for
freedom.

897 The Soviet commander Blücher, one of the leading figures of the revolutionary wars.

898 The Czech journalist Julius Fucik, executed by the Nazis.

899 Hero of the Soviet Union, Sergeant Miroshnichenko.

900 Karl Friedrich Goerdeler, one of the German resistance fighters against Hitler.

901 French stamp commemorating the anniversary of the liberation of Paris and Strasbourg by the Allies in the Second World War.

902 In 1964, twenty years after her liberation, France issued this stamp dedicated to the freedom fighters.

903 Stamp commemorating the liberation of Czechoslovakia.

904 United States stamp promoting the idea of the United Nations.

905 Official cover with Swiss official stamp for the European office of the United Nations in Geneva.

THE UNITED NATIONS

The postwar period saw the establishment of a great number of new nations. All new States immediately started to issue their own stamps. This was not only an outward sign of their sovereignty but also a very welcome source of income. These stamps are usually very attractive, and quite a number of collectors have taken them up. There is the great advantage that these countries are fairly new and that all the issued stamps are available. This makes it easy to form a good catalogue collection. Advanced philatelists choosing such a new country will probably want to go back further and collect also the previous period, i. e. the colonial stamps issued for that country.

One of the new philatelic countries, although without its own territory, is the United Nations. The UN stamps are issued in USA currency for the New York Offices and in Swiss currency for the

906 Some UN First Day covers.

907 Card with UN stamp and commemorative cancellation.

908 Cyprus stamp of 1964 overprinted with the arms of the United Nations.

Geneva centre. United Nations stamps came into existence not so long ago, they are readily available and the designs are most attractive. This is a very rewarding field for a catalogue collection.

MAXIMUM CARDS

For some time a new field of philately has been developing in France and many other countries: the collecting of *maximum cards*, or in French *cartes maximum*.

The collector tries to obtain, if possible, a picture postcard showing the same design as that on the issued stamp. The stamp is then affixed to the picture side of the card, where it impairs the

909 French maximum card showing the Palace of Justice at Rennes.

910 Maximum card featuring the bathyscaphe *Archimedes*.

911 Maximum card showing judo.

912 General de Gaulle's patriotic appeal on both stamp and maximum card.

design as little as possible, and is then cancelled with a commemorative postmark, first-day cancellation or another cancellation related to the design of the stamp and picture postcard.

As this is a new field of collecting the rules for a maximum card collection are not yet quite clear. There is not much sense in collecting just any maximum card. It is better to restrict yourself to one country or to a given theme. It is imperative to find good exchange partners to help. Generally it is more difficult to find a picture postcard that reflects the stamp design as far as possible than the stamp itself. In some places exact replicas of newly prepared stamps are issued in picture postcard form. This, of course, tends to lessen the interest. The exciting thing about such a collection is in finding old material.

913 German post in Turkey: in the bottom left corner is the arrival postmark of the German post office in Istanbul.

914 Austrian post in Turkey: registered letter from Salonika.

915 Austrian post in Jerusalem.

916 Russian newspaper stamp of 1863 for newspapers sent to Turkey.

917 Russian post in Turkey with overprint for Beirut.

918 Italian post in Turkey: registered letter from Smyrna.

MAIL FROM THE LEVANT

919 British post in Istanbul.

Before closing this chapter I should like to mention one more field of philately. Up to 1914 the so-called Capitulations were in force in Turkey. They were international treaties enforced upon the Ottoman Empire after its defeats during the nineteenth century. On the basis of these Capitulations some foreign powers were entitled to establish their own postal services on Turkish territory. These Capitulations were revoked by Turkey when the First World War began and only the Allied fieldposts (German, Austrian) were permitted. To commemorate this event Turkey issued on 20 September 1914 a set of overprinted stamps. After the First World War, when Turkey was defeated once more, some of these foreign postal services were in operation again for a short period. That is why British, French, German, Austrian, Russian, Italian, Polish, Rumanian, and Egyptian postal services were found on

920 German post in Shanghai, 1888.

921 'Wandering handstamp' used by Abbabis in German South West Africa in 1904.

922 A mark denomination for German New Guinea with two cancellations according to postal regulations.

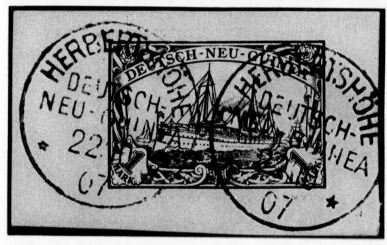

923 Mint 2 mark stamp for the Carolines.

Turkish territory. All these postal services are called *Levant Mail*.

At first these foreign post offices in Turkey used their own stamps which were cancelled with special postmarks using either a number, or a letter and a number, or, later, the name of the post office. Covers and postcards or even individual, used stamps can therefore be recognized as originating from the Levant. Later the stamps of the mother countries were overprinted with an appropriate text and a new value in Turkish currency, and finally proper stamps for the Levant were printed.

Levant stamps are mostly collected together with the stamps of the mother country but it is quite possible to form a separate, Levant collection.

These details apply also to some special sectors of European and overseas countries. General collectors sometimes omit colonial posts (postmarks and stamps), plebiscite issues, occupation issues, and so on. These are also well worth collecting.

Owing to their character, collections of Levant stamps and of other philatelic groupings mentioned above belong to catalogue collections. Nevertheless, a general collection of such a field will hardly prove satisfactory. You could not include all the postmarks which are the forerunners of colonial or Levant stamps, for instance. Therefore, it has to be a specialized collection.

IV. PHILATELIC LITERATURE

A very wide range of publications and printed accessories is issued for stamp collectors. We have already discussed in detail stamp albums and album leaves. Let us have a look now at the rest of philatelic literature.

STAMP CATALOGUES

A serious stamp collector cannot work without a catalogue. A catalogue is a list of stamps including illustrations and fairly detailed information about the stamps — the date of issue, size, perforation, colour and errors, for instance. Furthermore, catalogues also state for what occasion the stamps were issued; they sometimes give the name of the designer and engraver, how long the stamps were valid for postage, more information about the design on the stamps and other important facts for the use of the collector. To save space catalogues use all sorts of abbreviations and symbols for common terms. A philatelist must study the list of symbols and abbreviations given on the first pages of the catalogue.

The price quotations in catalogues are very important. Not all catalogues work to the same rules. The Stanley Gibbons catalogues, for instance, give prices at which stamps can be bought from them. Other catalogues give prices based on the real market prices, or prices based on the market situation, but not actual prices. The value of stamps is normally given in two columns, the first for mint stamps, the second for cancelled. Sometimes another column appears for stamps used on covers. Some catalogues have also introduced prices for unhinged mint stamps. The catalogue price is normally only a guideline. Take, for example, a classical stamp like the Penny Black. The state of preservation and quality of the stamp will obviously influence the price. A perfect copy might cost much more than the catalogue says and, on the other hand, a poor copy is bound to be cheaper. Other factors influence the price as well, such as postmark, supply and demand. If a collector wants to buy stamps he must be prepared to pay more than he can expect to get when selling the same stamps. If you buy a whole collection in an auction you should pay less than for individual stamps. There is always the chance of a good bargain and the more you know about your stamps the better your chances. Full catalogue prices are mostly used in exchange transactions between collectors. The prices of stamps naturally vary according to the situation on the stamp market.

The first stamp catalogue was printed in 1861 in France by Alfred Potiquet. It was a very simple little booklet giving a list of stamps without any reproductions. The catalogue had ten pages

924 Title page of the historic Stanley Gibbons catalogue of 1865.

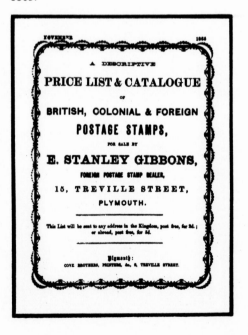

and listed all the stamps issued up to the date of printing in the whole world. Very similar was the first catalogue of Stanley Gibbons, issued in 1865. These old catalogues are very rare today. For instance, until recently the only known copy of the first Stanley Gibbons catalogue belonged to the British Museum. In 1965, the centenary year, another copy was discovered. It is owned by a well-known American philatelist.

The first catalogues were simply stamp dealers' price lists. Very soon, however, the catalogues acquired other, more important functions. They became lists of stamps for philatelists, the basis for new collections. In addition the pricing of stamps in catalogues enabled stamp collectors to exchange stamps according to their value. The original system of exchanging one stamp for another, a system still used nowadays by children, could not be upheld when it became evident that only a limited number of copies of some stamps exist and that they are rare and more valuable.

There are three main groups of catalogues: world catalogues, catalogues for individual countries and special catalogues.

a) World catalogues. These catalogues are important works of philately. They either include, in one or more volumes, the stamps of the whole world, or the stamps of one continent. They are called world catalogues, not only because they list stamps of the whole world but mainly because they are internationally recognized: on their basis stamps are sold and exchanged between philatelists of one particular country and also internationally. Most widely used are the following catalogues:

Stanley Gibbons — published in the United Kingdom
Scott — published in the United States
Michel — published in the Federal Republic of Germany

Yvert & Tellier — published in France
Lipsia — published in the German Democratic Republic
Zumstein — published in Switzerland (catalogue of Europe only)
Bolaffi — published in Italy

Originally these catalogues were printed in one volume and covered the whole world (with the exception of the Zumstein catalogue), but the growing number of newly issued stamps forced the publishers to split up their catalogues into two and even three volumes. Stanley Gibbons' catalogue, for instance, lists in Part I the British Commonwealth, in Part II Europe and Colonies and in Part III America, Asia and Africa; Yvert & Tellier have in Part I France and French-speaking countries, Part II Europe and Part III Overseas. These large catalogues are issued every year in a new edition, usually at the beginning of the philatelic season in the autumn. This means that a catalogue with the date 1970 will list stamps issued only until spring 1969. Stanley Gibbons have tried to overcome the problem of the large numbers of stamps by printing a Simplified Catalogue in one volume. This catalogue is useful for beginners and thematic collectors.

b) Single country catalogues. To publish a world catalogue is very expensive and cannot be undertaken if a large sale is not assured. Due to the rapidly growing numbers of newly issued stamps world catalogues have to limit the details and facts to an absolute minimum. That, obviously, cannot satisfy advanced and specialized stamp collectors. Therefore in practically all philatelically developed countries national catalogues are issued, which list all the stamps of the particular country in very great detail with varieties, colour shades, and so on. Such a catalogue is the most important accessory for philatelists who have decided to form a catalogue collection of a certain country or period.

The prices given in world catalogues are sometimes not satisfactory. They are good for an exchange of stamps, but the price level varies from country to country. Stamps are usually more highly valued in their country of origin, where they are most in demand. In London, for example, you might get French stamps cheaper than in Paris. Therefore, so-called *netto catalogues* are issued. These are straightforward, illustrated price lists based on realistic market prices. Every collector must always bear in mind that catalogue prices can be understood only as a guide-line and are meant for average stamps. Poorer copies should be cheaper (check in the table listing damaged stamps) and perfect copies will be more expensive.

Catalogue prices do not always reflect the scarcity of stamps. Some philatelic countries are more popular and more in demand; therefore the prices are bound to be higher. Other countries are neglected and so it happens that a stamp of a popular country, like Great Britain, will be listed at a higher price than a stamp of a less popular country which in actual fact is much rarer. This rule applies not only to countries but also to themes. Furthermore, covers and postcards of the first periods are very much in demand and fetch high prices. You might come across an old cover with a cheap stamp, but it might be very valuable due to the postmark, its history or other factors. Also bear in mind that most stamps were soaked off covers and quite a cheap stamp might be very rare on a letter simply because not many have survived.

Therefore it is impossible to make a general rule for the pricing of stamps. It will always depend on the experience and knowledge of the philatelist and it will be up to him to value the philatelic material offered to him.

926 Belgian philatelic magazine of 1863.

927 Philatelic magazine of 1893.

928 Colourful array of philatelic magazines.

c) Special catalogues. In addition to the above-mentioned catalogues, special catalogues are also printed; for instance, the airmail catalogues Sanabria or Silombra, catalogues for postal stationery, thematic catalogues, and so on.

Which catalogue a philatelist chooses is up to him and his requirements. The majority of stamp collectors will be satisfied with one of the world catalogues. If he is a beginner he does not need the latest edition. Stamp collectors concentrating on one country must have the specialized national catalogue.

One more point of importance: the listing of stamps in world and national catalogues is not identical. Some stamps or groups of stamps are listed in a different way under different headings; other stamps are listed in some catalogues and not in others. This is of great importance for philatelists forming general collections on numbered, printed album pages. The best advice for them is to buy an album which is available at home and also the appropriate catalogue which shows the fields for the stamps as they are numbered on the album sheets.

d) Auction catalogues. Philatelic auctioneers publish for their customers special catalogues listing and describing all lots put up for sale. Experienced philatelists are very interested in these auction catalogues, even if they do not intend to bid or cannot go to the auction. There are two reasons for this: first of all, auction catalogues published by large firms include photographs and sometimes colour plates of the best and most interesting items offered for sale. These photographs are most useful to specialized collectors and experts, who receive photographic documents of very rare stamps which are seldom seen. Furthermore, auctions serve as a gauge for the development and trend of stamp prices. It is interesting to note which lots were sold and which were not and to see what prices were reached.

PHILATELIC MAGAZINES

The first philatelic magazine made its appearance in 1862, in Liverpool. It was the *Monthly Advertiser*. Since then over one hundred years have passed and the number of philatelic magazines has grown tremendously. In the most important philatelic countries a number of magazines are published, weekly, fortnightly, or monthly; some are colour magazines or specialized philatelic magazines covering all fields of collecting. It would be impractical to list them all, but here are a few of the more important magazines:

United Kingdom — *Philatelic Magazine, Stamp Collecting, Stamp Magazine, Stamp Monthly, Stamp Weekly*
United States — *Linn's Stamp News, Stamps, SPA Journal, The American Philatelist*
Austria — *Austria-Philatelist, Die Briefmarke*
Belgium — *Balasse Magazine, Echo Philatélique, De Postzegel, La Revue du Timbre*
Czechoslovakia — *Filatelie, Merkur*
Denmark — *Dansk Filatelistik Tidsskrift*
Finland — *Philatelia Fennica*
France — *L'Echo de la Timbrologie, Le Monde des Philatélistes*
Germany (East) — *Der Sammler-Express*
Germany (West) — *Deutsche Zeitung für Briefmarkenkunde,*

Mauritius, Der Sammler-Dienst, Die Sammler-Lupe
Greece — *Philotelia*
Hungary — *Filatéliai Szemle*
Italy — *Il Collezionista, Il Bolletino Filatelico d'Italia, Filatelia Italiana*
Netherlands — *Nederlandsch Maandblad voor Philatelie*
Norway — *Norsk Filatelistisk Tidsskrift*
Poland — *Filatelista*
Russia — *Filateliya SSSR*
Spain — *Alhambra, Correo Filatelico, Eco Filatelico*
Sweden — *Nordisk Filateli, Svensk Filatelistisk Tidskrift*
Switzerland — *Berger Briefmarken-Zeitung, Philatelica, Schweizer Briefmarken-Zeitung*

Philatelic magazines are invaluable to all stamp collectors; although nowadays practically all magazines print many pages of advertisements, these too contain useful information.

All philatelic magazines give information about new stamp issues and print photographs of the stamps. This is of great importance, especially for thematic collectors. While they will find these stamps listed in the new editions of their catalogues, after several months there is a danger that some sets may be out of print. Furthermore, the magazines give a wealth of information which cannot be printed in catalogues for lack of space. Philatelic magazines contain articles on all recent developments, the use of new stamps and their validity, on commemorative postmarks, first flights, and so on. In addition, they print important studies and articles dealing with different sectors of philately.

PHILATELIC LITERATURE

Our great-grandfathers were hard up for philatelic information and professional knowledge. Nowadays the experience of generations of philatelists has been collected and concentrated into a great number of excellent books and monographs. Take, for instance, Stanley Gibbons' specialized stamp catalogue *Great Britain*, vol.1: Queen Victoria. When the catalogue was first issued in 1963 it was based on a number of detailed studies and listed all available information and facts. Since then it has been reprinted and re-edited as new details came to light. It has become an invaluable aid for specialized collectors. There exist, though, other works which go into even greater detail and sometimes deal with just one printing plate of one stamp.

An advanced philatelist who does not read philatelic literature is like a short-sighted man who refuses to wear spectacles. The sooner a specialized stamp collector reaches for a work of philately the better for him and his collection. Usually he is not interested in too wide a field but has to keep an eye on his sphere of philatelic interest, take account of all new works published in it, and never lose an opportunity to get hold of older publications. Not only large volumes are part of philatelic literature. Frequently outstanding specialized studies are found in *exhibition catalogues and bulletins*.

It is significant that a special class was included in national and international stamp exhibitions for philatelic literature; magazines, catalogues, albums and so on all compete within this class for the highest awards.

V. TO EXHIBIT OR NOT TO EXHIBIT

Every stamp exhibition is a philatelic event of great importance. Try never to miss an opportunity to visit an exhibition — and go more than once. Nowhere else can you find so much interesting material concentrated in one place. At an exhibition you can see the successes of your competitors; you can compare your collection with the very best exhibits in your particular field. You can see stamps that at any other time would be kept in bank vaults; you will get new ideas and tips for your own collection. This applies both to collectors forming a catalogue collection and thematic collectors.

It will be the healthy ambition of many philatelists to join the ranks of exhibitors and compete for a medal. The judges will evaluate your collection and give a verdict on its grade. It feels good to be able to accept a diploma and a medal. It does not matter if you do not win the Grand Prix at the first attempt. The highest awards are not given easily. To participate in a stamp exhibition is like taking part in the Olympic Games. There are not many winners, but it is a great honour for everyone who takes part, an excitement and experience never to be forgotten.

The competition in stamp exhibitions is not limited to hardy philatelists. In all great international and national exhibitions there are separate sections and competitions for young stamp collectors. In addition, special exhibitions for young collectors

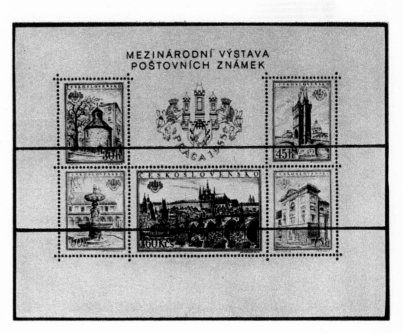

929 Special stamps and miniature sheets are issued for many stamp exhibitions. This is a miniature sheet commemorating the stamp exhibition in Prague, 1955.

only are being organized as well as separate exhibitions for thematic collectors and aerophilatelists.

The International Federation of Philately (FIP) has adopted a set of rules which apply to all international stamp exhibitions held under its patronage. Some international exhibitions are held without FIP patronage. National stamp exhibitions have also in most cases based their rules for the holding of an exhibition, for the participation and judging of exhibits on the international rules. Listed below is an excerpt of the most important points of these rules. After all, it is quite possible that today's beginner will in a few years' time win philatelic laurels in a great international stamp exhibition.

EXTRACT FROM THE FIP RULES FOR INTERNATIONAL STAMPS EXHIBITIONS

FIP accords its patronage to only one international stamp exhibition every year in the region of Europe, North Africa and the Near East and in the region of Africa, America, Asia and Oceania. The holding of such exhibitions has to be reported to FIP at least two years in advance and has to be approved by a majority at the FIP Congress.

International Exhibitions include the following classes:

a) Official Class. This class is reserved for postal administrations, postal museums and stamp printers. Exhibits are *Hors Concours* (not included in the competition).

b) Class of Honour. Exhibits which have previously been awarded

930 Invitation to the International Stamp Exhibition Melusina held in Luxembourg, 1963.

931 – 932 Two French stamps issued for the great International Stamp Exhibition Philatec held in 1964 in Paris.

932

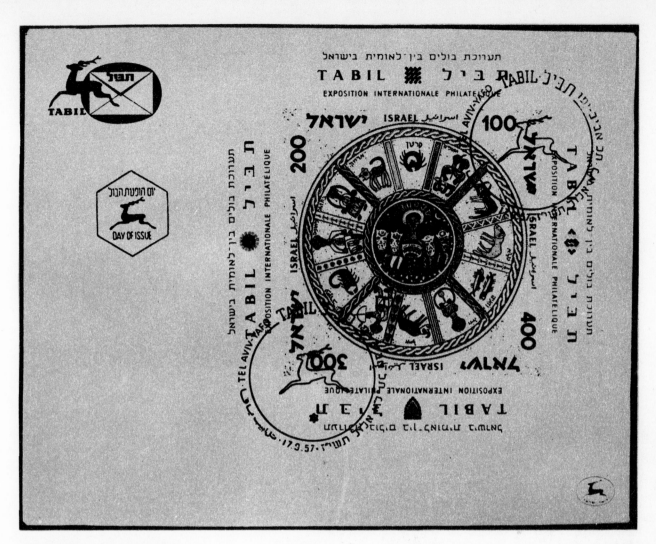

933 Miniature sheet issued for the International Stamp Exhibition Tabil held in 1957 in Tel Aviv.

two Large Gold Medals or a 'Grand Prix' and a Large Gold Medal or two 'Grand Prix' at an International Exhibition held under the patronage of FIP during the five years preceding this exhibition. In this class a Grand Prize is awarded consisting of an *Objet d'Art* or a Large Gold Medal. All other exhibitors in this class receive Gold Medals or an *Objet d'Art* and Diplomas. An exhibit which has been exhibited five times in the Class of Honour returns to the Competitive Classes.

c) Court of Honour. Exhibits of outstanding collectors displayed *Hors Concours* by invitation of the Executive Committee.

d) Competitive Class. This includes all exhibits competing for Exhibition Medals. It is usually divided as follows:

1. National Class (stamps of the country where the Exhibition is held)
2. Europe
3. America
4. Asia
5. Africa
6. Australia and Oceania
7. Thematic collections
8. Aerophilatelic collections

289

9. Junior class
10. Philatelic specialities
11. Philatelic literature
Exhibits are grouped into the following categories:
Category A: Classical (issues up to 1900)
Category B: Modern (issues since 1900)
Category C: Collections not confined to any one period of time
Category D: Literature

THE WORK OF THE JURY

The exhibits in the competitive class are judged by an international Jury composed of at least fifteen members, of which the majority must come from a country other than that of the organizing body. The Jury elects a Chairman from its midst. Usually the members of the Jury split up according to their qualification into smaller groups which judge certain parts of the competitive class (for instance a group of three members for junior exhibits).

The Jury judges the exhibits according to these obligatory qualities:

a) Philatelic knowledge and personal study shown in the collection
b) The level of progress
c) The condition of items displayed
d) The rarity of items displayed
e) The presentation, write-up and arrangement of the collection
The Jury makes the following awards:
a) The Grand Prix for the best exhibit in the Class of Honour. It can be an *Objet d'Art* or a Large Gold Medal
b) The National Grand Prix for the best exhibit in the National class. It can be an *Objet d'Art* or a Large Gold Medal
c) The International Grand Prix for the best exhibit in the Competitive class. It can be an *Objet d'Art* or a Large Gold Medal
d) Gold Medals (of pure gold)
e) Gold-Silver Medals (silver with a centre of gold) or Small Gold Medals
f) Silver-Gilt Medals
g) Silver Medals
h) Bronze-Silver Medals (or Small Silver Medals)
i) Bronze Medals
j) Diplomas
k) *Objets d'Art* as complementary awards in addition to Medals
l) Certificates of Participation

The Jury has the right to give some exhibitors their special felicitations.

Every exhibit which includes a certain number of forged or repaired stamps which are not marked as such is marked down.

THEMATIC AND SUBJECT COLLECTIONS

Special rules apply to thematic collections. They emphasize that stamps must be the centre and main object of every collection. Stamps must be genuine and in good condition. Philatelic documents must also be genuine. Cancelled stamps must have clean, legible postmarks which touch the design on the stamp as little as possible. It is recommended not to mix mint and cancelled stamps. The libretto should be clearly expressed and the texts and non-philatelic supplements should be kept to a necessary minimum.

With thematic and subject collections the Jury bases its judgment on the following criteria:

	Points	Overall number of points
1. Presentation:		
General impression of the collection	15	15
2. Theme, purpose of issue, subject:		
a) Development of the collection	25	
b) Extent of the collection	15	
c) Originality and elaboration of the theme	15	55
3. Philatelic elements:		
a) Philatelic knowledge	10	
b) Condition and rarity of stamps and philatelic items	20	30
	100	100

The FIP rules list three types of thematic collections, whereas we have spoken only of two: 1. Thematic collections; 2. Purpose of issue collections; and 3. Subject collections. There is very little difference between purpose of issue and subject collections. Examples of purpose of issue collections are 'Malaria' or 'Churchill'. That means that the collector collects stamp issues related to a given subject even if the design of the stamp does not show it. Examples of subject collections have been described ('Flowers,' 'Ships'). Both represent the lower level of thematic collecting.

On the basis of the number of points achieved according to the table given above the following medals are awarded to thematic exhibits:

Medals or other awards	Minimum points awarded International exhibition	National exibition
Large Gold Medal	95 %	90 %
Small Gold Medal	90 %	85 %
Silver-Gilt Medal	85 %	80 %
Silver Medal	75 %	70 %
Bronze-Silver Medal	70 %	60 %
Bronze Medal	60 %	50 %
Diploma	50 %	40 %
Certificate of Participation		

JUNIOR COLLECTIONS

The International Federation of Philately has also adopted special rules for the Junior class in international stamps exhibitions.

The Junior class is divided into two categories: a) individual exhibits and b) joint exhibits entered by youth groups. In each of these categories there are three age groups: 1. Exhibitors not older than 15 up to 31 December of the year of the exhibition; 2. Exhibitors 15-18; 3. Exhibitors 19-21.

Only stamps and other philatelic items must form the basic and predominant element of the collection. Exhibitors must declare that the exhibit is their own property and that they have formed it by their own means. Stamps and philatelic items must be genuine and in good condition. Cancelled stamps should have clean and legible postmarks, so that their design may be clearly distinguished. Stamp issues declared by FIP to be abusive cannot be exhibited. The following rules apply for the judging of junior exhibits:

	Up to 15 years	From 15 to 18 years	From 19 to 21 years
a) General impression (presentation, write-up)	45 points	30 points	20 points
b) Basis and development of the collection	15	20	25
c) Condition of stamps, cancellations and philatelic knowledge	35	40	45
d) Size of the collection	5	10	10
Total:	100 points	100 points	100 points

Exhibitors participating in the competition can win the following awards:

a) Silver Medal	90—100 points
b) Silver-Gilt Medal	75—89 points
c) Bronze Medal	60—74 points
d) Diploma	45—59 points
e) Certificate of Participation	less than 45 points

In addition material awards can be given.

PHILATELISTS FIGHT BACK

During the last ten or more years there have been a number of cases of certain postal administrations trying to exploit philatelists and make easy money out of them. They issued unnecessarily long sets of stamps, stamps with exorbitant surcharges, stamps of the same set perforated and imperforate, miniature sheets in different colours and perforated as well as imperforate, changes of colours, artificial errors, and so on. Therefore the International Federation of Philately took decisive action. A special Commission set up by the FIP for this purpose has declared some sets of stamps and individual stamps to be harmful, abusive or undesirable. Such items must not be shown in exhibitions held under the patronage of the FIP. The special Commission of the FIP publishes from time to time lists of issues which cannot be exhibited.

Issues or stamps are known as *harmful* when sold in bulk or in part to private speculators who can then dictate their prices; also issues comprising stamps which are not available for free sale at post office counters or sold only under special conditions; issues comprising some values with surcharges representing more than fifty per cent of the franking value (this does not apply if a set of stamps is issued after a natural disaster or in support of a philatelic exhibition); sets of stamps, stamps and miniature sheets perforated or overprinted by private persons; private issues; parts of normal issues which are not on sale at post offices — these are all harmful.

Issues comprising perforated and imperforate stamps and miniature sheets where the numbers printed have not been disclosed; issues sold only together with other stamps; issues sold in several sets of different colours and miniature sheets printed in different colours; and issues or their parts reprinted for profit reasons, are all called *abusive*.

The category *undesirable* relates to commemorative sets which are far too long; issues where the values are too high; miniature sheets of overlarge size; and issues printed on purpose in inadequate numbers.

This action of the FIP has already brought good results. Some governments (that of Panama, for instance), have changed their stamp issuing policy and have given undertakings to abide by the principles laid down by the FIP. This, of course, is just the beginning and much more has to be done in this field.

The fight of the FIP has been joined by the philatelic press. Also some of the greatest publishers of world catalogues have introduced most important measures. Stanley Gibbons and Yvert & Tellier, to mention but two, have decided not to include harmful, abusive and undesirable issues in their normal lists of stamp issues. Such issues are listed in an appendix of the catalogue without illustrations, detailed descriptions or prices.

HOW Mr BURRUS OUTWITTED Mr HIND

An auction is an auction. It is not very easy to describe the atmosphere loaded with tension. Whispered remarks, sighs, unseen duels and the pretended calm of experienced bidders '. . . going, going, gone!' One knock from the wooden gavel and the battle is decided.

Philatelic history was made on 5 April 1922. The giants of philately met in the rue Drouot in Paris; the greatest stamp collectors, dealers, experts and millionaires, were all present. On a little table in front of the auctioneer's desk under a glass cover rested a stamp which attracted the attention of the entire hall: British Guiana 1856, One Cent black on magenta, the only copy in the world.

When the bidding reached 150,000 francs the situation was still not clear. A number of philatelists were interested, and bids were made from left and right. As soon as the figure reached 200,000, though, the outsiders dropped back and among them was the representative of His Majesty King George V.

In the end only two equally strong competitors remained in the fight — Maurice Burrus, from Alsace, and the American Arthur Hind. It is difficult to say which millionaire was the richer. Hugo Griebert, the representative of Arthur Hind, offered 280,000 francs. Burrus raised him to 290,000. Then Griebert added another ten thousand. 'Three hundred thousand francs for the first time, for the second time . . . going, going, gone!' The British Guiana One Cent had found a new home — Utica, USA.

All eyes in the room turned to Maurice Burrus, the loser. He smiled, seeming not to mind having been outbid.

If it had not been for philatelic greenhorns many a stamp treasure would be forgotten or destroyed; take this British Guiana One Cent, for example.

L. Vernon Vaughan was almost thirteen. He collected stamps and was very keen on them. One day, in about 1872, he discovered a box of old letters, in the attic, and amongst them was a dirty magenta stamp. He did not like it at all and furthermore there was no space reserved for this particular stamp in his album. Nevertheless, he stuck it in.

The stamp dealer in Bath had just received a new shipment of colourful stamps and they were just the thing the young stamp collector wanted. His pocket money was not sufficient, and so he decided to sell some of his stamp supplies. He chose a few, including the ugly magenta British Guiana, and went to see Mr N. R. McKinnon, whom he knew as a great stamp collector. Mr McKinnon inspected the dark red bit of paper with cut-off corners from all sides, and then gave the boy six shillings for it. Mr McKinnon had a lot to say about stamps but the boy did not listen. He was in

934 The rarest stamp in the world: British Guiana 1 cent, 1856.

a great hurry to get to the stamp dealer before someone else bought the colourful new stamps.

The magenta beauty stayed with Mr McKinnon for five years. Then he sold the stamp together with his whole collection to the stamp dealer Mr Thomas Ridpath of Liverpool for £120. Ridpath sold the British Guiana shortly afterwards for £150 to the famous philatelist Count Philippe de la Rénotière von Ferrari.

Ferrari was a great philatelist but not a politician, or he would not have acquired German nationality. He was a nobleman from an old Italian family and lived in France. Count Ferrari could spend more money on stamps than anybody else. He started to collect stamps at the right time, when a Post Office Mauritius could be bought for a handful of francs. Finally he had five copies of the rare Mauritius stamps in his collection including the famous cover with both the One Penny and Two Pence Post Office Mauritius. He also owned the British Guiana One Cent.

When Ferrari died in 1917 he bequeathed his whole stamp collection to the Berlin Postal Museum; that was his greatest mistake. The French government confiscated the stamps as enemy property and after the war the collection was sold in fourteen auctions as part of war reparations, and thus the magenta British Guiana One Cent landed in the rue Drouot.

Mr Arthur Hind enjoyed his treasure for eleven years. One day he had a visitor. The man, so the story goes, offered him for sale another copy of the One Cent. Hind could not believe his eyes. He scrutinized the stamp closely, measured it, compared it with his unique copy and studied it under a strong magnifying glass. There could be no doubt, it really was identical. Hind was not short of money and did not think twice. He paid the huge price asked by the owner. As soon as the stamp became his property, and while the flabbergasted philatelist was still with him, he burned the stamp: 'Right, now there is still just the one copy!'

Whether this story is true or not will probably never be known. Hind died in 1933 and the secret went with him to his grave.

After Arthur Hind's death his collection was sold by auction, but the British Guiana One Cent was not included in the sale. The stamp was claimed in court by his widow, and she almost lost it. When the stamp was returned to her after an exhibition in Europe she mislaid the envelope with the stamp and discovered it only after some time by sheer luck. Perhaps this was the reason she decided to sell it. It is said that she was offered £10,000 in 1935 but did not consider this offer to be sufficient. Finally she sold the stamp in 1940 for approximately £15,000. The name of the new owner was for 30 years the most closely kept secret in philately and was disclosed only on the day he parted with the stamp. He was Frederic T. Small, an Australian living in Fort Lauderdale, Florida, USA.

The sale was preceded by much publicity and the stamp was expected to reach a record price. Although it was sold for $280,000 the auctioneers were a bit disappointed. It was the highest figure ever paid for a single stamp but was still a full $100,000 short of the price fetched by the Mauritius cover with two copies of the orange-red Post Office Penny.

The auction was a great event and the room was crowded. The bidding started at $100,000 and very soon reached $200,000. At that stage competitors started to drop off. To the surprise of all present, among the bidders who gave up were the Weill brothers of New Orleans, the buyers of the Mauritius cover. In the end the stamp was bought for $280,000 by Irving Weinberg of Pennsylvania on behalf of a consortium of eight businessmen who put up the money as an investment. After the sale Mr. Weinberg admitted that he did not know much about the stamp, only what he had read in the auction catalogue. In his opinion the stamp will double its value in ten years time. Maybe he is right.

Philatelists had few opportunities to see the stamp. It was exhibited in 1965 at the Royal Festival Hall in London in an exhibition commemorating the centenary of the first catalogue of Stanley Gibbons. It is rumoured though, that the real stamp was on show only on the first day and was later replaced by an exact copy. Shortly before the 1970 auction it was again exhibited at the Interpex exhibition in New York.

Although few stamp collectors had a chance to see the stamp, Maurice Burrus did manage to inspect and study it very closely prior to the exciting Paris sale on 5 April 1922. He also went to see an expert who had checked the genuineness of the lots in the Ferrari sale. When Burrus scrutinized the stamp under a strong magnifying glass he noticed that on the right, where the text 'one cent', appears, the structure of the paper was disturbed and that this spot was overpainted with practically the same colour as the original. He therefore came to the conclusion that somebody probably took a Four Cent stamp (incidentally also very expensive) and cleverly removed from the text the first 'f' and replaced the last 's' by a dot. Then the 'u' in the first word was overpainted to 'n' and the 'r' to 'e', thus changing 'four', to 'one', and the rarity was completed. If you have a close look at the photograph you will notice that the shape of the letters 'n' and 'e' in the word 'one' is different from the shape of the same letters in the word 'cent'.

This was probably the reason why Mr Burrus had such a cunning smile on his face when he raised Hind up to the then fantastic figure of 300,000 francs. It seems he found out before the sale that the American millionaire had instructed his agent Mr Griebert to buy the stamp at any price.

Why is this stamp so rare, and how was it produced? British Guiana issued its first stamps in 1850. They are the famous Cotton-reels, simple printings of a circle looking like a postmark with the name of the country and the value on coloured paper. Six years after the first stamps were issued the supply of stamps ran out and the boat bringing new stamps from London was late. The postmaster therefore asked the printers of the local paper, the *Official Gazette*, Joseph Baum and William Dallas, to print an emergency issue of stamps. It was supposed to be similar to the second stamp issue featuring a sailing ship. As time was short and nothing else was available they took from the printing press a block of a sailing ship usually used in the paper as a heading to the column with news about arrivals and departures of ships. From newspaper letter-type the text and the quotation from Horace, *damus petimusque vicissim*, was composed and the black stamp rectangles were printed first on magenta and later on blue surface-coloured paper. Since these stamps were so primitive every single copy was signed or initialled by one of the four post office officials to exclude the possibility of forgery.

No postal documents or archives survived from those days and for many years nobody knew that, in addition to the known Four Cent stamps, One Cent stamps had also been printed. This did not emerge until Master Vaughan made his discovery.

There is one more unexplained puzzle. One Cent stamps were used to pay the postage for newspapers, which is why they did not survive; for not many people keep copies of old newspapers and the *Official Gazette* was a small, local paper with an insignificant circulation. Vaughan, though, tells us in his memoirs that he took this rare One Cent stamp off a letter. Can he be trusted? The postage for a letter was higher, and required a Four Cent stamp. Besides, every copy of these stamps was initialled by a postal clerk, so it could hardly have passed for a Four Cent stamp on a letter. Or was it a printing error?

The truth will probably never be known. Vaughan died long ago; Ferrari, Hind and Burrus are also dead. Only the mysterious little bit of paper remains, certainly the only one of its kind. Hardly anybody has access to it today. Nevertheless, take a good look at the reproduction of the unique stamp. You would not see very much on a colour print, for the magenta colour is too dark; a black and white illustration is better. On the left are the initials EDW, the signature of the postal clerk E. D. Wright. Then there are traces of a hardly legible postmark 'Demerara, Ap 4 1856', of 4 April 1856.

If you should get a chance to inspect the stamp you would find on the back the signs of its owners. There is Ferrari's lily, Hinds' quatrefoil of clover and a comet, the sign of Mr Small.

935 One of the three Tiflis stamps from the Fabergé collection sold in an H. R. Harmer auction in London, 1939, and (below) a drawing of the embossed design of the stamp.

THE FORGOTTEN NOAH'S ARK

The number of philatelists all over the world is thought to be over one hundred million. Generations of stamp collectors have searched attics and gone through old correspondence and archives to discover details about stamps and their history. Not all the mysteries have been solved, however; new and surprising finds are being made, as shown by the following story.

The ten kopek stamp of 1858 was generally considered to be the first stamp used in Russia. As early as the 1880s there were, though, stories circulating about another stamp, older than that of 1858, used somewhere in the Caucasus. The first concrete facts were published as late as 1924 in the philatelic press.

In 1889 Mr J. B. Moens, the editor of the Belgian philatelic magazine *Timbre Poste*, wrote to the Director of Posts in Tiflis (Tbilisi), the capital of Georgia, asking whether he knew anything about a stamp once issued by the local post of Tiflis. The Director replied that such a stamp really had existed but he could not say when it had been in use. Nobody in Russia had seen it. The first examples of this stamp were found shortly before the outbreak of the First World War, and one was acquired by the great collector of Russian stamps, K. K. Schmidt, who set out to discover all the facts about its use. He published an announcement in the press asking the inhabitants of Tiflis for information about this stamp and for copies if they had any. War, revolution and civil war stopped all further research and the stamp was again forgotten. Not until 1924 did Mr Schmidt describe the Tiflis local stamp in the philatelic magazine *Sovietskiy Filatelist* and publish a photograph.

The local stamp of Tiflis is most interesting. It was printed in colourless embossing in strips of five in the official printing shop of the Governorship at Tiflis. In the centre of the stamp is a circle with the double-headed tsarist eagle surmounted over the arms of Tiflis and the Gubernia of Tiflis. The emblems of the arms are difficult to discern. At the top is Mount Ararat with Noah's Ark, a river and George the Victorious on horseback, and at the bottom is the winged staff of Mercury. The circle is placed in the centre of a double square with the following text running from left to right: 'Tiflis Gorods. Pochta 6 Kop' (City Post of Tiflis. 6 kopeks). The size of the stamp is 22×22 millimetres (about $\frac{7}{8}$" square). It is imperforate and printed on white or yellowish paper without watermark. The paper is 0·2 millimetres thick, and the thick gum is a yellowish colour.

Philatelists in Russia were naturally very excited about this interesting stamp and started a search for more facts and information about its issue and use. In the end details were discovered in the Caucasian Calendar for 1858. The stamp was issued by order of the tsarist Governor of the Caucasus in November or December 1857, and was used for the payment of postage in the territory of Tiflis and Kodzhory. It could not be bought in single copies but only in strips of five. Since normal letters could be handed in at the post office and paid for there, only very few people bought strips of five stamps at once. Furthermore, the stamp was in use for only about four months, which explains why it was forgotten and why it is so very rare. It must be borne in mind that on 1 January 1858 the normal Russian stamps were issued.

This stamp was shown for the first time by Mr Schmidt in 1930 at the Berlin stamp exhibition IPOSTA and caused a small sensation. There were some people who said it was not a stamp at all, but the answer to that is quite clear. The Governor naturally had the right to order the printing of the stamp. It was produced in the official printing shop, was on sale normally at the post office and was used for the franking of mail.

The local stamp of Tiflis is not as famous as the Post Office Mauritius but there exist far fewer copies, less than six, and perhaps there exists only one copy on a cover. Three Tiflis stamps were in the collection of Agathon Fabergé and were auctioned in 1939 by H. R. Harmer. Nobody in Russia is known to possess the stamp. The whereabouts of the copy originally shown by Mr Schmidt is also unknown. Perhaps the stamp was destroyed during the Second World War. Or perhaps there are some more forgotten copies, waiting for discovery somewhere in the mountains of Georgia.

A POLAR TRAGEDY

The fate of the *Chelyuskin* Expedition, many years before the outbreak of the Second World War, electrified the world. In August 1933 a Soviet expedition led by Professor O. I. Schmidt left port aboard the steamer *Chelyuskin*. It was to have been the first attempt by normal steamer to pass through the north-east passage (from Murmansk eastwards along the coast of Siberia to Vladivostok) unaccompanied by an icebreaker. At first everything went well, but in October the *Chelyuskin* was caught in the Bering Straits in a cold embrace of ice. The pressure of the ice mounted until at last it crushed the sides of the ship, and in February 1934 the *Chelyuskin* sank.

The crew, though, did not lose their presence of mind. By an almost superhuman effort they managed to salvage everything possible from the doomed ship. Under the leadership of the

936 Rare error: the Levanevski stamp with inverted overprint and small 'f' in the word San Francisco.

experienced polar explorer Professor Schmidt, an emergency camp was built on an ice floe. The commander of the expedition and his party knew well enough that there was not enough food or equipment for very long. Their only hope was help from the mainland which had been informed of the disaster by radio.

It was the start of a rescue operation watched with great interest by the whole world. No ship could get to the survivors, and to cross the ice was impossible. There was only one way to help them — by air. Seven of the best Russian fliers were chosen and planes and supplies were moved to the Far East. Although the conditions of the Arctic winter were hard and the planes in those days were not very advanced, they managed to save all the members of the expedition. The shipwrecked crew built an emergency landing strip on the ice floe and the fliers picked them up group by group. Professor Schmidt, the captain of the ship V. Voronin and the seven pilots were awarded the title of Hero of the Soviet Union for their bravery. To commemorate the rescue of the *Chelyuskin* Expedition Russia issued, in January 1935, a set of ten stamps showing the portraits of the heroes and scenes from the rescue operation.

In the same year one of the pilots who had taken part in the rescue operation, S. A. Levanevski, was chosen to undertake a direct flight from Moscow to San Francisco via the North Pole. Ten thousand copies of the sepia brown ten kopek stamp of the *Chelyuskin* set showing the portrait of Levanevski were overprinted with a red text of five lines reading: 'Flight Moscow-San Francisco over the North Pole 1935' and the new value of one rubel. The overprinted stamp was issued on 2 August 1935 to be used for the franking of mail carried by Levanevski on his flight. Levanevski started as planned, but the next day he had to interrupt his flight because of dangerous icing-up. All mail carried aboard was turned over to the post, and was either returned to the sender or received a blue cachet with a text explaining that the flight was postponed and that all the mail was therefore travelling normally.

The flight was repeated in 1936 and again the overprinted Levanevski stamps were used for the franking of mail carried by the plane. Somewhere over the Arctic Ocean the plane crashed for reasons unknown. It disappeared into the icy waters and the crew and cargo were lost.

This is the moving tragedy of the Polar Sea as told by the Levanevski stamp. The number of copies originally overprinted was small. In addition a large part of these stamps was lost in the sea together with the plane. It is therefore not surprising that this airmail stamp is in great demand and that covers from the first interrupted flight in particular are highly valued.

Philatelists discovered on this expensive stamp an interesting overprint error. A sheet consisted of twenty-five stamps (five rows of five stamps each). When the sheets were overprinted one row of overprints had the word Francisco spelt with a small 'f' instead of a capital 'F'. Therefore on a sheet of twenty-five there are five copies with the error. It is obvious that this error is more valuable than the stamp with the normal overprint.

That is not all. After some time it was discovered that one, perhaps even two sheets were issued with the overprint inverted. That, of course, is a great rarity. In February 1945 the famous Crimean Conference was held at Yalta. Stalin knew very well that Roosevelt was an ardent philatelist and therefore presented him with a copy of the Levanevski stamp with overprint inverted. President Roosevelt was very pleased.

In theory it can therefore be assumed that there must have existed five or even ten copies of this stamp with a combination of both errors, i. e. with the overprint inverted and with the small 'f'. All over Russia and also abroad stamp collectors were checking their copies. Nobody in Russia had the combination of errors, not even the Postal Museum, and there were doubts whether it existed at all. It is, though, reported that such a copy turned up in the early sixties in New York at an auction and was sold for a four-figure sum.

Doubts were dispelled fairly recently when a copy of this quite outstanding airmail rarity was discovered by the well-known collector of Russian stamps, Dr Peter Lavrov, in Prague. How many copies of this double error exist nobody knows. After all, some might have been among the stamps lost together with Levanevski's plane; not even the stamp President Roosevelt brought home from Yalta was one of these. It was a copy of the overprint inverted but with a capital 'F' in the word Francisco.

THE EMPEROR'S BIRTHDAY

New Orleans is a gay city, a city of gorgeous colours, flowers, carnivals and music. Here, on the shores of the Mississippi, jazz was born, the music which conquered the world. The German colony of New Orleans decided to celebrate the birthday of Emperor Wilhelm II by giving a grand party with music and dancing. This evening was always a great social event, but in 1901 it had a special splendour. Out there on the waves the German cruiser *Vineta* was riding at anchor. The warship was on a friendly tour, visiting ports of North and South America. Naturally the whole crew of the cruiser was invited to the ball, and only a small guard remained on board.

The ball was a great success. The supplies of whisky and wine were ample and the handsome sailors spun the elegantly dressed ladies on the parquet. All the notables of the city came to the ball and reporters and photographers swarmed everywhere. The *Vineta* had to leave port the morning after the ball, and many a sailor left his heart in New Orleans.

When the ship dropped anchor at the Brazilian port of Pernambuco great sacks of post were brought on board. They were full of mail from fellow countrymen in New Orleans and also contained numerous copies of newspapers with detailed descriptions of the great ball and many photographs of the German sailors. The sailors carefully folded the newspapers to send home to Germany.

At this stage a problem arose. The purser of the ship had a sufficient supply of German stamps for postcards, letters and higher values, but there were not sufficient three-pfennig stamps for newspapers. The purser therefore took a piece of rubber from a scrubbing-brush and cut a handstamp. Then he took some five pfennig stamps, bisected them vertically, and overprinted each half of the green stamp neatly in violet with the new value '3 PF'.

The first mail with this provisional stamp was posted on 17 April 1901. It caused a great row in Berlin. The Ministry of Posts and the Admiralty held a conference and finally, on 28 June, it was officially announced that it was forbidden to produce and use such provisional stamps. Five months passed, however, before this decision reached the *Vineta* and before the warship received a sufficient

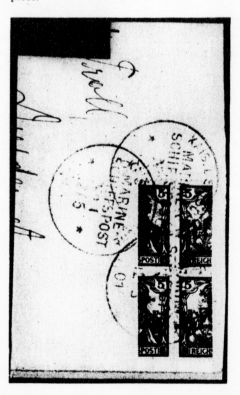

937 Block of four of the *Vineta* provisional stamp with overprint '3 Pf' on piece.

938 Pair of the rare unissued stamp of New Brunswick with the portrait of Charles Connell.

supply of three-pfennig stamps. The provisional bisected and overprinted stamps were used until September 1901.

Philatelists, especially stamp collectors in Germany, started to look for the *Vineta* stamps. True, it was a provisional issue produced without permission, but it arose out of a real need, it was used postally and therefore is listed as a normal stamp in all catalogues.

There were just 600 bisected stamps with the overprint, as the purser had only had a supply of three sheets of the five-pfennig stamp. Stamp forgers soon saw their chance and started to produce their own 'provisionals'. The genuine bisects were used only on board the *Vineta* and all of them are cancelled with a circular postmark with the text 'Kais. deutsche Marine Schiffs-post No 1' and the date. A certain part of the provisionals remained mint.

Still more valuable are copies of the provisional stamp on which the purser had by mistake applied the overprint inverted.

THE AMBITIOUS MINISTER

If it were not for its interesting and rare stamps the Canadian Province of New Brunswick might not command much attention.

New Brunswick issued its first stamps in 1851 but collectors normally see them only in stamp exhibitions or auctions. They are rather scarce and were frequently used bisected and sometimes even quartered. Such covers are very much in demand.

In 1859 Canada replaced British currency by Canadian dollars and cents and it was therefore necessary to print new stamps in decimal currency. In the province of New Brunswick this was a task entrusted to the Postmaster General, Charles Connell.

The Postmaster General was a man of great ideas and high ambitions. He ordered the new stamps from a printing firm in the United States. Well before the planned date of issue he laid before his colleagues in the government samples of the new stamps for their approval. Their reaction was of such a nature that he had no choice but to resign, for the Postmaster General had presented his provincial government with a set of six stamps among which there was a brown five-cent stamp with the portrait of Charles Connell.

The Postmaster General resigned, the brown five-cent stamps went to the paper mill and a new five-cent stamp in green with the portrait of Queen Victoria was ordered. Because of this delay the new stamps were not issued on 1 May as originally intended but on 15 May, and the green five-cent stamp was not on sale until July. No five-cent stamps were available, and bisected ten-cent stamps were therefore used on letters.

Not all the brown five-cent stamps with the portrait of Charles Connell were destroyed. The former Postmaster General, and perhaps others, probably kept a few hundred. They never had to regret this investment. Although the stamps were never issued or used, and are therefore not proper postage stamps, they are still very popular because of the interesting story behind them, and their price is correspondingly high.

A RARE ERROR

Postal administrations nowadays print stamps in fantastic quantities. In all printing works there is strict supervision and the authorities do their best to prevent errors and rarities from slipping through. To err is human, though, and there are plenty of misprints even today. In many cases some of the commonest stamps suddenly become terribly rare — due to a misprint.

When Czechoslovakia was founded in 1918 stamps for the new nation were hurriedly printed. They feature Hradčany, the royal castle of Prague. These surface-printed stamps were not very satisfactory, and therefore a new set of definitives was issued in 1920. The stamps show two designs: a pigeon carrying a letter, and a symbolic figure of a woman breaking her chains, known among philatelists as the 'Allegory of the Republic'.

These stamps were in use for five years. When they were replaced by a new set of definitives large quantities of remainders were sent to Prague from post offices all over the country. It was decided to overprint all the remainders of the 'Allegory of the Republic' stamps and also of the Hradčany stamps and to use them as postage dues. Altogether three values of the 'Allegory of the Republic' were printed in the same red colour: 20, 50 and 150 heller. Since 50 heller was the postage for a postcard and not many red 50-heller stamps were left, it was decided to overprint only the red 20 and 150-heller stamps with the diagonal text 'Doplatit' (postage due) and the new value of 50 heller.

To the great surprise of the philatelic public in Czechoslovakia a red 50-heller 'Allegory of the Republic' stamp was discovered with the overprint '50 Doplatit 50'. This error was discovered at a time when the provisional postage-due stamps had been withdrawn from use and a new, definitive set of postage-due stamps had been issued.

It was obviously an error. The red 50-heller stamp was not intended for overprinting at all; the word 'Doplatit' as used on the brown 100-heller stamp would have been quite sufficient. There would have been no sense in printing the value '50' on a 50-heller stamp.

How this error originated is quite clear. At the printer's a sheet of the red 50-heller 'Allegory of the Republic' stamps must have been mixed up with the sheets of red 20 and 150-heller stamps. On the other hand, it is quite possible that it was not a complete sheet of one hundred stamps but only half a sheet or just a quarter sheet used by a printer to complete a sheet returned by one of the post offices with a part missing.

Stamp collectors immediately started an extensive search for the stamp with the error on it. A few copies were found in collections and a number of copies were discovered on some old correspondence of a large department store. Nevertheless, only about twenty copies of this error are known to exist and it is unlikely that further copies will be found. All the copies are cancelled and all of them bear the postmark 'Praha 14'. Not one mint copy of the error has been found.

All these facts confirm beyond any doubt that all known copies of the error come from just one large unit delivered to the post office Prague 14. The overprinted stamp was a postage due and was not on sale at normal post office counters.

939 Error on a Czechoslovak postage-due stamp with overprint '50 Doplatit 50' on a 50 heller stamp.

PHILATELIC ODDITIES

Do you want to accumulate a million stamps? Even if you acquire fifty stamps a day it would take you almost fifty-five years to reach one million, and should you succeed, your accumulation would still not be a stamp collection.

All sorts of animals have been put into postal service, horses and camels, dogs and reindeer. Probably the most interesting experiment, though, was to employ bees for the transmission of news. Towards the end of the last century the French bee-keeper Taynac established a bee post line to a friend who was also a bee-keeper. From time to time they exchanged a certain number of bees. On a given day they gave the hungry bees a dish of honey and whilst they were feeding the bee-keepers stuck little pieces of cigarette paper with agreed code numbers on the bees' backs. Then the bees were released and they started their journey home. On arrival at the bee-hive they had to crawl through a narrow hole and the bits of cigarette paper with the message were stripped off their backs.

On the eve of the First World War German spies also used bees. From the French frontier areas bees came flying into Germany carrying coloured threads tied to their bodies by German agents. A red thread meant that French infantry units were moving towards the frontier; a green thread signified artillery, a blue thread stood for cavalry.

It has been disclosed that attempts are being made today to use bees for espionage purposes. A microdot is applied to a bee's wing and on arrival at the destination the microdot is enlarged and decoded.

Numerous portraits of famous personalities are to be found on stamps — pictures of heads of State, scientists, artists, soldiers and politicians. Sometimes stamps also show portraits of ordinary people. In 1956 a stamp was issued in the Soviet Union with the portrait of the Azerbaijan collective farmer M. B. Eyvazov. The stamp commemorated his 148th birthday. Incidentally, this stamp exists in two types. The first issue incorrectly gave his first name as Muhamed, the second issue gave the right name, Mahmud. The second type with the correct name is more valuable.

The record of the Soviet Methuselah was beaten by Colombia. This country issued in 1957 two stamps with the portrait of Xavier Pereira, born in the year of the great French Revolution of 1789! It is not known whether Mr Pereira is still alive . . .

It is the fate of the rarest stamps that they are bought by people who can afford them — by millionnaires. Frequently they are not stamp collectors at all but people looking for sound investments. The stamps are kept in a safe and nobody gets a chance to admire them. Such a collector was the American Alfred H. Caspary. Not until 1958, when his collection was sold after his death in a series of large auctions, could the world learn how fantastic his 'stamp supplies' really were.

The first years after the First World War was the time of pioneer flights. The London *Daily Mail* offered an award of £10,000 for the first transatlantic flight. In 1919 the pilots Hawker and Grieve tried the crossing in a Sopwith plane. They were lucky. When they were forced to make an emergency landing in mid-ocean after a flight of about 11,000 miles the Danish boat *Mary* happened to be nearby and picked them up. Another ship saved the wreck of the plane and the mailbag.

Newfoundland overprinted a three cent stamp for this flight with the text 'First Transatlantic Air Post April, 1919'. There were only 200 copies of this overprint, of which eighteen were damaged and destroyed. Each stamp was signed on the back J.A.R., the initials of J. A. Robinson, the Postmaster of Newfoundland. Several other airmail issues were printed in very small numbers in Newfoundland for special flights. These airmail stamps are among the greatest rarities and are sometimes more expensive than the first Newfoundland stamps of 1857.

Are stamps poisonous? Experts tested samples of gum used and came to the conclusion that it does not contain any poison. There is, though, another danger threatening people who lick stamps — the possibility of infection. This is true not only when moistening stamps before affixing them to mail but also when collectors re-use old stamp hinges. Therefore, be careful.

In 1935 a special stamp issue was being prepared in the United Kingdom to commemorate the Silver Jubilee of the reign of King George V. When the first sheets of the newly printed stamps were shown to him, his Majesty King George V did not like the colour of the $2\frac{1}{2}$d, the highest value in the set. Instead of Prussian blue he preferred a normal blue. The King's wish was respected, the sheets already printed in Prussian blue were destroyed and the top value reprinted in blue.

Three sheets of the Prussian blue stamp, of 120 copies each, were overlooked and arrived at the Post Office in Fore Street, Upper Edmonton in north London. The postal clerk did not notice that he was handling stamps of a different colour and shortly after the post office was opened in the morning he sold forty-one copies to a young girl. She was not a philatelist either and used some of the stamps for mail to Australia.

Soon after the first customer had left a businessman came to buy a supply of stamps. He noticed the unusual colour of the $2\frac{1}{2}$d stamps and bought all the remaining 319 copies. Later in the day he went into central London and sold all his $2\frac{1}{2}$d stamps to a stamp dealer for a pound each. He should not have been in such a hurry to make a quick profit. A block of four Prussian blue $2\frac{1}{2}$d was sold on 28 March 1969 at Stanley Gibbons' auction for £950, and a good single copy fetched £325.

Post offices always have great problems with wrongly addressed letters. As time passes hundreds and thousands of undeliverable mail items accumulate. Some time ago there were great problems with mail addressed to Sherlock Holmes. It was decided to deliver such mail to the son of Conan Doyle, the deceased author of Sherlock Holmes' adventures.

Another flood of letters reaches post offices shortly before Christmas from children writing to Father Christmas. In many countries such mail is opened and passed on to the parents and children sometimes get a nice card from 'Father Christmas'. In Scandinavia children get a picture book as a present from the Post Office.

The British Post Office has introduced a special Christmas Card signed by Santa Claus. The cover bears a postmark 'Reindeerland'.

About 50,000 of these Christmas cards are sent to children each year.

Several years ago a New York Sunday paper carried an advertisement offering for sale a large stamp collection valued at $300,000 which was to be sold in smaller lots. Prices of some items were given and were very cheap indeed. Interested buyers were asked to send money in advance and if somebody ordered stamps for $200 or more he would be given a discount. The American Stamp Dealer's Association notified the authorities of this suspicious advertisement.

The first day some 400 letters with orders were intercepted and within a week there were several thousand. It is unbelievable how much money unsuspecting collectors were willing to sacrifice. The whole affair was investigated and it was found that the advertisement was a practical joke invented by a boy.

Stamps were already being used for espionage activities during the First World War. In 1915 perfect copies of the German ten- and fifteen-pfennig stamps were printed in England. The paper used for the stamps showing the symbolic figure of Germania was chemically treated. With the help of a special ink it was possible to write invisible messages on the backs of these forgeries. The message came to light only after treatment with special chemicals. The spy stamps were issued to British agents working inside Germany. They wrote their messages on the stamps which were then affixed to inconspicuous letters and postcards addressed to neutral countries. The secret of these stamps was disclosed many years after the war. It is not known if philatelists managed to get hold of some of these most interesting official forgeries.

'Next time you issue stamps with my portrait, ask my barber to approve them first.' Those were the words of King Christian X of Denmark when he was shown, in 1924, the new commemorative stamps issued for the three hundredth anniversary of the founding of the Danish post by King Christian IV. The stamps were printed in blocks of four in such a way that the portraits of the two kings are repeated in a tessellated arrangement so that they are alternately looking to the right and to the left. When the printers produced the blocks for printing they simply turned the portrait of the King around. Therefore on one stamp he has his hair parted on the left and on the other it is parted on the right.

On 13 January 1957 the Yugoslav post in Rieka (Fiume) delivered a postcard posted in nearby Pirano on 20 January 1918. It took this mail item almost thirty-nine years to reach its destination. The addressee had died many years before and so the card was handed to his brother. Most interesting is the fact that, although an eight heller stamp with the portrait of the Austro-Hungarian Emperor Franz Joseph I, which had become invalid for postage in 1918, was printed on the postcard, the Yugoslav post did not charge any postage due.

When the famous painting of the French Impressionist Paul Cézanne *The Cardplayers* was stolen the French Ministry of Posts included in the first set of art stamps a reproduction of this painting. The 'detective stamps' travelled all over the world and really assisted in the recovery of the painting.

The French idea was adopted by the German Democratic

Republic. Numbers of stamps were issued showing works of art lost or stolen during the Second World War.

A British philatelist decided to find out which post office was listed first in an alphabetical list of all post offices and which was the last. Out of some 500,000 post offices all over the world the first place is held by Norway. There is a post office in a fishing village called A in the region of Afjord, about thirty-five miles north of Trondheim. The last place in alphabetical order is held by the post office of the railway station at Zyznow in Poland, in the region of Rzeszow.

The postal service of the Thurn and Taxis family ceased to exist in 1867, when Prussia bought the whole network for three million thalers. It was also the end of the Thurn and Taxis stamps. According to this deal, though, later confirmed by a law passed on 7 May 1872, the Thurn and Taxis family were granted the right to use postal services free of charge for their family correspondence. They had special labels printed for use on their correspondence. The label shows a simple, rectangular frame with a text stating that this mail item is free of postage on the basis of the law of 1872. Such labels on mail and also entires with such a text printed on them were used by the Thurn and Taxis family up to the beginning of the First World War.

Thus the Thurn and Taxis stamps in a way continued their existence for a further forty-seven years. Mail items with the Thurn and Taxis labels are collectors' items of great interest and value.

TABLE SHOWING THE EVALUATION OF STAMPS

THE VALUATION OF STAMPS ACCORDING TO THEIR STATE OF PRESERVATION

Value in %		Quality	Imperforate Stamp (Margin)	Perforated Stamp		Colour	Cancellation Stains
				Centred	Perforations		
100	1st CHOICE	Faultless	Full margins	Design in centre of stamp	Complete	Fresh	Light and clean
90		Very light fault in appearance	Full margins	Design slightly off centre	1 short perforation	Good	Clean
80		Light quality fault	¾ of width	Design slightly off centre	½ perforation missing	Good	Small stain on reverse
70	2nd CHOICE	Small defect	½ of width	Design displaced upwards or downwards	2 perforations short	Small stain caused by dampness	Heavy cancellation
60			One side narrow	Design displaced to left or right	1 perforation missing	Not very fresh	Stain on reverse
50			Design slightly touched	Design displaced into corner	Short perforations on one side	Partly oxidized	Small stain on design
40	3rd CHOICE	Visible defect	Design touched	Perforation slightly touches design	2 perforations missing	Oxidized	Smudged cancellation
30			Part of design margin missing	Perforation in margin of design	Several perforations cut off	Slightly faded	Cancellation very smudged
10	4th CHOICE	Heavy defect	Design cut into	Perforation in design	3—4 perforations missing	Large stains caused by dampness	Ink stain
5			Whole edge of design cut off	Perforation in design	4—5 perforations missing	Faded to great extent	Cancellation just large stain
1			Part of design cut off	Perforation deep in design	Perforations cut off on one side	Undefinable	Cancellation just large stain

EXPLANATIONS TO THE TABLE: *If you find more than one fault on a stamp you must multiply the percentage value of the defects. The resulting figure has to be divided for each additional fault (except the first) by* **100**. *The easiest way is simply to delete two noughts for the second and every additional defect.*

Tears	Thinnings, Hole	Fold, Crease	Repaired	Gum (on unused stamps)	Remark
—	—	—	—	Mint	In every respect perfect
—	—	—	—	Traces of old hinge	
—	—	Slight trace of fold	—	Traces of old hinge	
In margin ½ millimetre	Margin slightly thin	Corner folded	½ perforation added	Traces of old hinge	Collect stamps of 2nd choice if stamps of 1st choice are unobtainable or too expensive
In margin 1 millimetre	Pinhole, margin thin	Folded	1 perforation added	Partly missing	
In margin 1 millimetre	Thinning in design	Light fold on reverse	Covered pinhole	Partly missing	
Into design 1 millimetre	Thinning 2 square millimetres	Fold on face of stamp	2 perforations added	Missing	Whenever possible replace by 1st or 2nd choice
Into design 1 millimetre	Thinning 2—3 square millimetres	Creased	Thinnings covered	Missing	
Into design 2 millimetres	Large thinning	Folded and creased	Margin added	Regummed	Can be used as sample for comparison
Into design 3 millimetres	Large thinning	Crumpled	Whole top of stamp on new layer	—	
More than 3 millimetres	Hole	Crumpled	Fitted together from pieces	—	

EXAMPLES: *On the stamp you are scrutinizing half a perforation is missing (**80%** of the full value) and the stamp is folded (**60%**):*
$$80 \times 60 = 4.800 \div 100 = \mathbf{48\%} \text{ of the value of a perfect copy.}$$
*It is found on a stamp that half a perforation is missing (**80%**), it is folded (**60%**) and the design is displaced into a corner (**50%**) $\div$ **80** $\times$ **60** $\times$ **50** =*
$$= \mathbf{240.000} \div \mathbf{100} \times \mathbf{100} = \mathbf{24\%} \text{ of the value of a perfect copy.}$$

A

Abusive stamps   87, 292
Accountancy stamps   93, 97, 111
Acetic acid   228
Aerophilately   75, 194, 247, 252
Airgraphs   57, 254
Airletters   57
Airmail   258
Airmail cancellations   194
Airmail labels   95
Airmail stamps   93, 95, 258, 262
Albums   117, 208, 224, 233, 245, 282, 285, 286
Album leaves   224, 239, 282, 285
Alexander the Great   11, 15
Alhambra   286
Allegory of the Republic   135, 302
Alphons X   17
American Philatelic Society   88
American Philatelist, The   285
American Stamp Dealer's Association   305
Amundsen, Roald   263
Angareion   15
Annulato   188
Approval booklets   222, 229
Arab Postal Union   59
Arc roulette   137
Association Internationale des Experts Philatéliques (AIEP)   219
Association Internationale des Journalistes Philatéliques (AIJP)   63
Auction catalogues   285
Augustus   16
Austria-Philatelist   285
Auxiliary cancellation   197
Avis de paiement   103
Avis de réception   103, 195

B

Balasse Magazine   285
Balloon mail   75, 194, 254, 270
Barnard, Joseph   7
Baum, Joseph   296
Benzine   145, 222
Berger Briefmarken-Zeitung   286
Billets de Port Payé   38
Bisect   218, 300, 301
Bishop, Henry   36
Black blot   88
Black print   150
Blair, Montgomery   58

Blind perforations   182

Blocks   120, 230
Blocked stamps   87
Bolaffi   284
Bolaffi, Giulio   9
Bolitho, Henry   254
Bolletino Filatelico d' Italia, Il   286
Boyd Dale, Louise   8
Briefmarke, Die   285
British Philatelic Association   114, 213, 219
Brushes   222
Bulk postage   203
Burrus, Maurice   8, 294
Bypost   113
Byrd, Richard Evelyn   263

C

Cachets   259, 261, 263, 266, 268
Caesar   16
Canadian provinces   48
Cancellation date stamps (CDS)   194
Cancellation of local and private posts   200
Cancellations   60, 116, 126, 188, 217, 279, 281, 301, 302
Cancelled by favour   207
Cancelled-to-order   104, 123, 207
Capitulations   280
Carcier, François   38
Cartes maximum   278
Caspary, Alfred H.   303
Catalogues   69, 73, 232, 234, 245, 262, 282, 286, 293, 296, 301
Catalogue collections   69, 287
Catapult flights   258
Censor labels   270
Censored mail   74, 268
Census stamps   111
Cézanne, Paul   305
Chalmers, James   42
Charity stamps   39, 90, 261
Charlemagne   18
Chelyuskin Expedition   298
Christian IV   305
Christian X   305
Christmas seals   111
Cinderella   81
Cito; citissimo   100
Clapper Post   38
Class of Honour   288
Classical period   49, 120
Clay tablets   13
Clichés   164, 173, 174
Coated paper   122, 141